8

High School Prodigies Have It Easy Even in Another World!

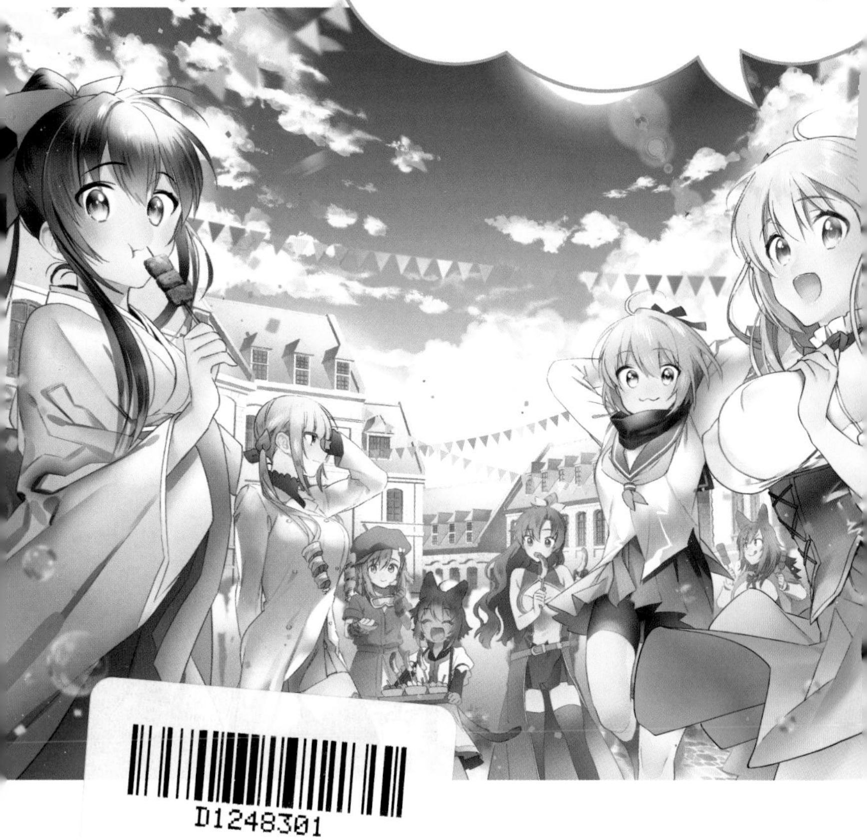

STORY BY
Riku Misora
ART BY
Kotaro Yamada
CHARACTER DESIGN BY
Sacraneco

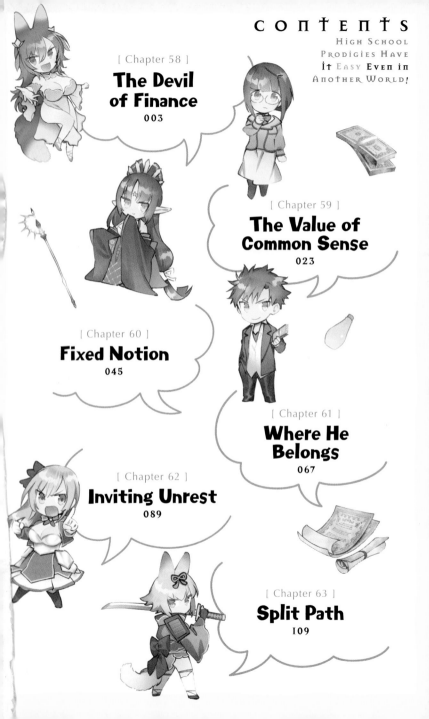

CONTENTS

HIGH SCHOOL PRODIGIES HAVE IT EASY EVEN IN ANOTHER WORLD!

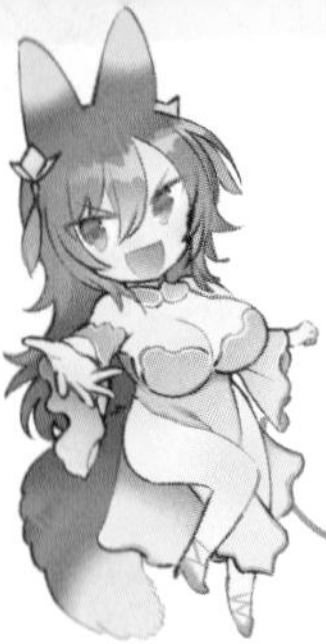

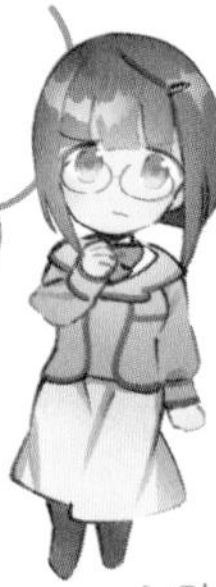

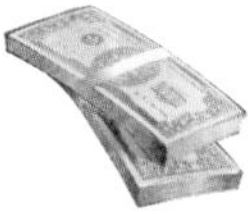

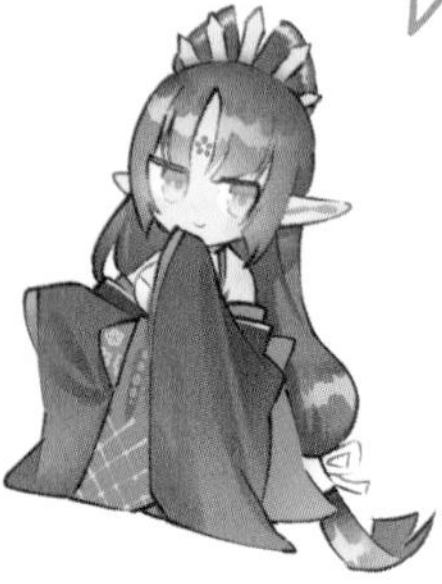

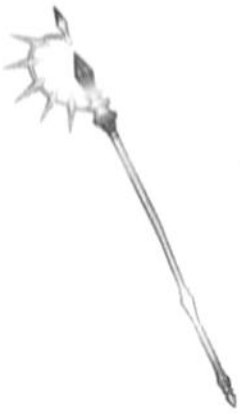

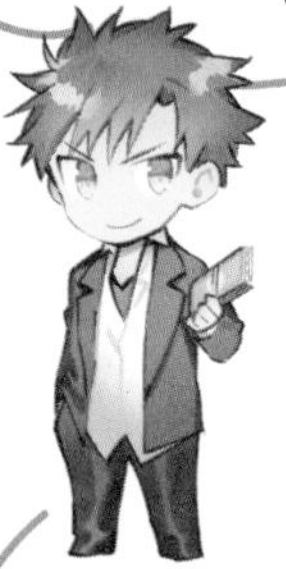

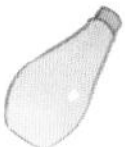

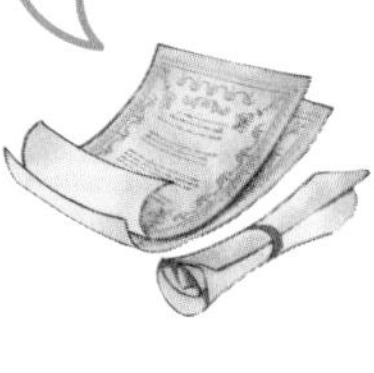

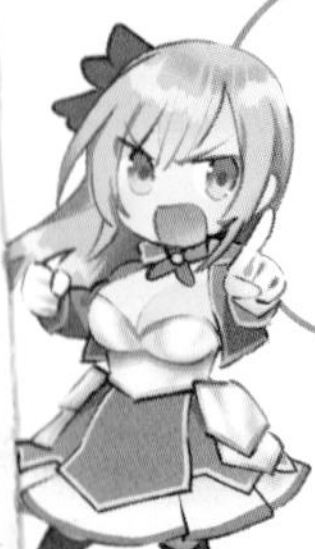

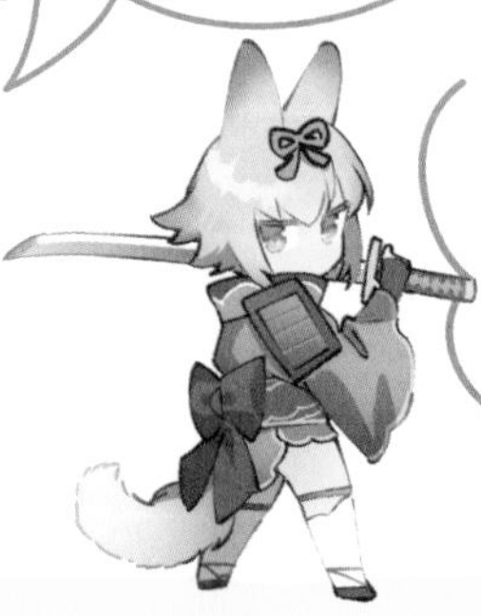

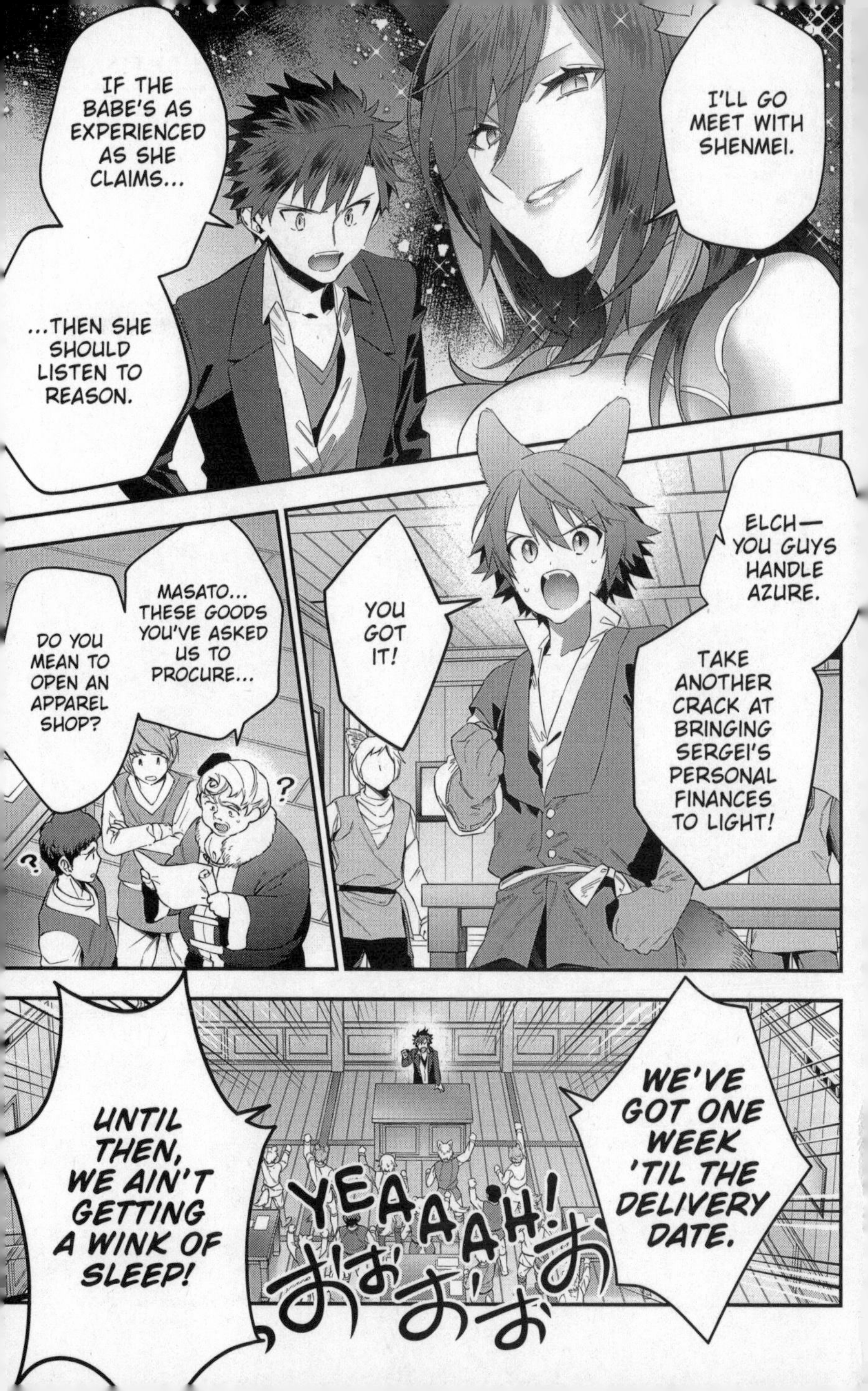
I'LL GO MEET WITH SHENMEI.
IF THE BABE'S AS EXPERIENCED AS SHE CLAIMS...
...THEN SHE SHOULD LISTEN TO REASON.
ELCH— YOU GUYS HANDLE AZURE.
TAKE ANOTHER CRACK AT BRINGING SERGEI'S PERSONAL FINANCES TO LIGHT!
YOU GOT IT!
MASATO... THESE GOODS YOU'VE ASKED US TO PROCURE...
DO YOU MEAN TO OPEN AN APPAREL SHOP?
WE'VE GOT ONE WEEK 'TIL THE DELIVERY DATE.
UNTIL THEN, WE AIN'T GETTING A WINK OF SLEEP!
YEAAAAH!

CHAPTER 58: THE DEVIL OF FINANCE

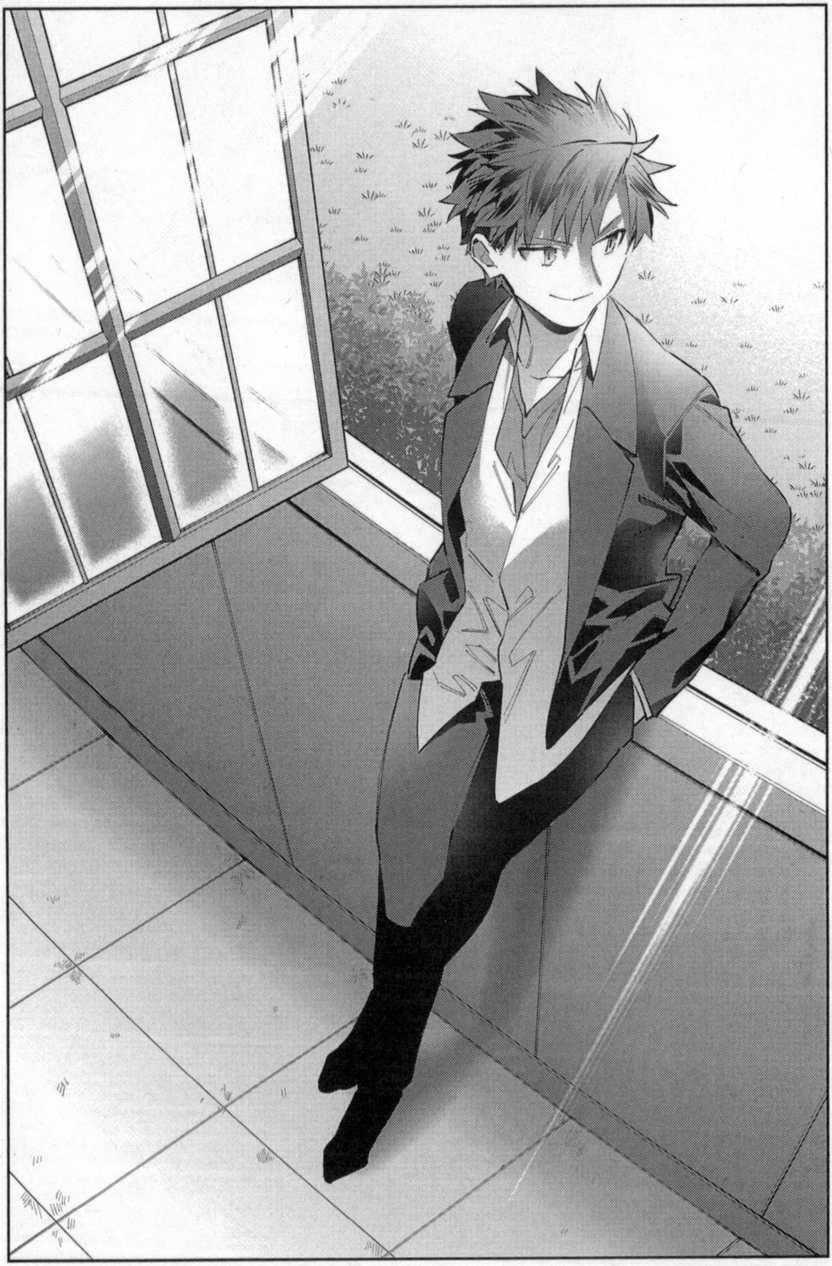

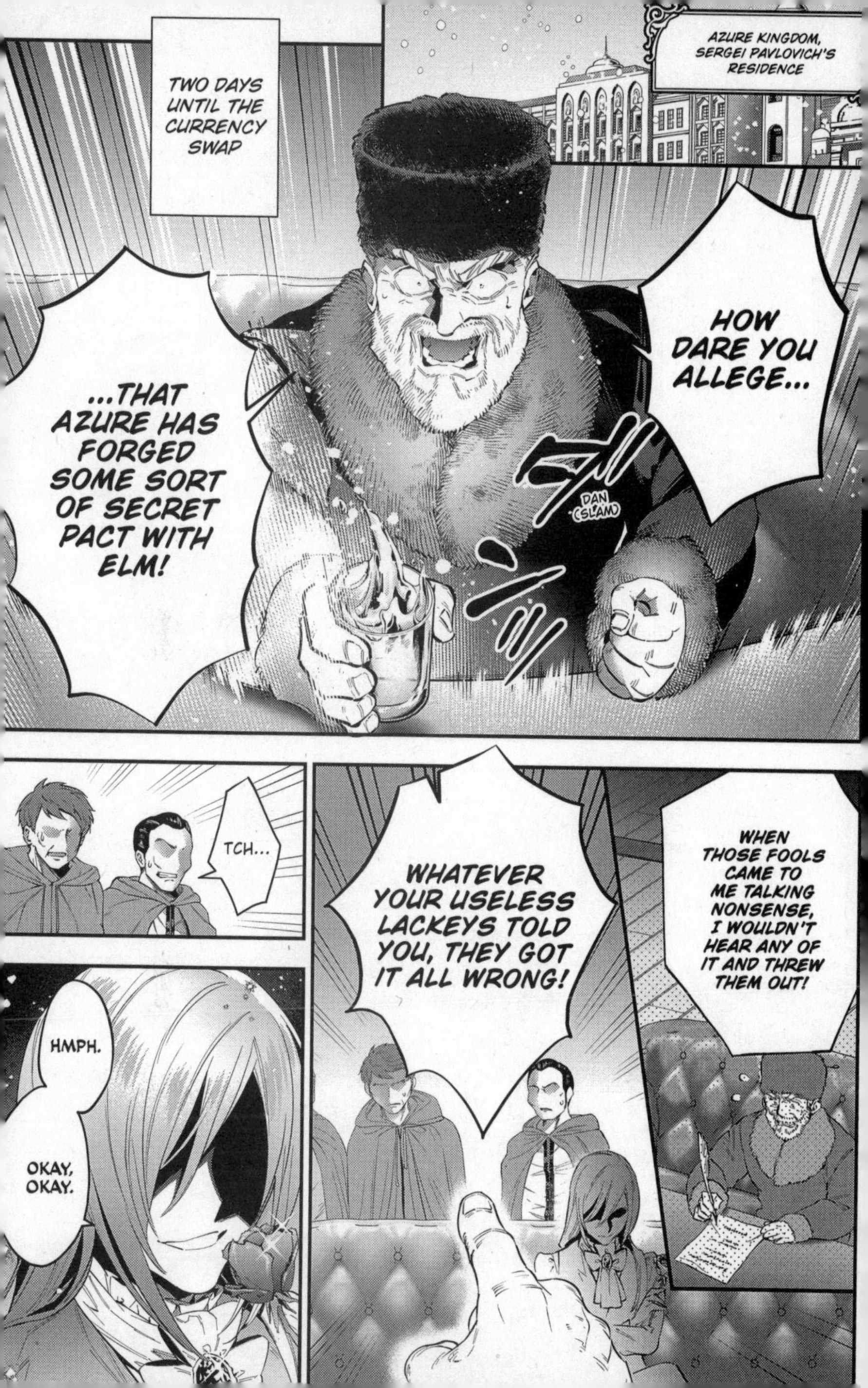
AZURE KINGDOM, SERGEI PAVLOVICH'S RESIDENCE
TWO DAYS UNTIL THE CURRENCY SWAP
HOW DARE YOU ALLEGE...
DAN (SLAM)
...THAT AZURE HAS FORGED SOME SORT OF SECRET PACT WITH ELM!
WHEN THOSE FOOLS CAME TO ME TALKING NONSENSE, I WOULDN'T HEAR ANY OF IT AND THREW THEM OUT!
WHATEVER YOUR USELESS LACKEYS TOLD YOU, THEY GOT IT ALL WRONG!
TCH...
HMPH.
OKAY, OKAY.

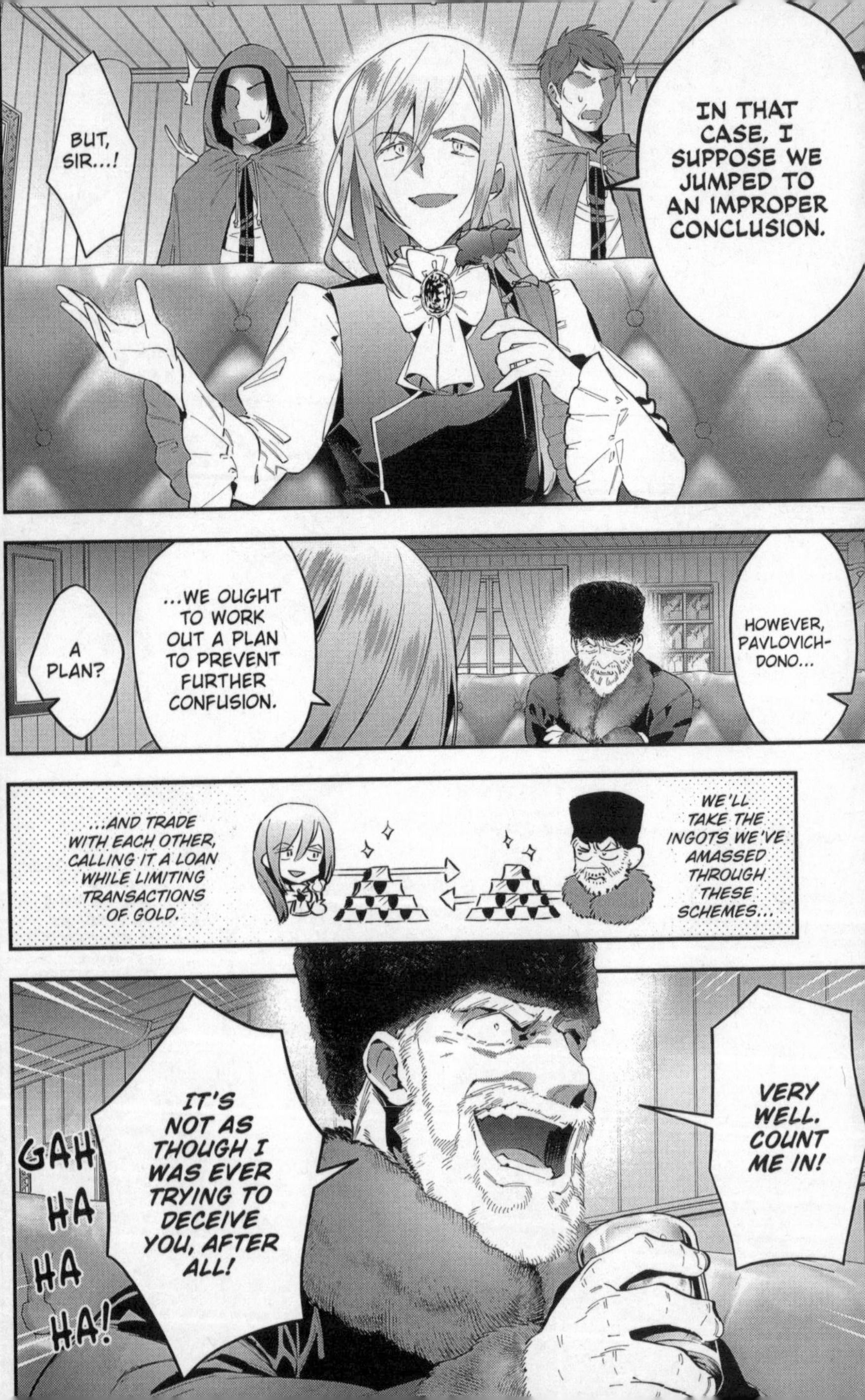
IN THAT CASE, I SUPPOSE WE JUMPED TO AN IMPROPER CONCLUSION.
BUT, SIR...!
HOWEVER, PAVLOVICH-DONO...
...WE OUGHT TO WORK OUT A PLAN TO PREVENT FURTHER CONFUSION.
A PLAN?
WE'LL TAKE THE INGOTS WE'VE AMASSED THROUGH THESE SCHEMES...
...AND TRADE WITH EACH OTHER, CALLING IT A LOAN WHILE LIMITING TRANSACTIONS OF GOLD.
VERY WELL. COUNT ME IN!
IT'S NOT AS THOUGH I WAS EVER TRYING TO DECEIVE YOU, AFTER ALL!
GAH HA HA HA!

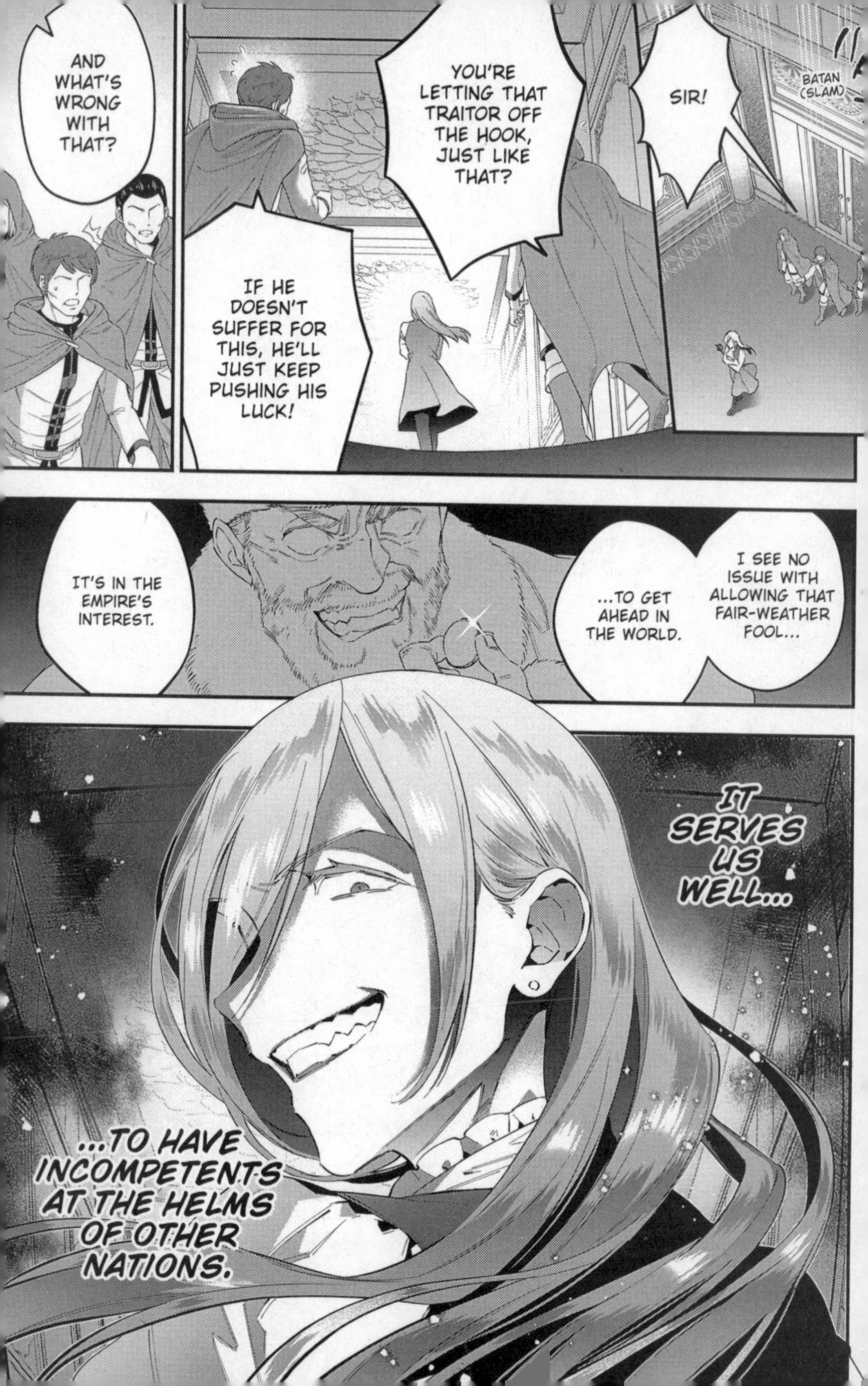
BATAN (SLAM)
SIR!
YOU'RE LETTING THAT TRAITOR OFF THE HOOK, JUST LIKE THAT?
IF HE DOESN'T SUFFER FOR THIS, HE'LL JUST KEEP PUSHING HIS LUCK!
AND WHAT'S WRONG WITH THAT?
I SEE NO ISSUE WITH ALLOWING THAT FAIR-WEATHER FOOL...
...TO GET AHEAD IN THE WORLD.
IT'S IN THE EMPIRE'S INTEREST.
IT SERVES US WELL...
...TO HAVE INCOMPETENTS AT THE HELMS OF OTHER NATIONS.

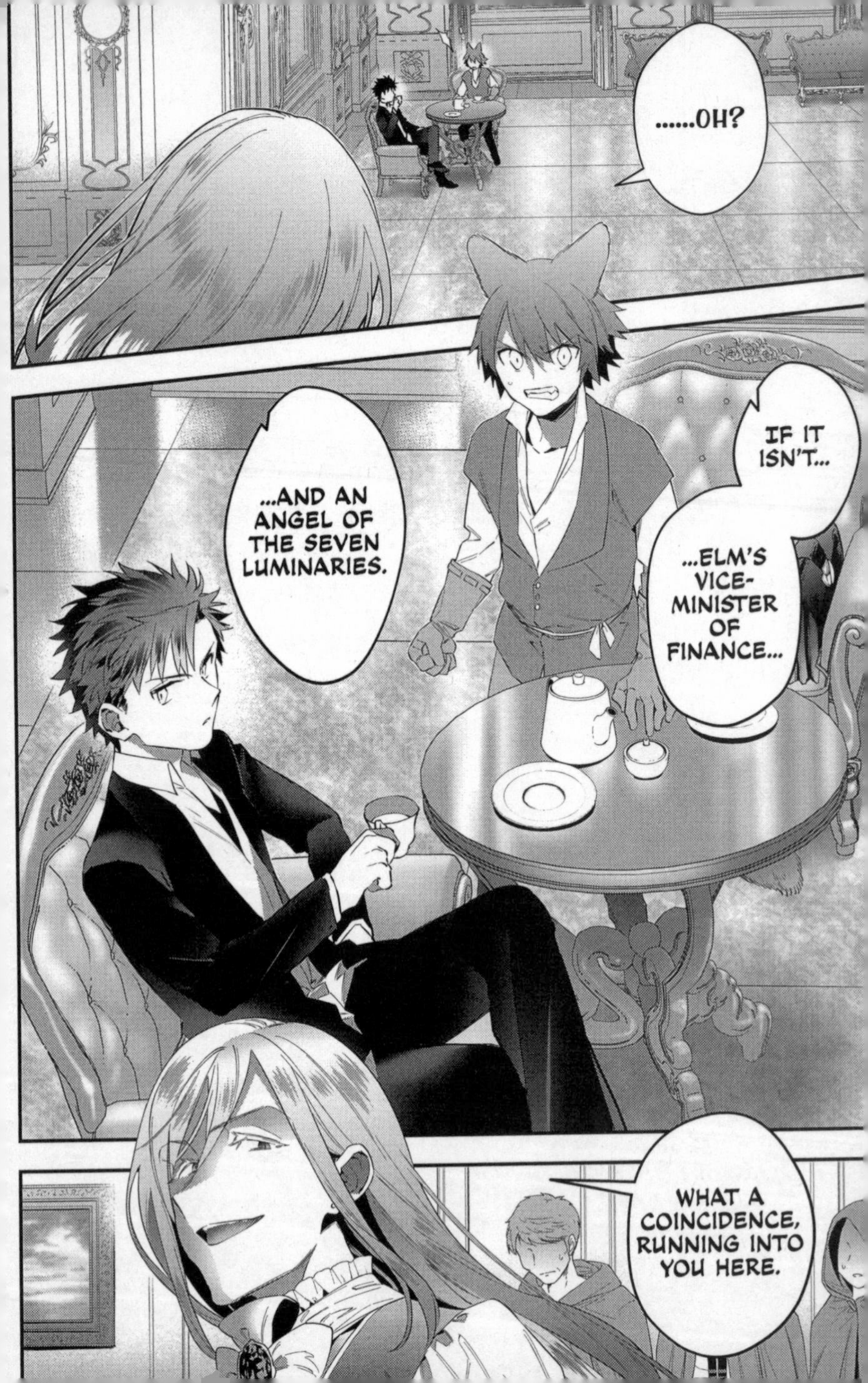
......OH?
IF IT ISN'T...
...ELM'S VICE-MINISTER OF FINANCE...
...AND AN ANGEL OF THE SEVEN LUMINARIES.
WHAT A COINCIDENCE, RUNNING INTO YOU HERE.

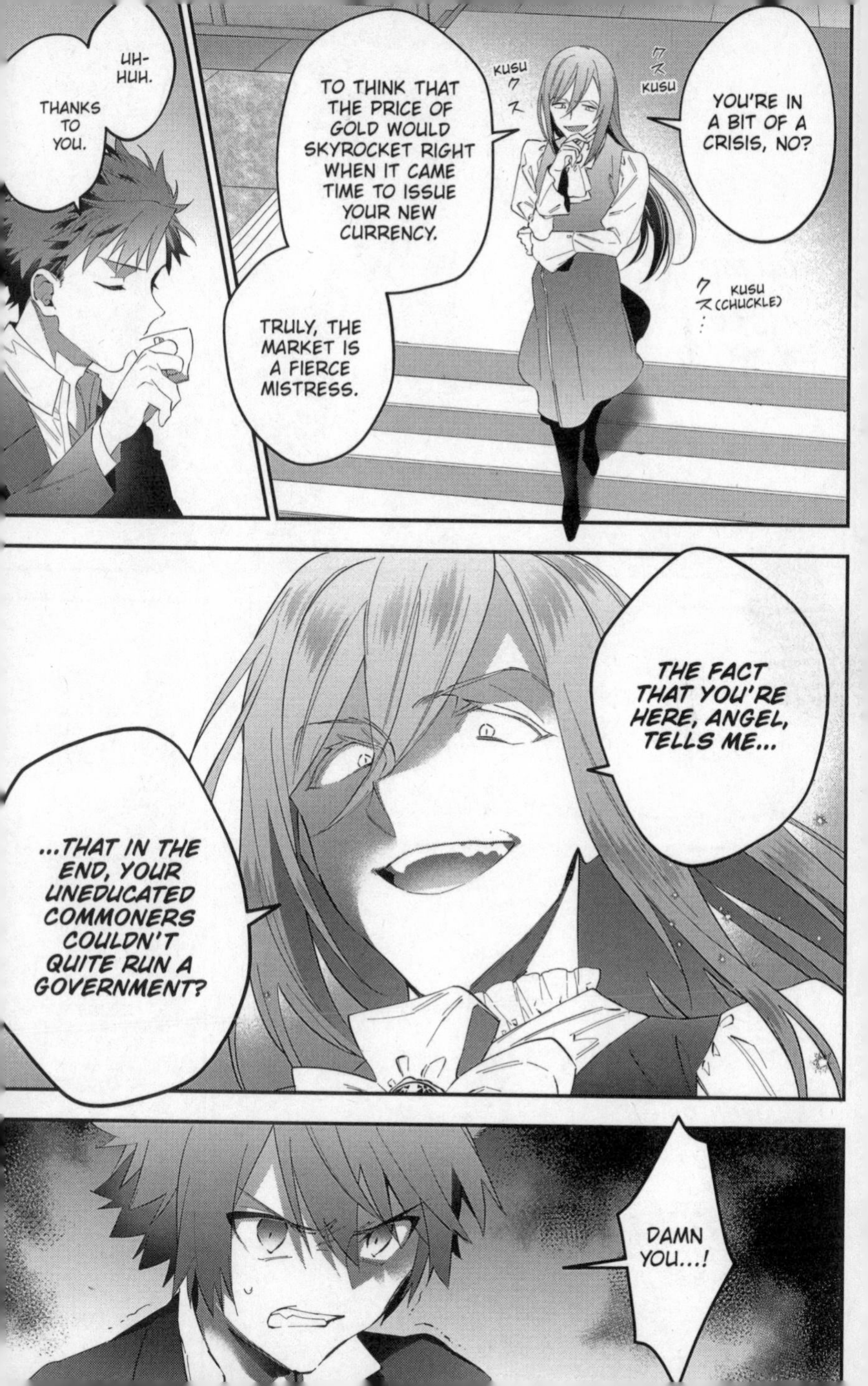
YOU'RE IN A BIT OF A CRISIS, NO?
クス KUSU
KUSU クス
TO THINK THAT THE PRICE OF GOLD WOULD SKYROCKET RIGHT WHEN IT CAME TIME TO ISSUE YOUR NEW CURRENCY.
TRULY, THE MARKET IS A FIERCE MISTRESS.
クス KUSU (CHUCKLE) ...
UH-HUH.
THANKS TO YOU.
THE FACT THAT YOU'RE HERE, ANGEL, TELLS ME...
...THAT IN THE END, YOUR UNEDUCATED COMMONERS COULDN'T QUITE RUN A GOVERNMENT?
DAMN YOU...!

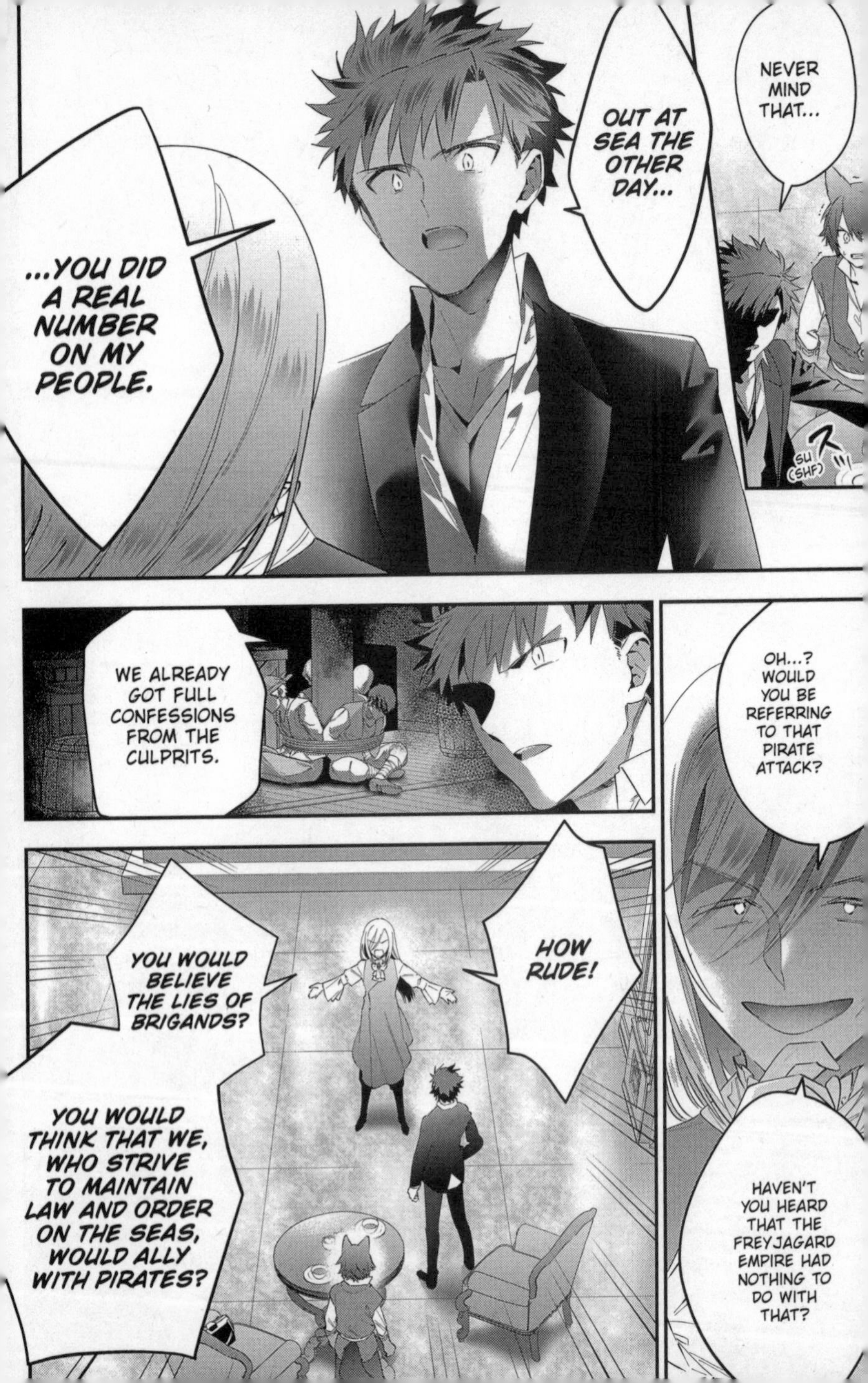
NEVER MIND THAT...
SU (SHF)
OUT AT SEA THE OTHER DAY...
...YOU DID A REAL NUMBER ON MY PEOPLE.
OH...? WOULD YOU BE REFERRING TO THAT PIRATE ATTACK?
HAVEN'T YOU HEARD THAT THE FREYJAGARD EMPIRE HAD NOTHING TO DO WITH THAT?
WE ALREADY GOT FULL CONFESSIONS FROM THE CULPRITS.
HOW RUDE!
YOU WOULD BELIEVE THE LIES OF BRIGANDS?
YOU WOULD THINK THAT WE, WHO STRIVE TO MAINTAIN LAW AND ORDER ON THE SEAS, WOULD ALLY WITH PIRATES?

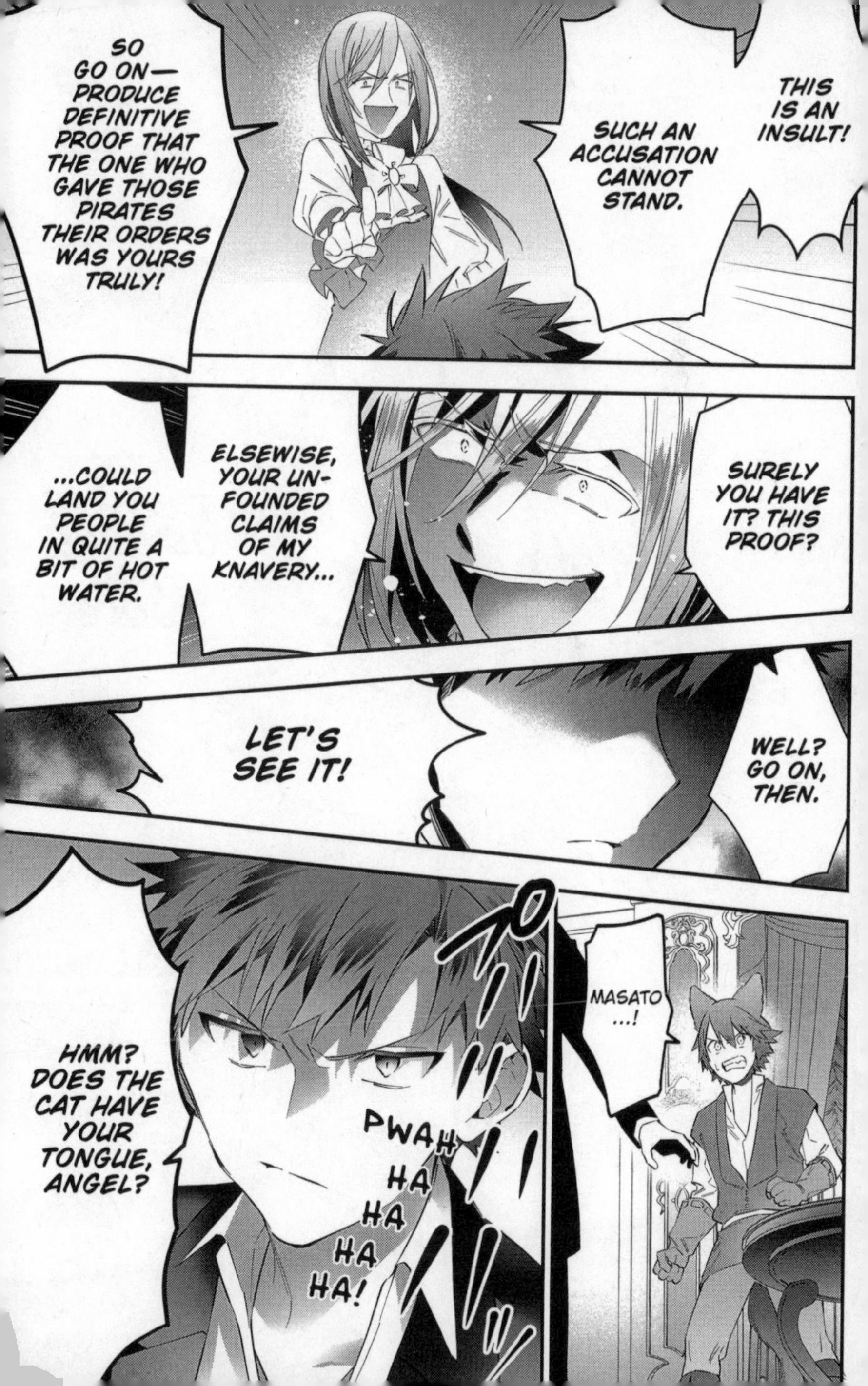
THIS IS AN INSULT!
SUCH AN ACCUSATION CANNOT STAND.
SO GO ON—PRODUCE DEFINITIVE PROOF THAT THE ONE WHO GAVE THOSE PIRATES THEIR ORDERS WAS YOURS TRULY!
SURELY YOU HAVE IT? THIS PROOF?
ELSEWISE, YOUR UN-FOUNDED CLAIMS OF MY KNAVERY...
...COULD LAND YOU PEOPLE IN QUITE A BIT OF HOT WATER.
WELL? GO ON, THEN.
LET'S SEE IT!
MASATO ...!
PWAH HA HA HA HA!
HMM? DOES THE CAT HAVE YOUR TONGUE, ANGEL?

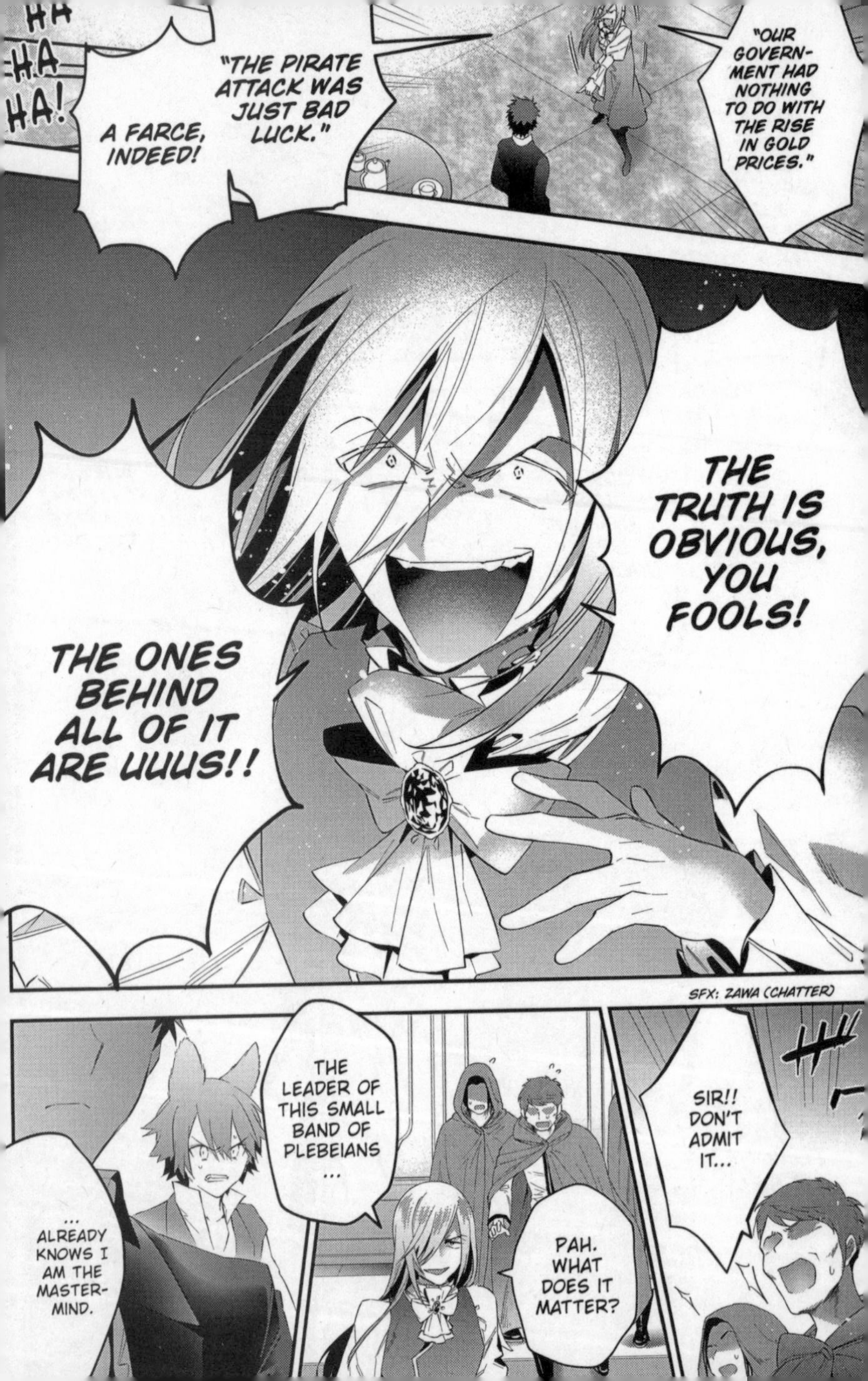
"OUR GOVERNMENT HAD NOTHING TO DO WITH THE RISE IN GOLD PRICES."
"THE PIRATE ATTACK WAS JUST BAD LUCK."
A FARCE, INDEED!
HA HA HA!
THE TRUTH IS OBVIOUS, YOU FOOLS!
THE ONES BEHIND ALL OF IT ARE UUUS!!
SFX: ZAWA (CHATTER)
SIR!! DON'T ADMIT IT...
PAH. WHAT DOES IT MATTER?
THE LEADER OF THIS SMALL BAND OF PLEBEIANS...
...ALREADY KNOWS I AM THE MASTERMIND.

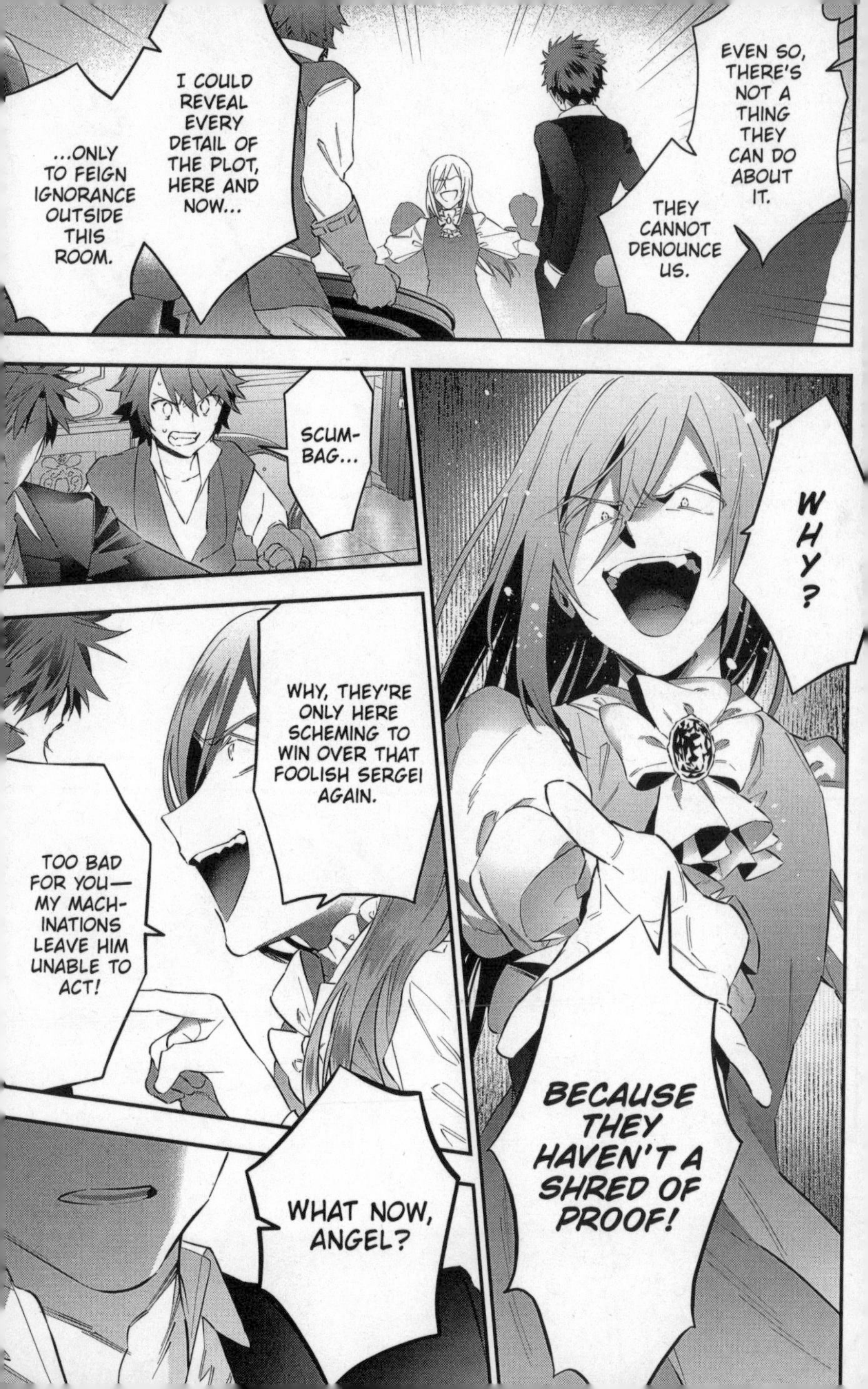
EVEN SO, THERE'S NOT A THING THEY CAN DO ABOUT IT.
THEY CANNOT DENOUNCE US.
I COULD REVEAL EVERY DETAIL OF THE PLOT, HERE AND NOW...
...ONLY TO FEIGN IGNORANCE OUTSIDE THIS ROOM.
WHY?
BECAUSE THEY HAVEN'T A SHRED OF PROOF!
SCUM-BAG...
WHY, THEY'RE ONLY HERE SCHEMING TO WIN OVER THAT FOOLISH SERGEI AGAIN.
TOO BAD FOR YOU— MY MACH-INATIONS LEAVE HIM UNABLE TO ACT!
WHAT NOW, ANGEL?

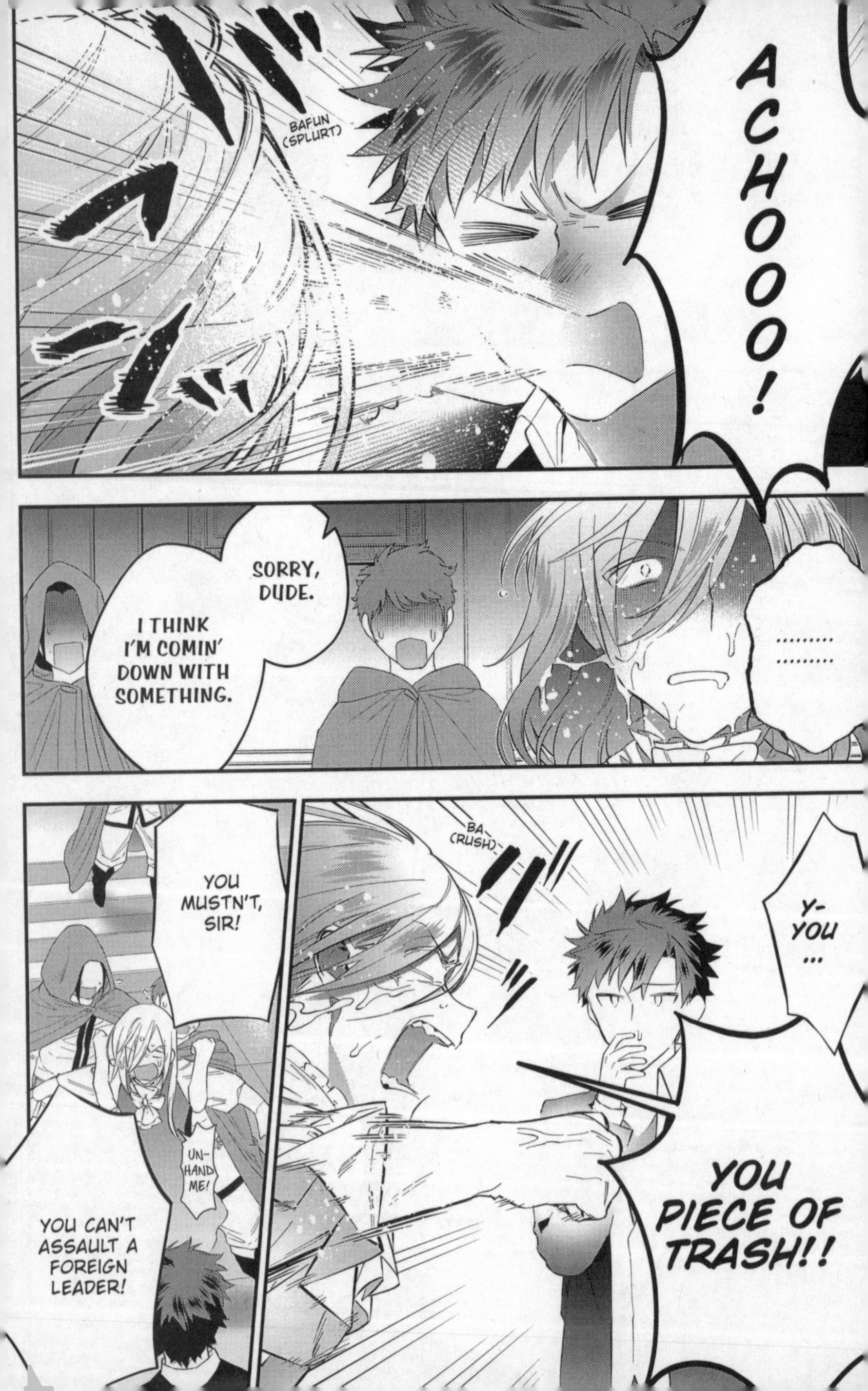
ACHOOOO!
BAFUN (SPLURT)
....
SORRY, DUDE.
I THINK I'M COMIN' DOWN WITH SOMETHING.
Y-YOU...
YOU PIECE OF TRASH!!
BA (RUSH)
YOU MUSTN'T, SIR!
UN-HAND ME!
YOU CAN'T ASSAULT A FOREIGN LEADER!

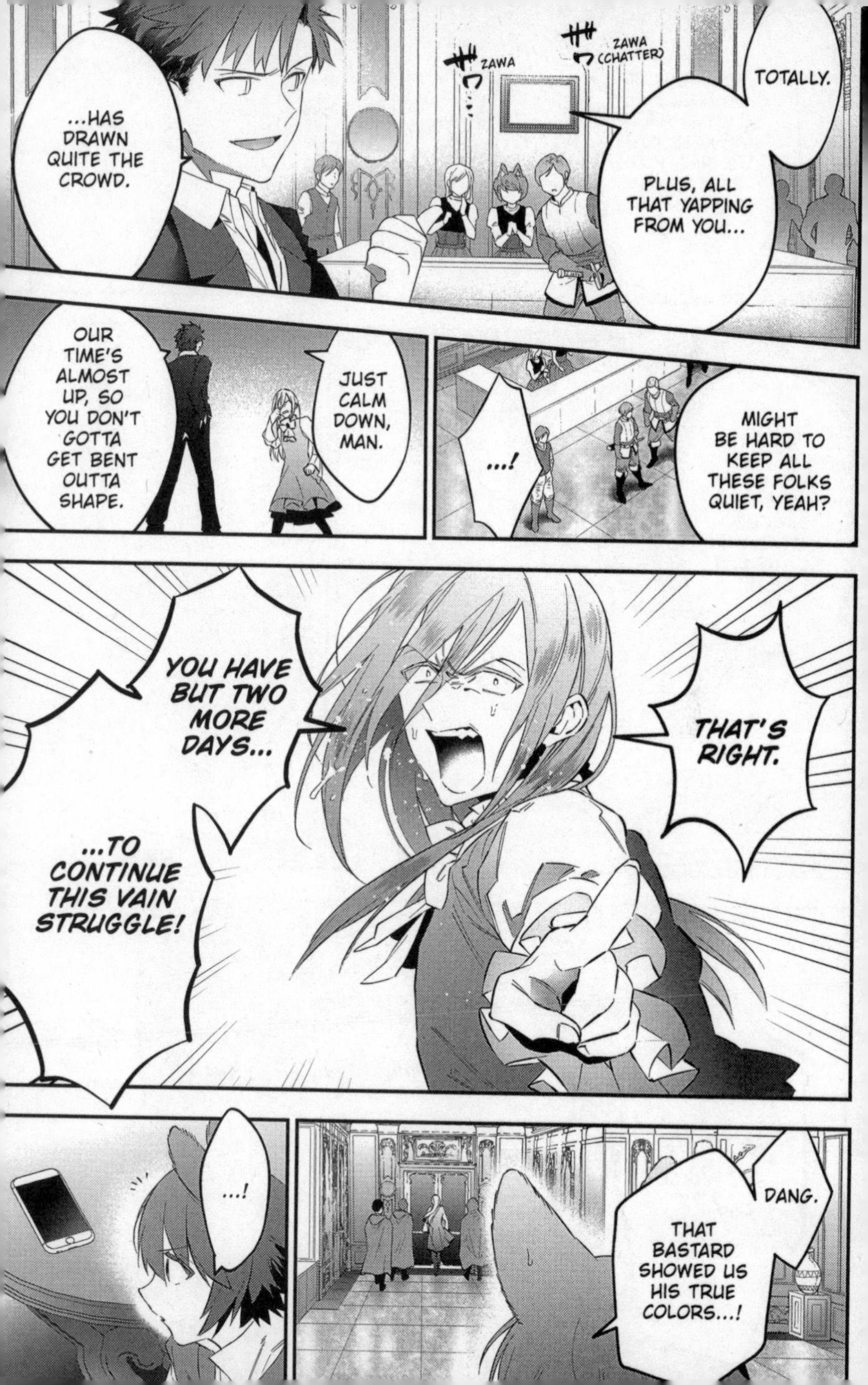
ZAWA (CHATTER)
ZAWA
TOTALLY.
PLUS, ALL THAT YAPPING FROM YOU...
...HAS DRAWN QUITE THE CROWD.
MIGHT BE HARD TO KEEP ALL THESE FOLKS QUIET, YEAH?
...!
JUST CALM DOWN, MAN.
OUR TIME'S ALMOST UP, SO YOU DON'T GOTTA GET BENT OUTTA SHAPE.
THAT'S RIGHT.
YOU HAVE BUT TWO MORE DAYS...
...TO CONTINUE THIS VAIN STRUGGLE!
DANG.
THAT BASTARD SHOWED US HIS TRUE COLORS...!
...!

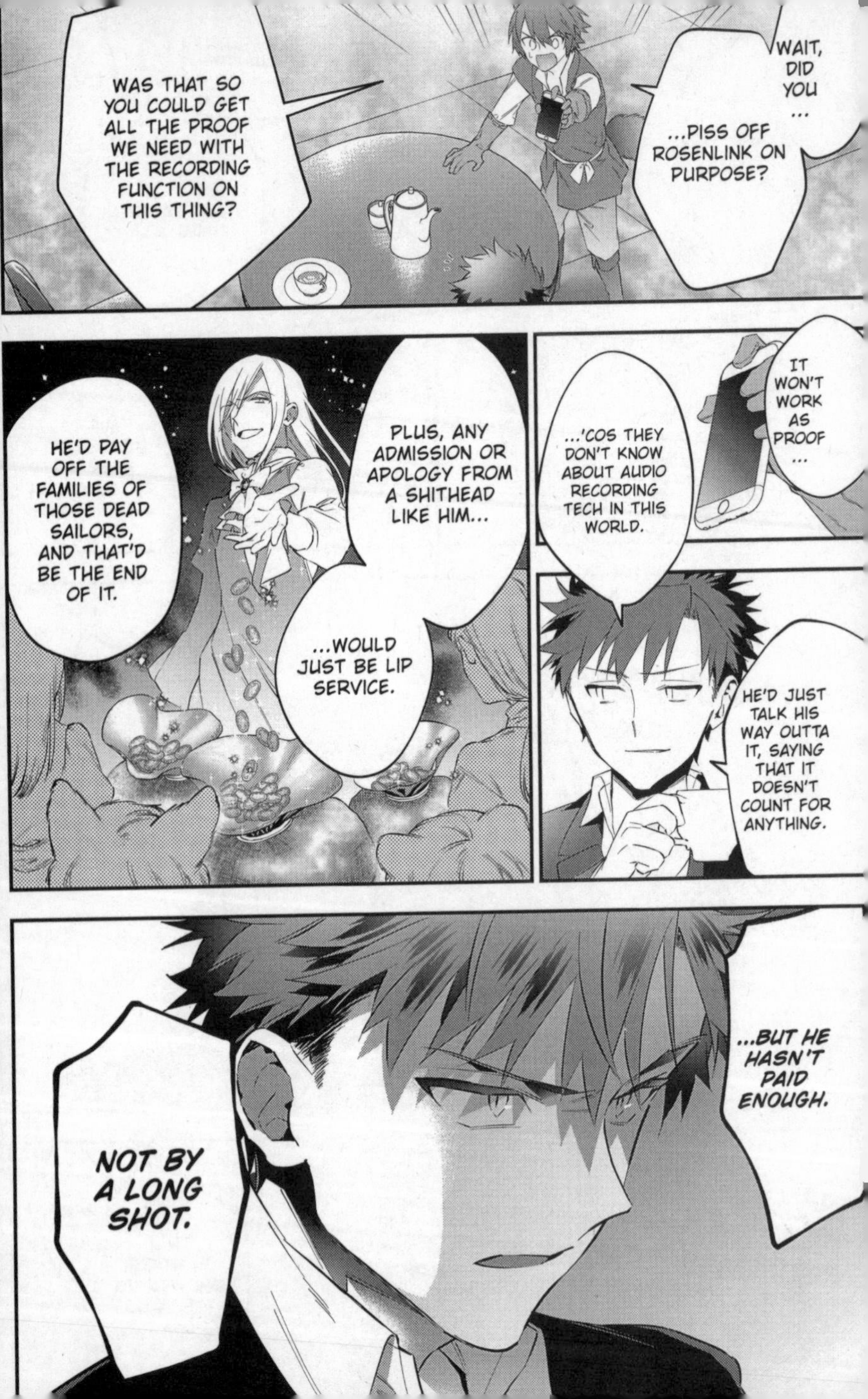
WAIT, DID YOU ...
...PISS OFF ROSENLINK ON PURPOSE?
WAS THAT SO YOU COULD GET ALL THE PROOF WE NEED WITH THE RECORDING FUNCTION ON THIS THING?
IT WON'T WORK AS PROOF ...
...'COS THEY DON'T KNOW ABOUT AUDIO RECORDING TECH IN THIS WORLD.
HE'D JUST TALK HIS WAY OUTTA IT, SAYING THAT IT DOESN'T COUNT FOR ANYTHING.
PLUS, ANY ADMISSION OR APOLOGY FROM A SHITHEAD LIKE HIM...
...WOULD JUST BE LIP SERVICE.
HE'D PAY OFF THE FAMILIES OF THOSE DEAD SAILORS, AND THAT'D BE THE END OF IT.
...BUT HE HASN'T PAID ENOUGH.
NOT BY A LONG SHOT.

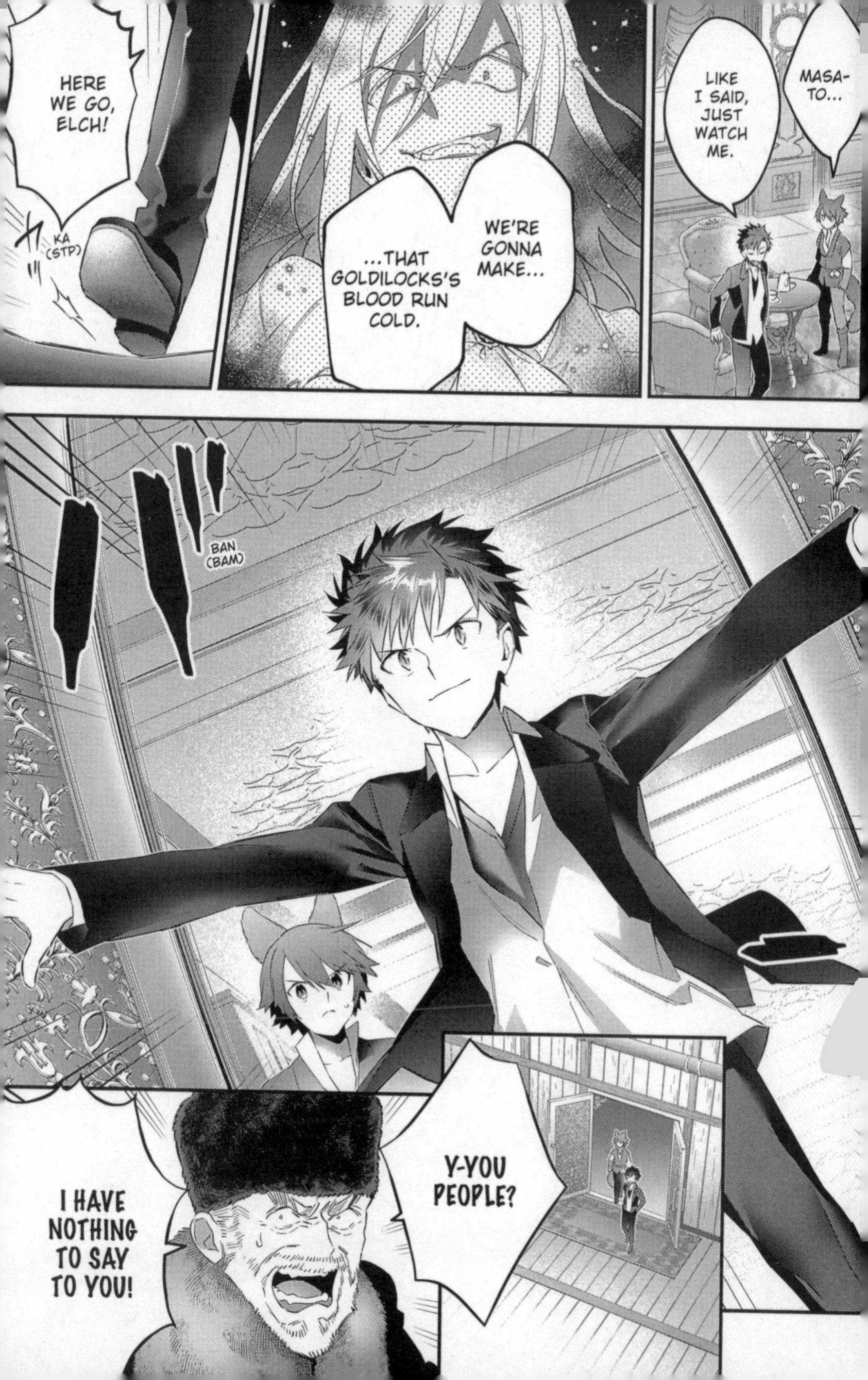
MASA-TO...
LIKE I SAID, JUST WATCH ME.
WE'RE GONNA MAKE...
...THAT GOLDILOCKS'S BLOOD RUN COLD.
HERE WE GO, ELCH!
KA (STP)
BAN (BAM)
Y-YOU PEOPLE?
I HAVE NOTHING TO SAY TO YOU!

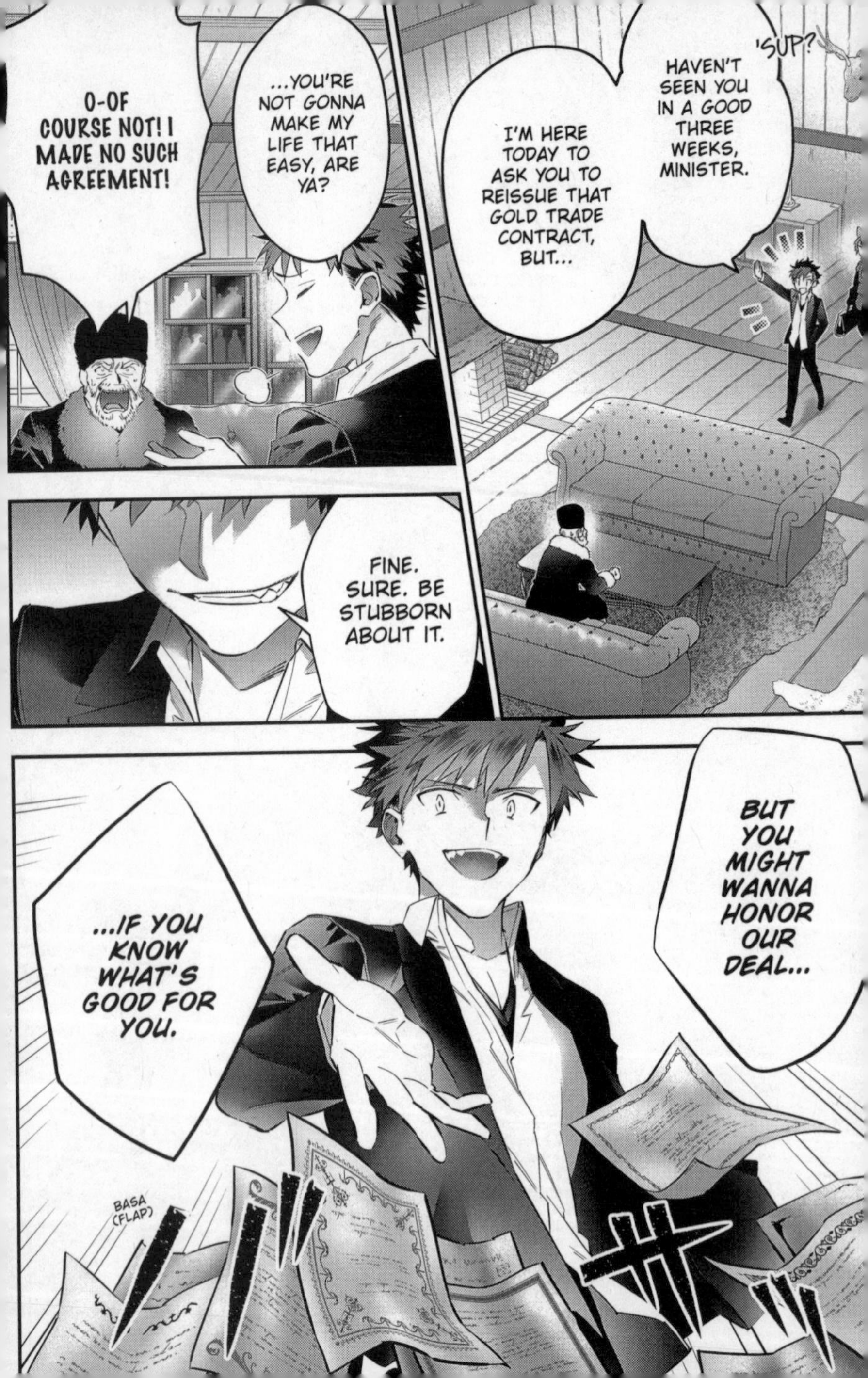
'SUP?
HAVEN'T SEEN YOU IN A GOOD THREE WEEKS, MINISTER.
I'M HERE TODAY TO ASK YOU TO REISSUE THAT GOLD TRADE CONTRACT, BUT...
...YOU'RE NOT GONNA MAKE MY LIFE THAT EASY, ARE YA?
O-OF COURSE NOT!! I MADE NO SUCH AGREEMENT!
FINE. SURE. BE STUBBORN ABOUT IT.
BUT YOU MIGHT WANNA HONOR OUR DEAL...
...IF YOU KNOW WHAT'S GOOD FOR YOU.
BASA (FLAP)

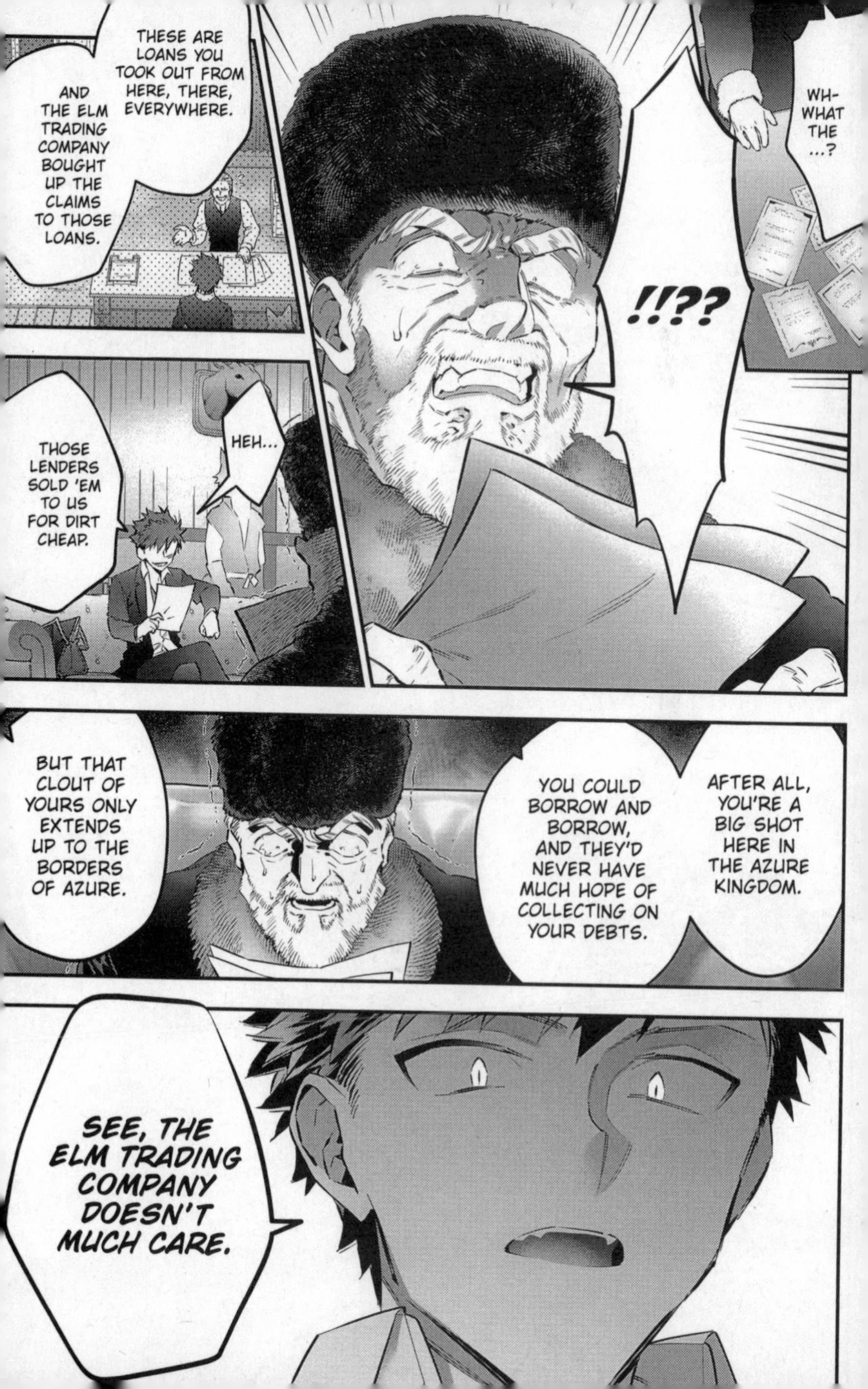
WH- WHAT THE ...?
!!??
THESE ARE LOANS YOU TOOK OUT FROM HERE, THERE, EVERYWHERE.
AND THE ELM TRADING COMPANY BOUGHT UP THE CLAIMS TO THOSE LOANS.
HEH...
THOSE LENDERS SOLD 'EM TO US FOR DIRT CHEAP.
AFTER ALL, YOU'RE A BIG SHOT HERE IN THE AZURE KINGDOM.
YOU COULD BORROW AND BORROW, AND THEY'D NEVER HAVE MUCH HOPE OF COLLECTING ON YOUR DEBTS.
BUT THAT CLOUT OF YOURS ONLY EXTENDS UP TO THE BORDERS OF AZURE.
SEE, THE ELM TRADING COMPANY DOESN'T MUCH CARE.

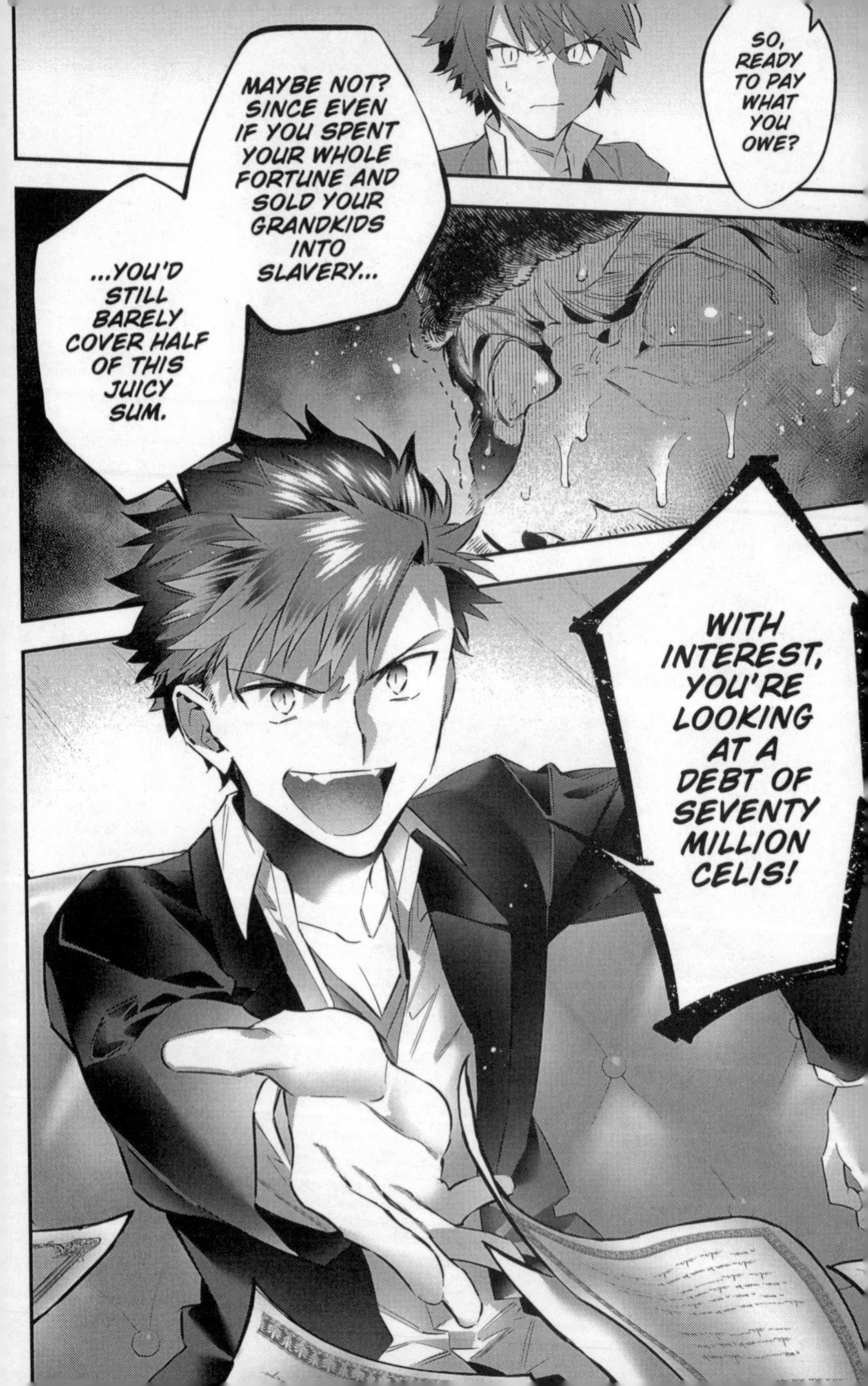
SO, READY TO PAY WHAT YOU OWE?
MAYBE NOT? SINCE EVEN IF YOU SPENT YOUR WHOLE FORTUNE AND SOLD YOUR GRANDKIDS INTO SLAVERY...
...YOU'D STILL BARELY COVER HALF OF THIS JUICY SUM.
WITH INTEREST, YOU'RE LOOKING AT A DEBT OF SEVENTY MILLION CELIS!

HIGH SCHOOL PRODIGIES HAVE IT EASY EVEN IN ANOTHER WORLD!

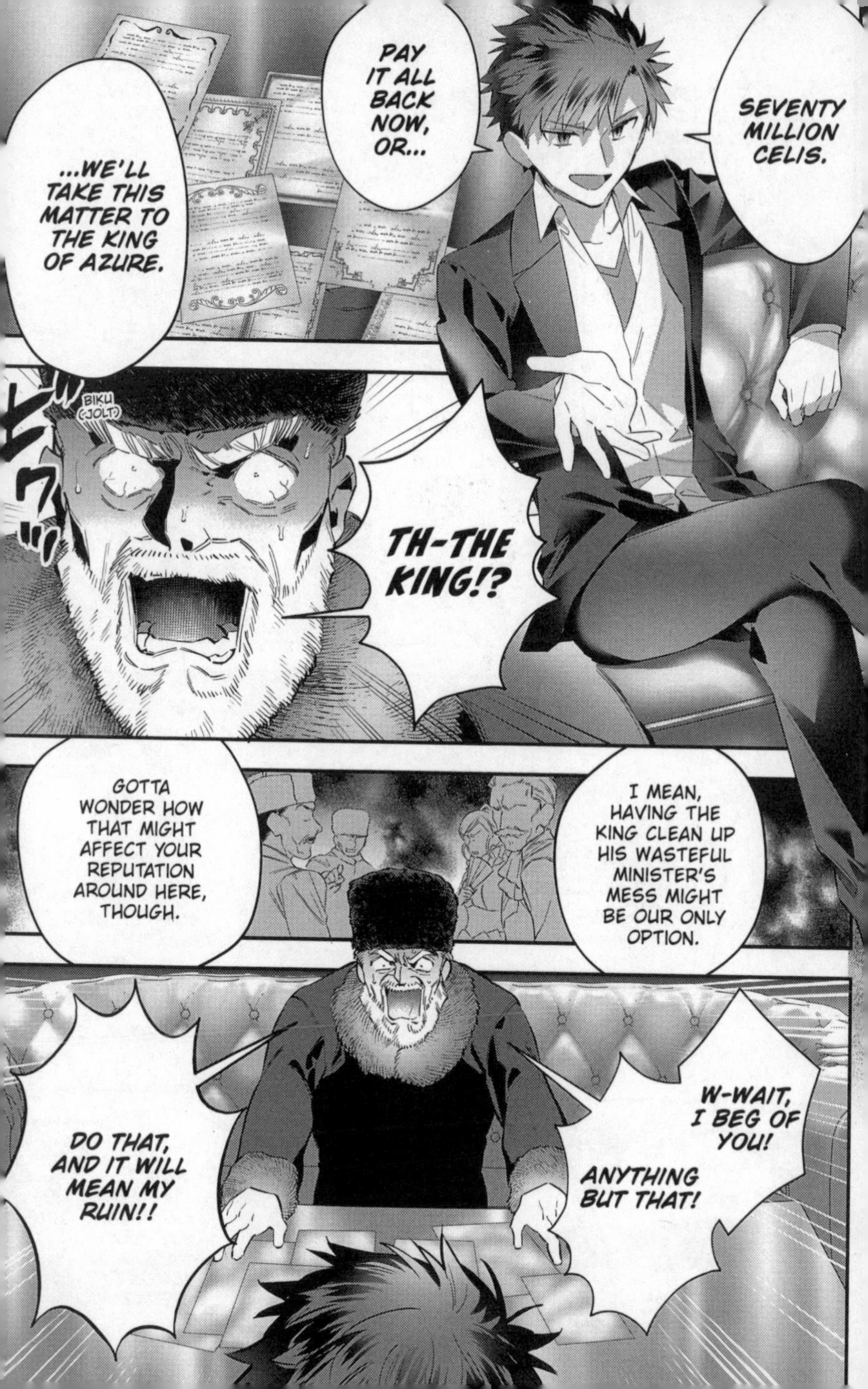
SEVENTY MILLION CELIS.
PAY IT ALL BACK NOW, OR...
...WE'LL TAKE THIS MATTER TO THE KING OF AZURE.
BIKU (-JOLT-)
TH-THE KING!?
I MEAN, HAVING THE KING CLEAN UP HIS WASTEFUL MINISTER'S MESS MIGHT BE OUR ONLY OPTION.
GOTTA WONDER HOW THAT MIGHT AFFECT YOUR REPUTATION AROUND HERE, THOUGH.
W-WAIT, I BEG OF YOU!
ANYTHING BUT THAT!
DO THAT, AND IT WILL MEAN MY RUIN!!

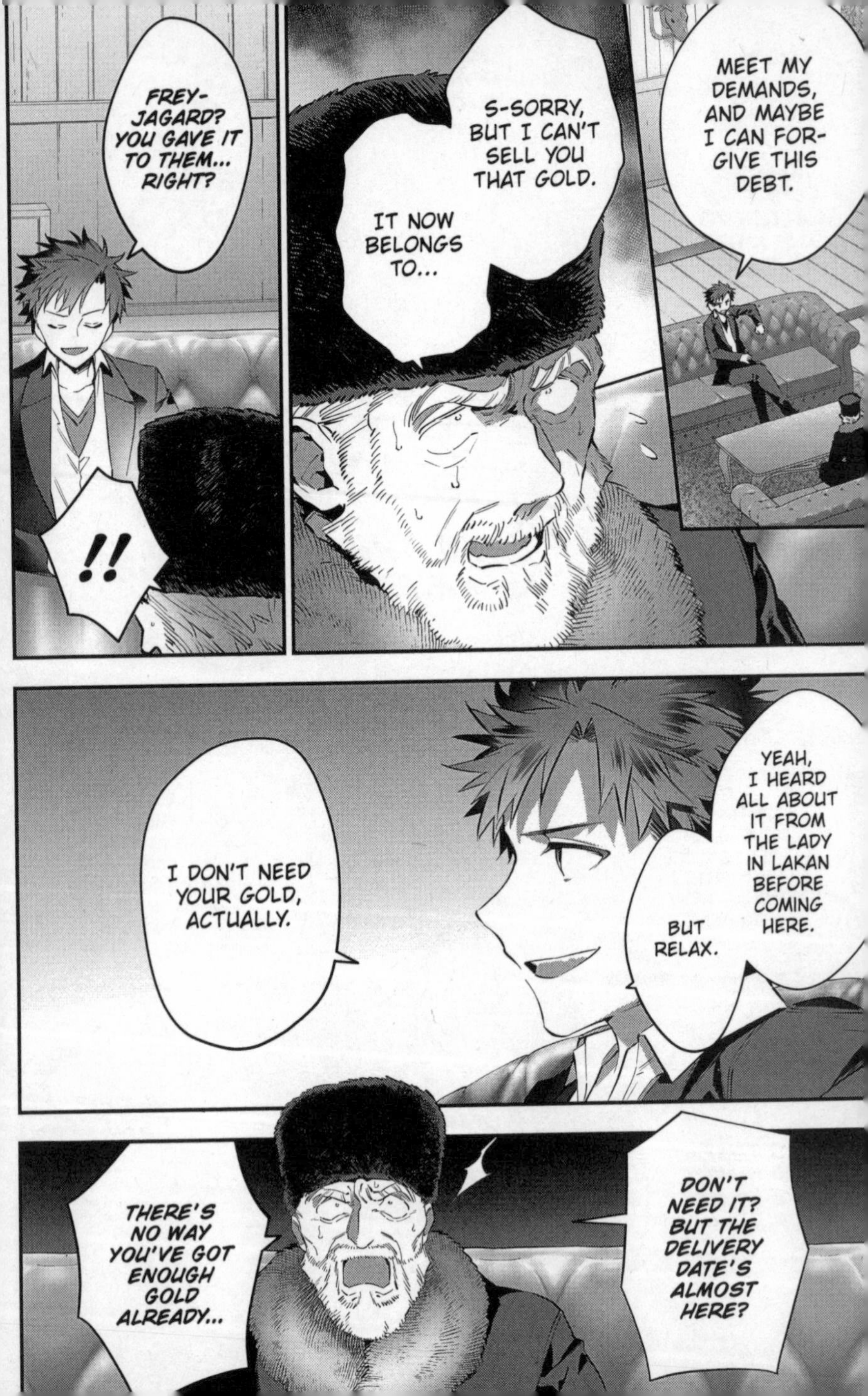
MEET MY DEMANDS, AND MAYBE I CAN FORGIVE THIS DEBT.
S-SORRY, BUT I CAN'T SELL YOU THAT GOLD.
IT NOW BELONGS TO...
FREY-JAGARD? YOU GAVE IT TO THEM... RIGHT?
!!
YEAH, I HEARD ALL ABOUT IT FROM THE LADY IN LAKAN BEFORE COMING HERE.
BUT RELAX.
I DON'T NEED YOUR GOLD, ACTUALLY.
DON'T NEED IT? BUT THE DELIVERY DATE'S ALMOST HERE?
THERE'S NO WAY YOU'VE GOT ENOUGH GOLD ALREADY...

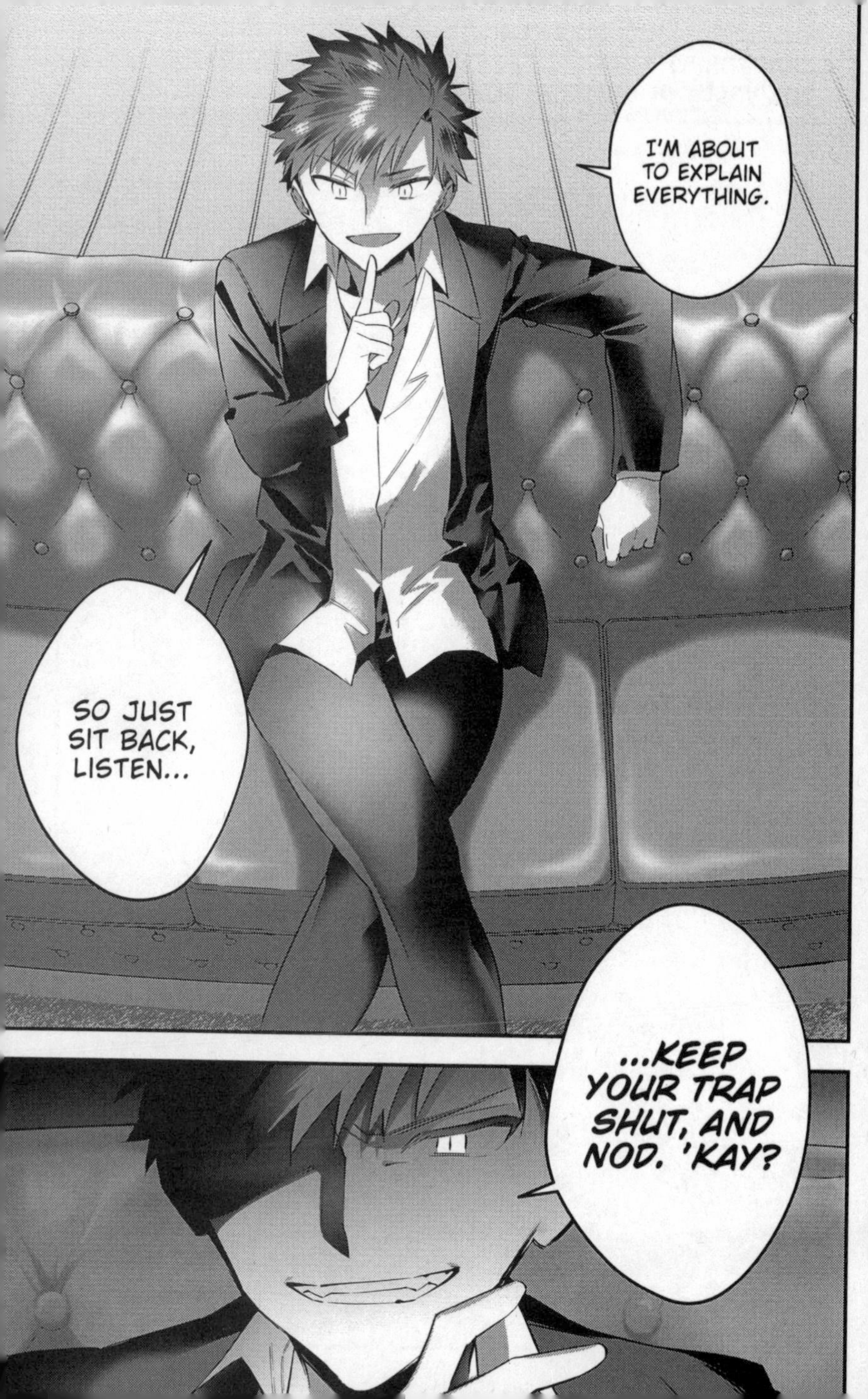
I'M ABOUT TO EXPLAIN EVERYTHING.
SO JUST SIT BACK, LISTEN...
...KEEP YOUR TRAP SHUT, AND NOD. 'KAY?

CHAPTER 59:
THE VALUE OF COMMON SENSE

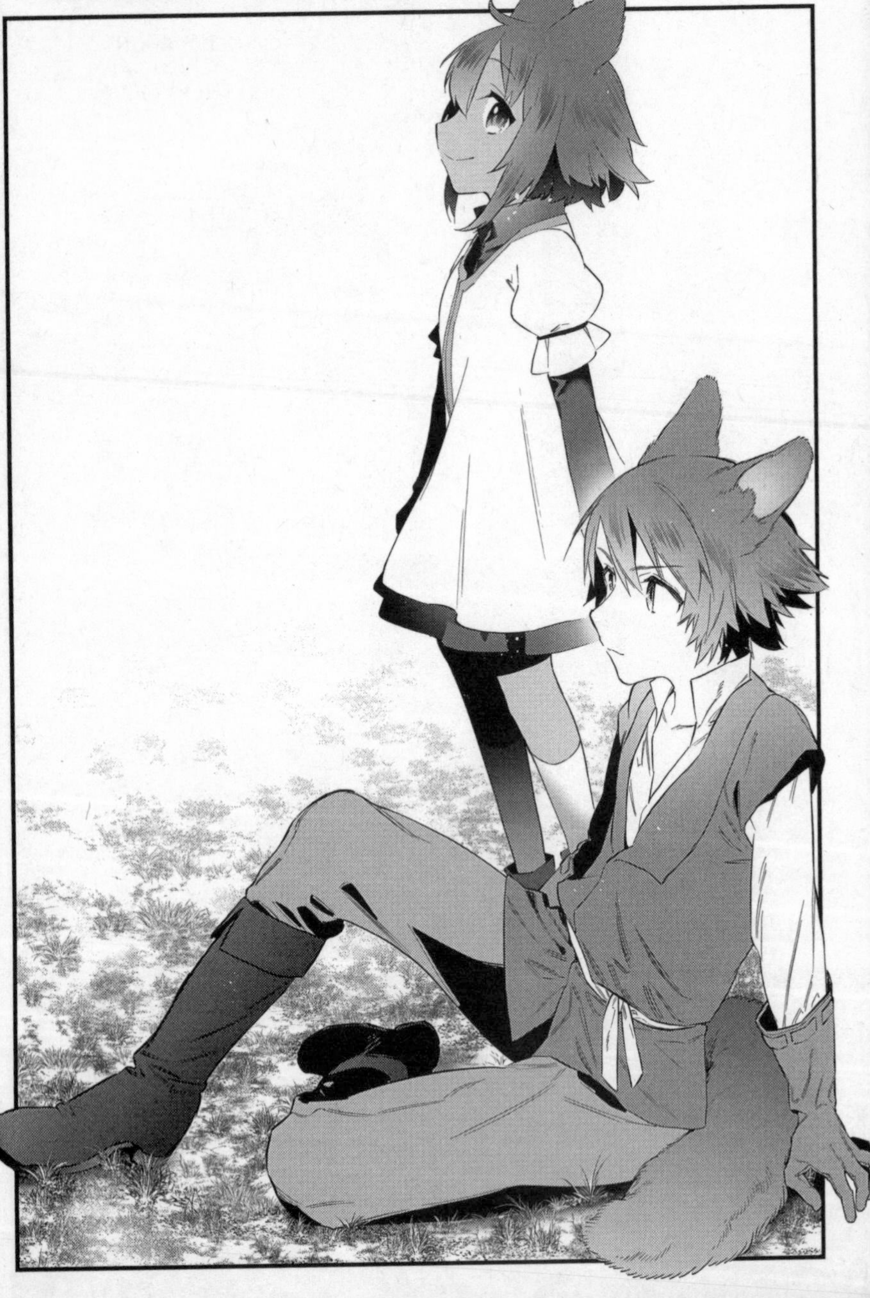

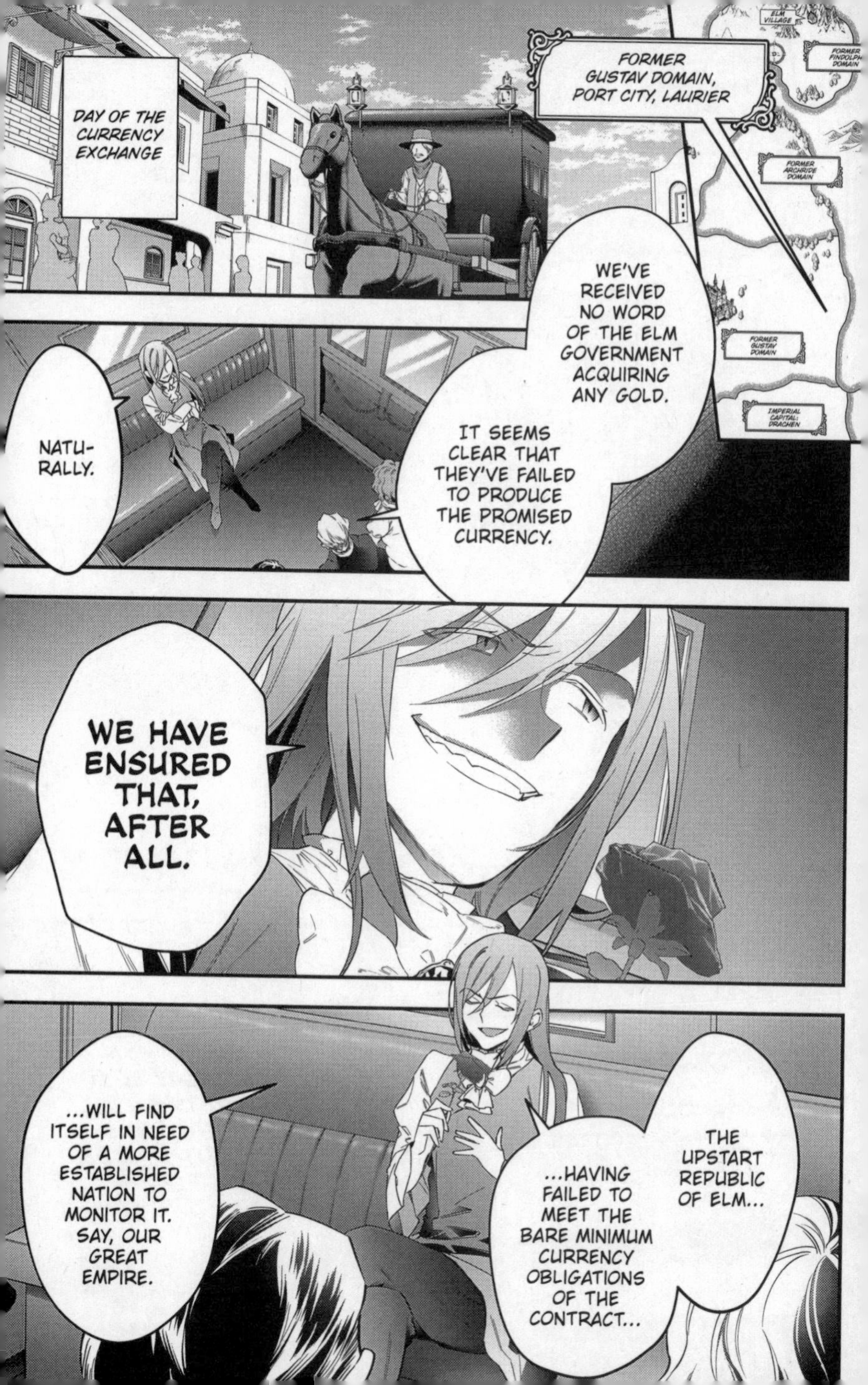
ELM VILLAGE
FORMER FINDOLPH DOMAIN
FORMER ARCHRIDE DOMAIN
FORMER GUSTAV DOMAIN
IMPERIAL CAPITAL: DRACHEN
FORMER GUSTAV DOMAIN, PORT CITY, LAURIER
DAY OF THE CURRENCY EXCHANGE
WE'VE RECEIVED NO WORD OF THE ELM GOVERNMENT ACQUIRING ANY GOLD.
IT SEEMS CLEAR THAT THEY'VE FAILED TO PRODUCE THE PROMISED CURRENCY.
NATU-RALLY.
WE HAVE ENSURED THAT, AFTER ALL.
THE UPSTART REPUBLIC OF ELM...
...HAVING FAILED TO MEET THE BARE MINIMUM CURRENCY OBLIGATIONS OF THE CONTRACT...
...WILL FIND ITSELF IN NEED OF A MORE ESTABLISHED NATION TO MONITOR IT. SAY, OUR GREAT EMPIRE.

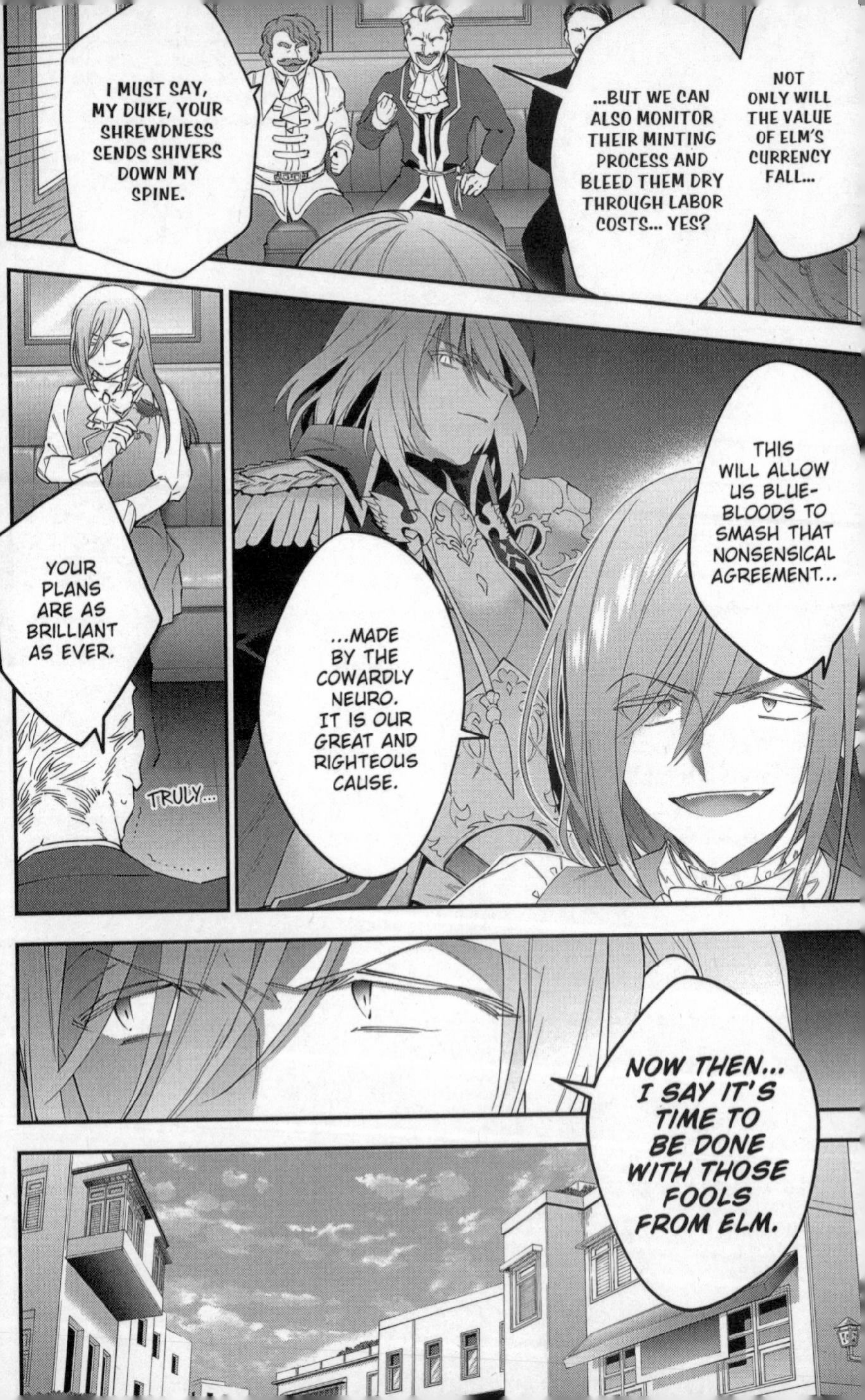
NOT ONLY WILL THE VALUE OF ELM'S CURRENCY FALL...
...BUT WE CAN ALSO MONITOR THEIR MINTING PROCESS AND BLEED THEM DRY THROUGH LABOR COSTS... YES?
I MUST SAY, MY DUKE, YOUR SHREWDNESS SENDS SHIVERS DOWN MY SPINE.
THIS WILL ALLOW US BLUE-BLOODS TO SMASH THAT NONSENSICAL AGREEMENT...
...MADE BY THE COWARDLY NEURO. IT IS OUR GREAT AND RIGHTEOUS CAUSE.
YOUR PLANS ARE AS BRILLIANT AS EVER.
TRULY...
NOW THEN... I SAY IT'S TIME TO BE DONE WITH THOSE FOOLS FROM ELM.

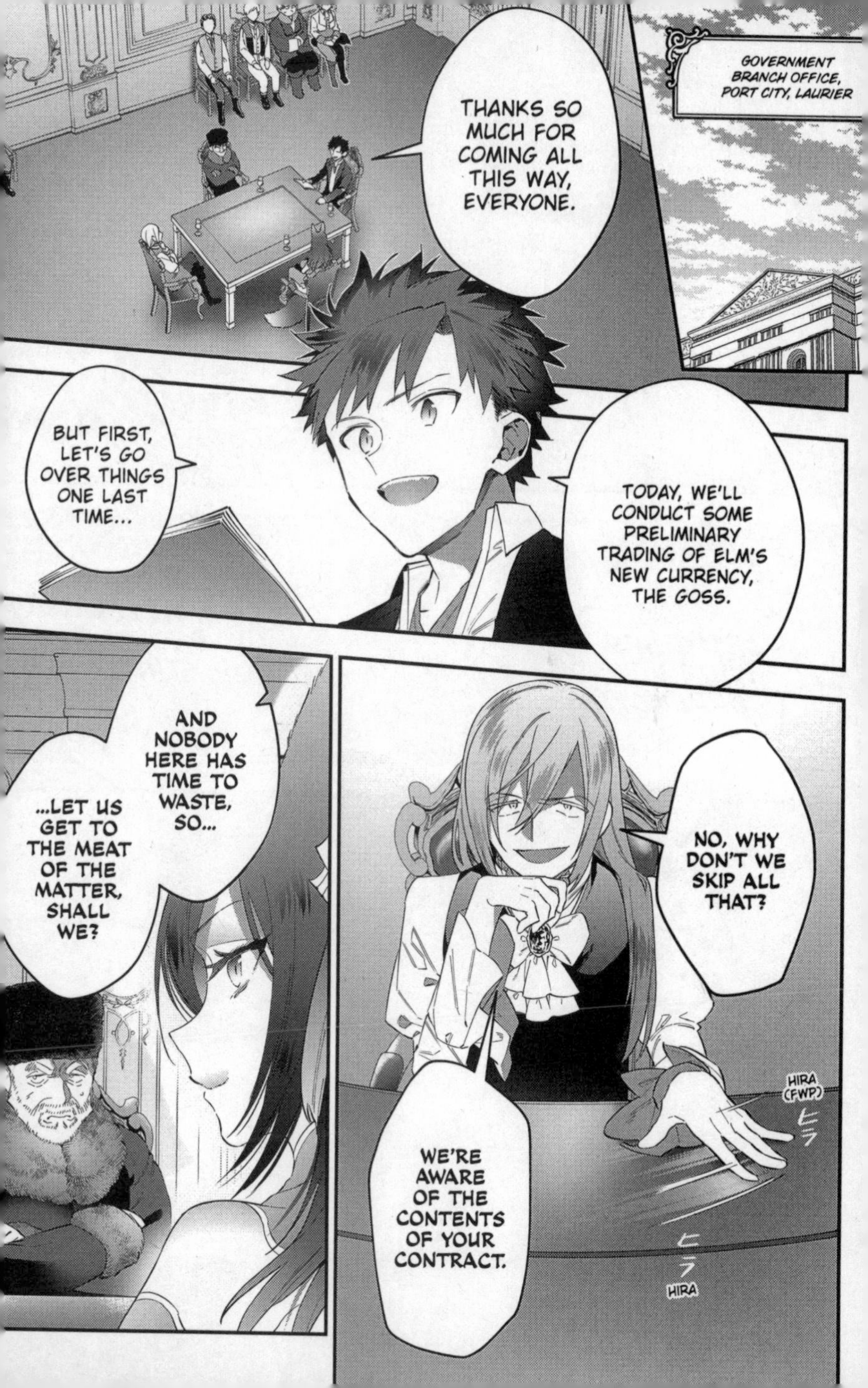
GOVERNMENT BRANCH OFFICE, PORT CITY, LAURIER
THANKS SO MUCH FOR COMING ALL THIS WAY, EVERYONE.
TODAY, WE'LL CONDUCT SOME PRELIMINARY TRADING OF ELM'S NEW CURRENCY, THE GOSS.
BUT FIRST, LET'S GO OVER THINGS ONE LAST TIME...
NO, WHY DON'T WE SKIP ALL THAT?
HIRA (FWP)
HIRA
WE'RE AWARE OF THE CONTENTS OF YOUR CONTRACT.
AND NOBODY HERE HAS TIME TO WASTE, SO...
...LET US GET TO THE MEAT OF THE MATTER, SHALL WE?

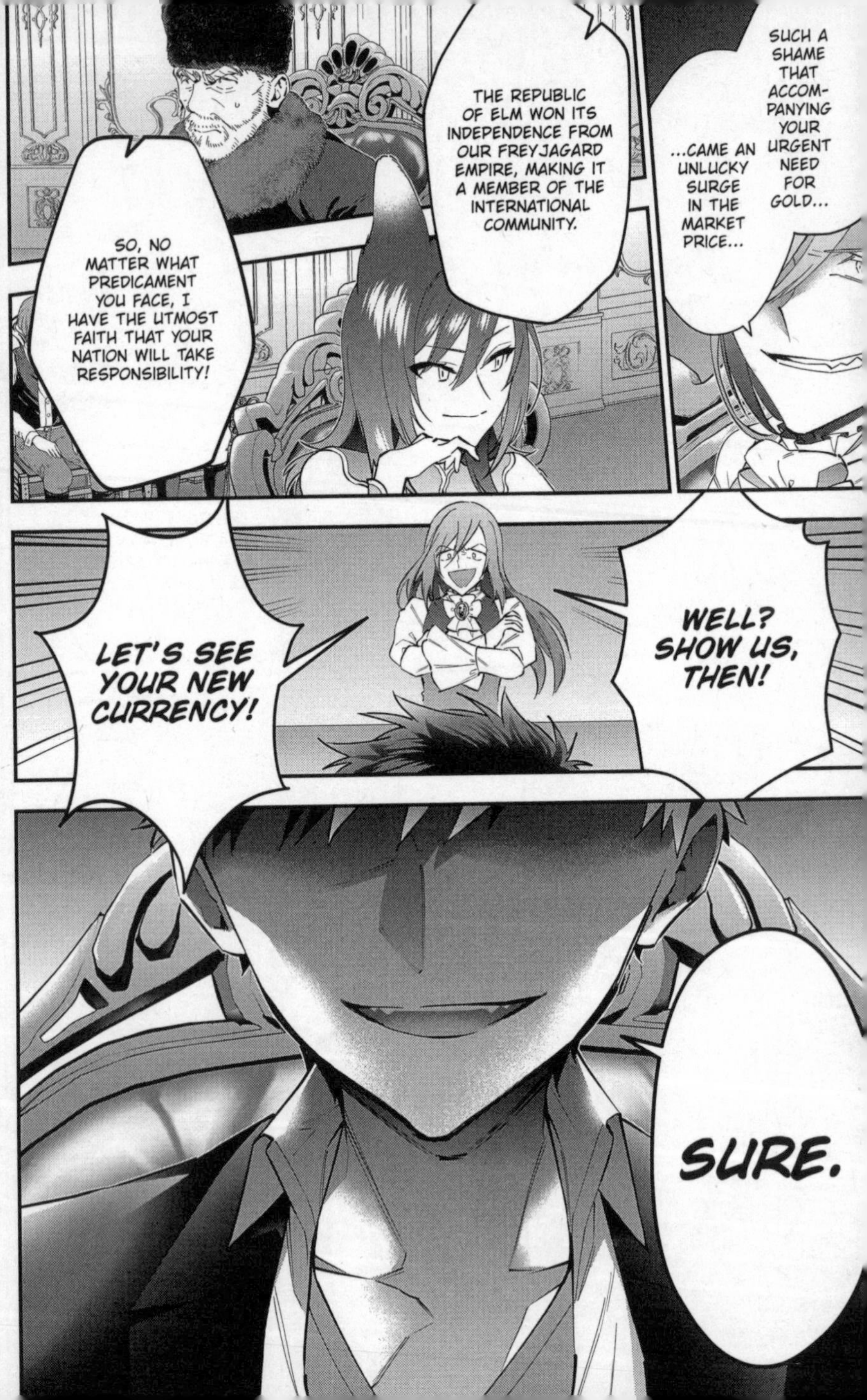
SUCH A SHAME THAT ACCOMPANYING YOUR URGENT NEED FOR GOLD...
...CAME AN UNLUCKY SURGE IN THE MARKET PRICE...
THE REPUBLIC OF ELM WON ITS INDEPENDENCE FROM OUR FREYJAGARD EMPIRE, MAKING IT A MEMBER OF THE INTERNATIONAL COMMUNITY.
SO, NO MATTER WHAT PREDICAMENT YOU FACE, I HAVE THE UTMOST FAITH THAT YOUR NATION WILL TAKE RESPONSIBILITY!
WELL? SHOW US, THEN!
LET'S SEE YOUR NEW CURRENCY!
SURE.

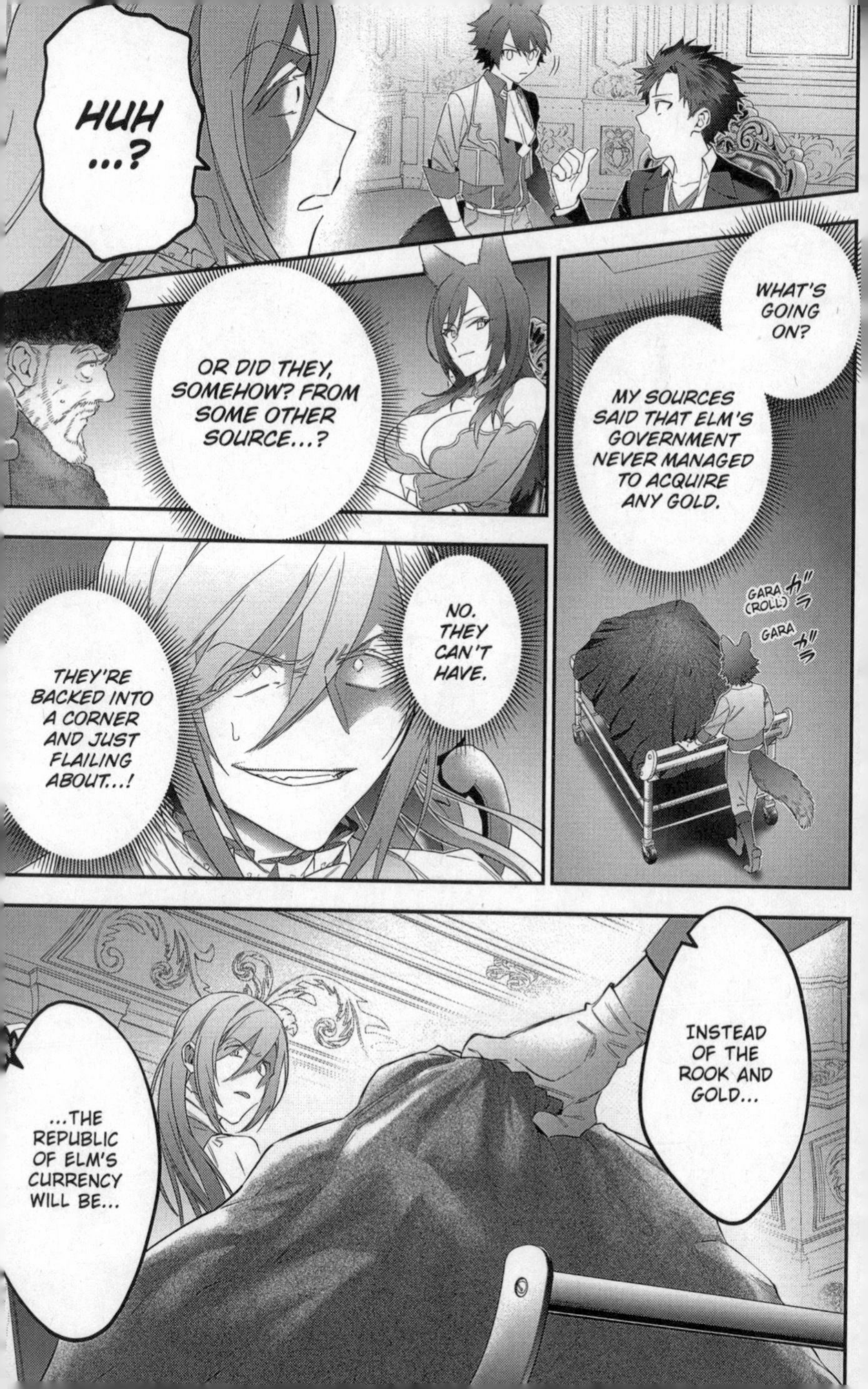
HUH ...?
WHAT'S GOING ON?
MY SOURCES SAID THAT ELM'S GOVERNMENT NEVER MANAGED TO ACQUIRE ANY GOLD.
GARA (ROLL) ガラ
GARA ガラ
OR DID THEY, SOMEHOW? FROM SOME OTHER SOURCE...?
NO. THEY CAN'T HAVE.
THEY'RE BACKED INTO A CORNER AND JUST FLAILING ABOUT...!
INSTEAD OF THE ROOK AND GOLD...
...THE REPUBLIC OF ELM'S CURRENCY WILL BE...

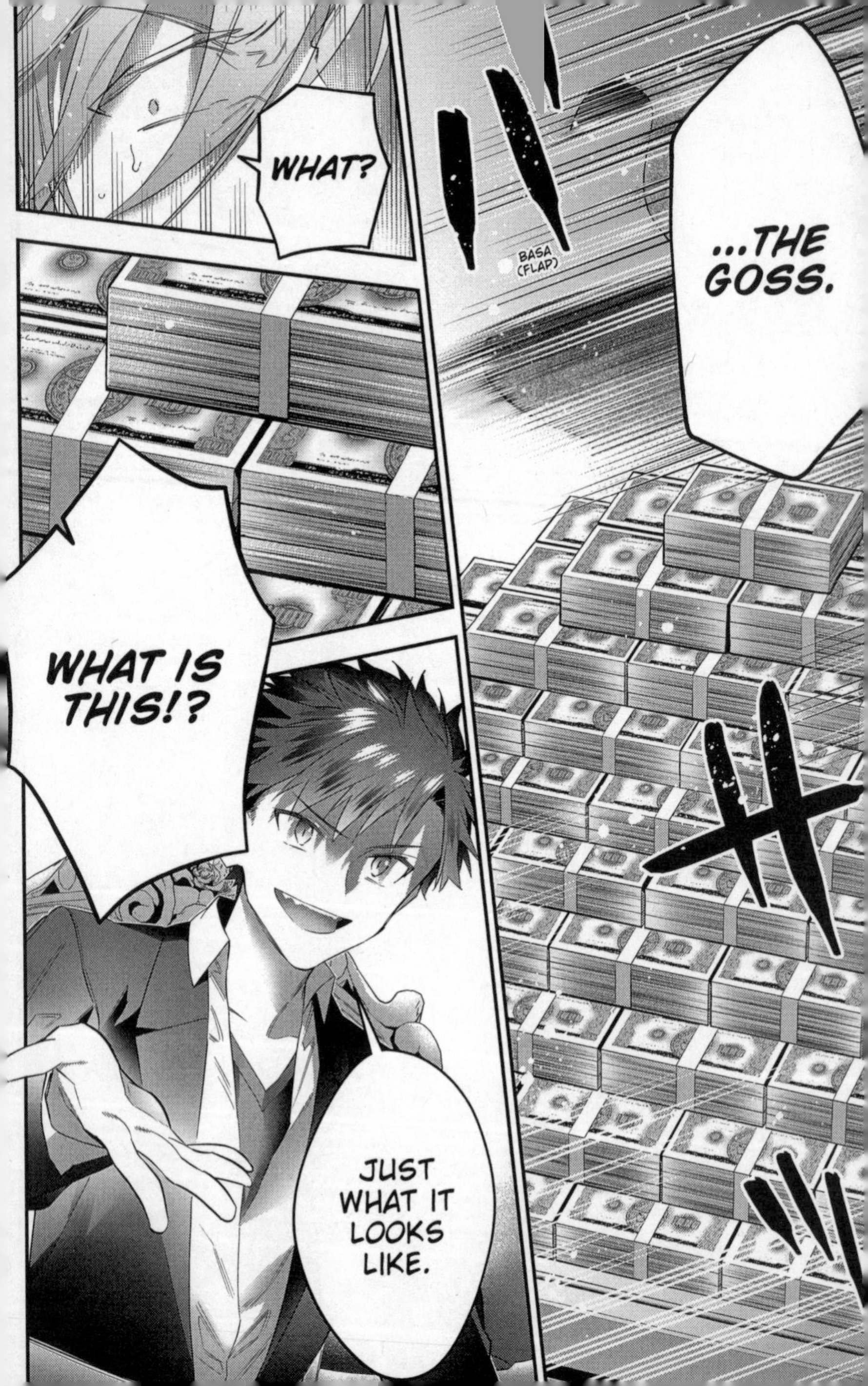

BASA (FLAP)
...THE GOSS.
WHAT?
WHAT IS THIS!?
JUST WHAT IT LOOKS LIKE.

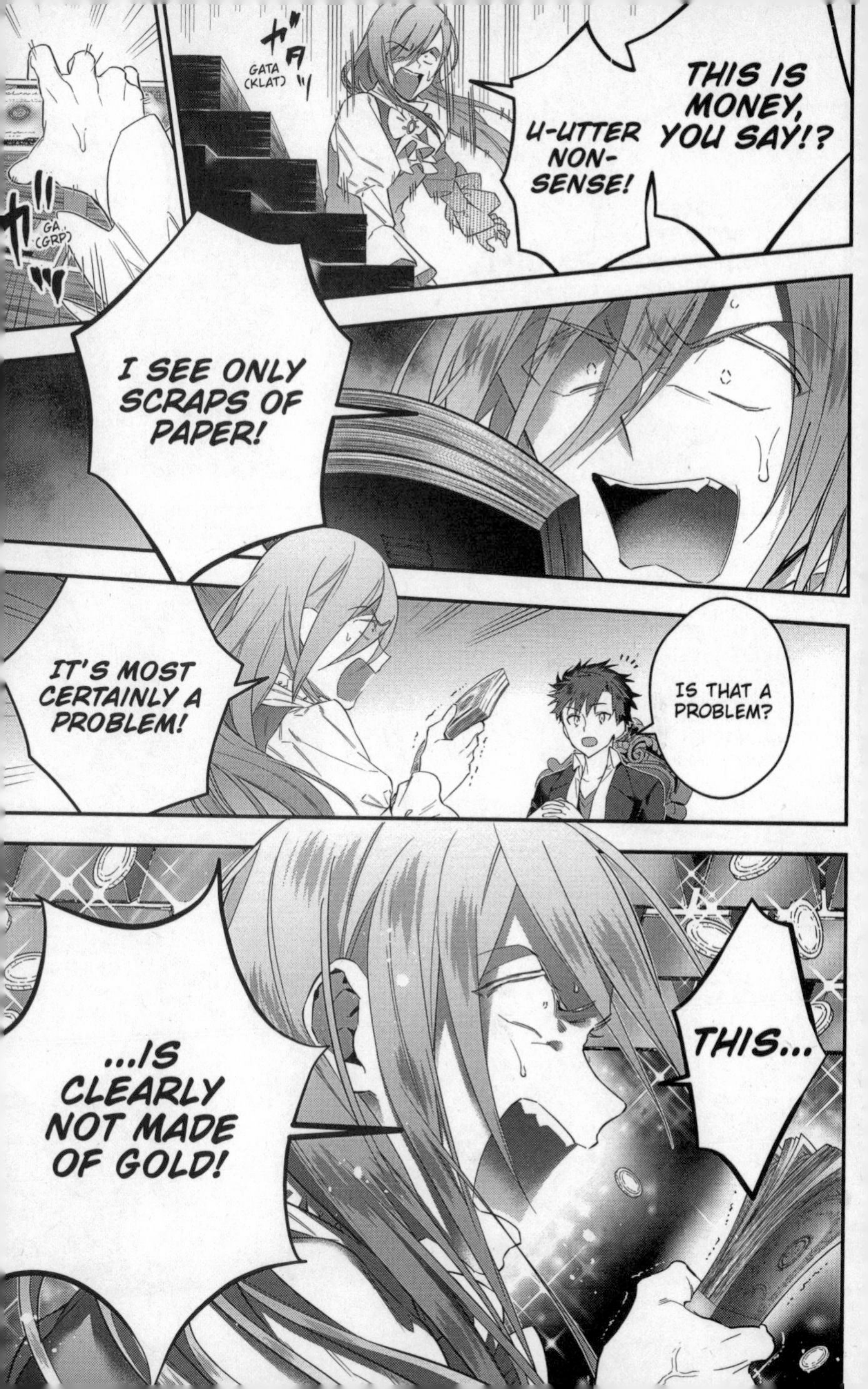
THIS IS MONEY, YOU SAY!?
U-UTTER NON-SENSE!
GATA (KLAT)
GA (GRP)
I SEE ONLY SCRAPS OF PAPER!
IS THAT A PROBLEM?
IT'S MOST CERTAINLY A PROBLEM!
THIS...
...IS CLEARLY NOT MADE OF GOLD!

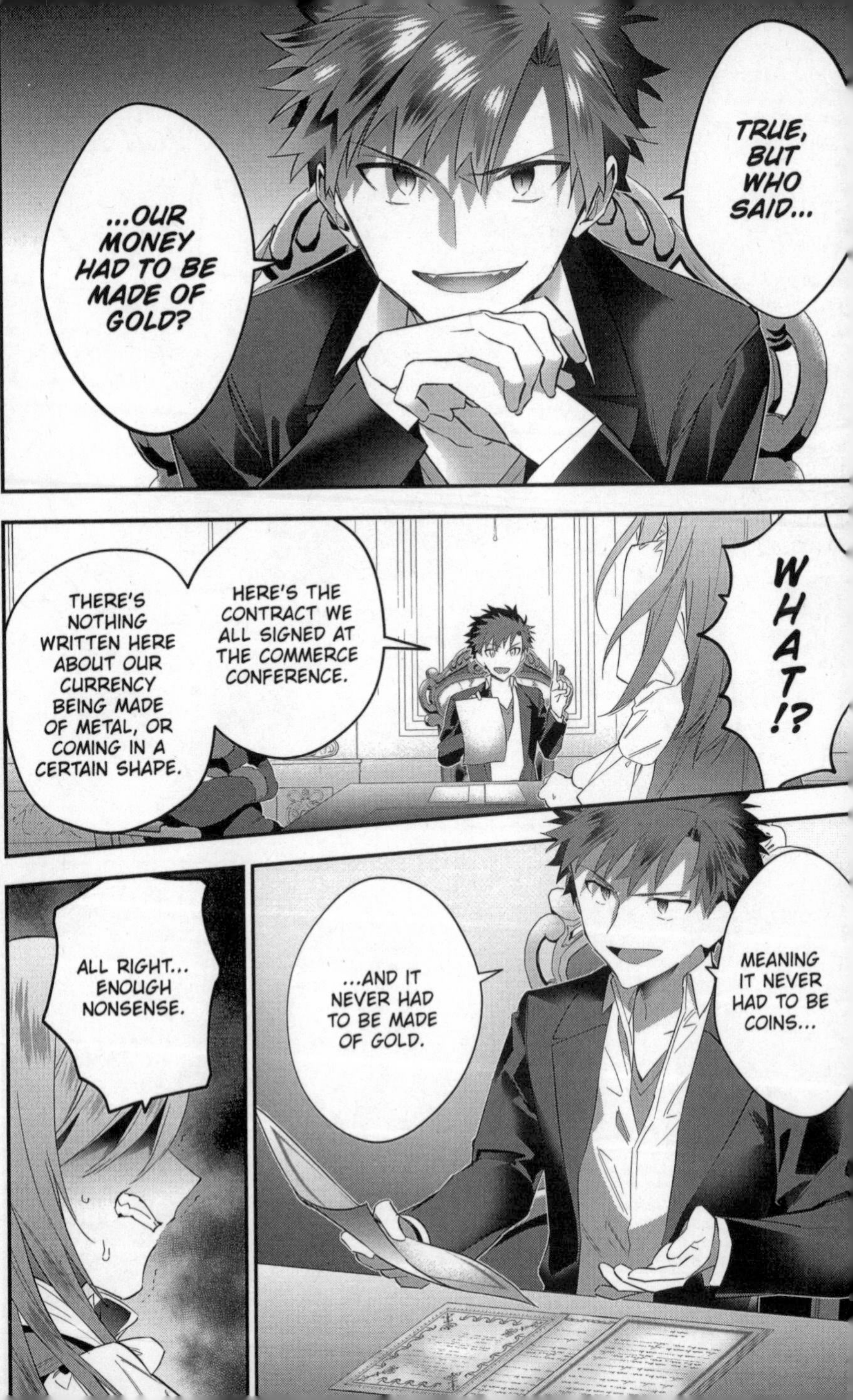
TRUE, BUT WHO SAID...
...OUR MONEY HAD TO BE MADE OF GOLD?
WHAT!?
HERE'S THE CONTRACT WE ALL SIGNED AT THE COMMERCE CONFERENCE.
THERE'S NOTHING WRITTEN HERE ABOUT OUR CURRENCY BEING MADE OF METAL, OR COMING IN A CERTAIN SHAPE.
MEANING IT NEVER HAD TO BE COINS...
...AND IT NEVER HAD TO BE MADE OF GOLD.
ALL RIGHT... ENOUGH NONSENSE.

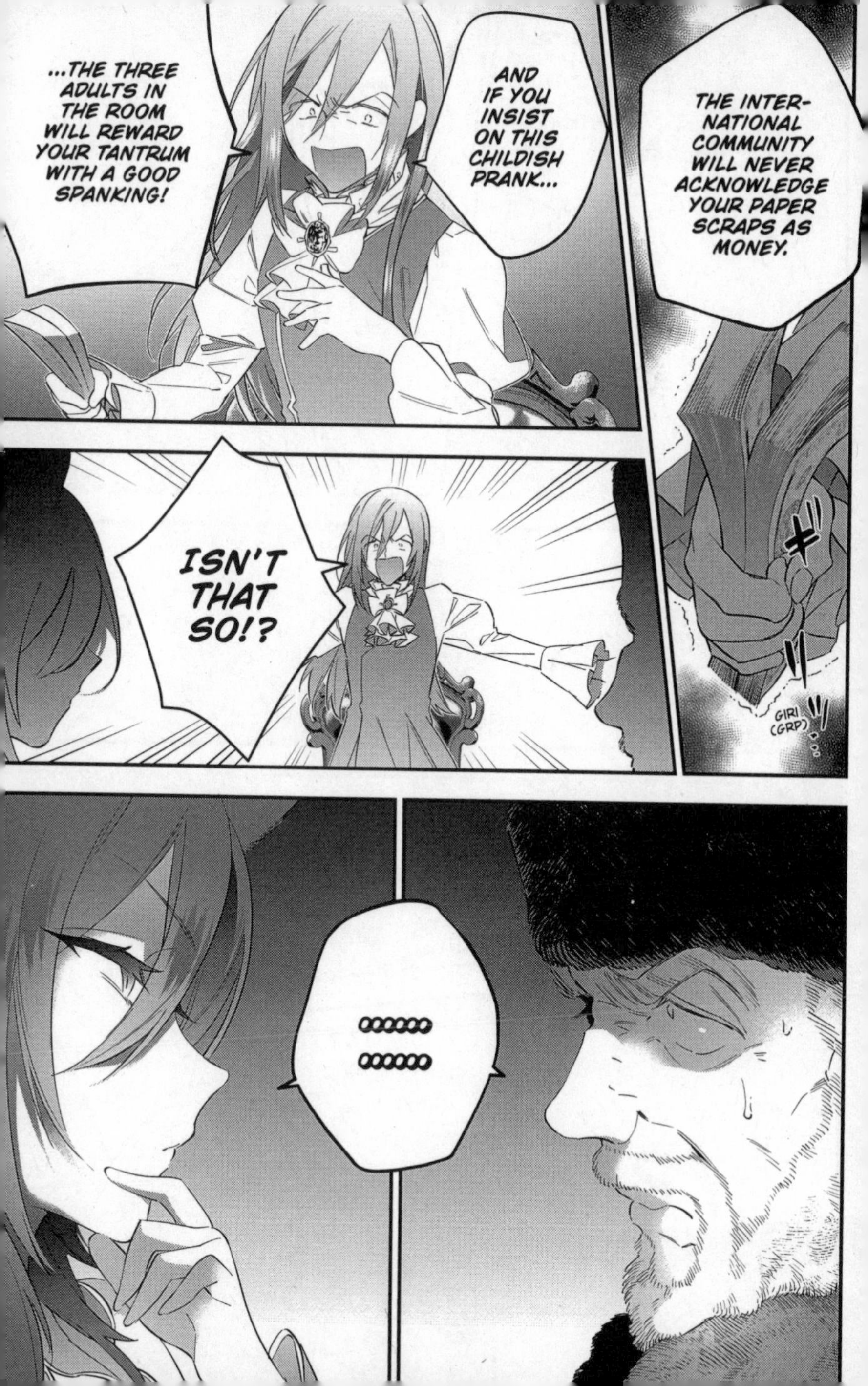
THE INTERNATIONAL COMMUNITY WILL NEVER ACKNOWLEDGE YOUR PAPER SCRAPS AS MONEY.
GIRI (GRP)
AND IF YOU INSIST ON THIS CHILDISH PRANK...
...THE THREE ADULTS IN THE ROOM WILL REWARD YOUR TANTRUM WITH A GOOD SPANKING!
ISN'T THAT SO!?
......
......

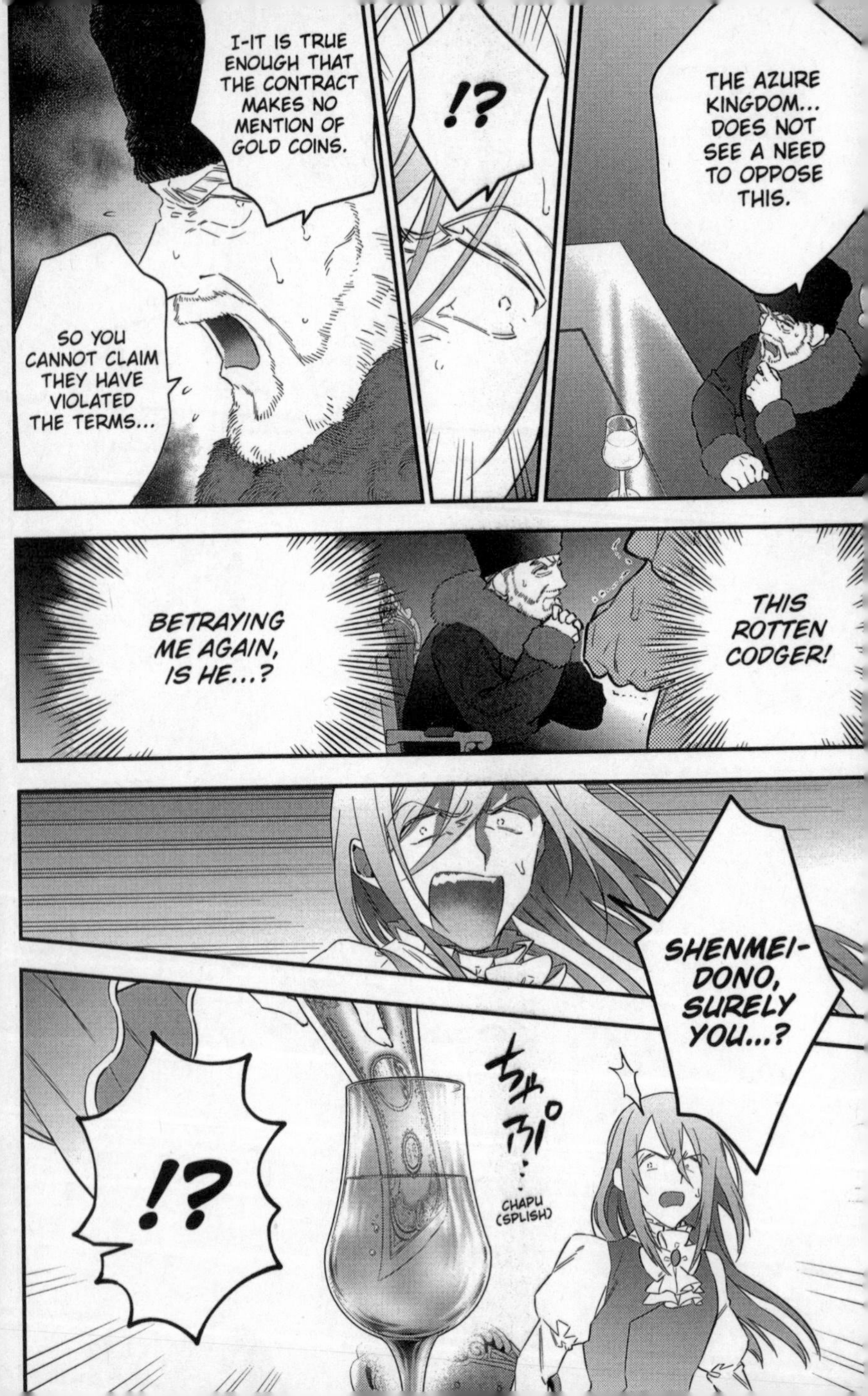
THE AZURE KINGDOM... DOES NOT SEE A NEED TO OPPOSE THIS.
!?
I-IT IS TRUE ENOUGH THAT THE CONTRACT MAKES NO MENTION OF GOLD COINS.
SO YOU CANNOT CLAIM THEY HAVE VIOLATED THE TERMS...
THIS ROTTEN CODGER!
BETRAYING ME AGAIN, IS HE...?
SHENMEI-DONO, SURELY YOU...?
ちゃぷ...
CHAPU (SPLISH)
!?

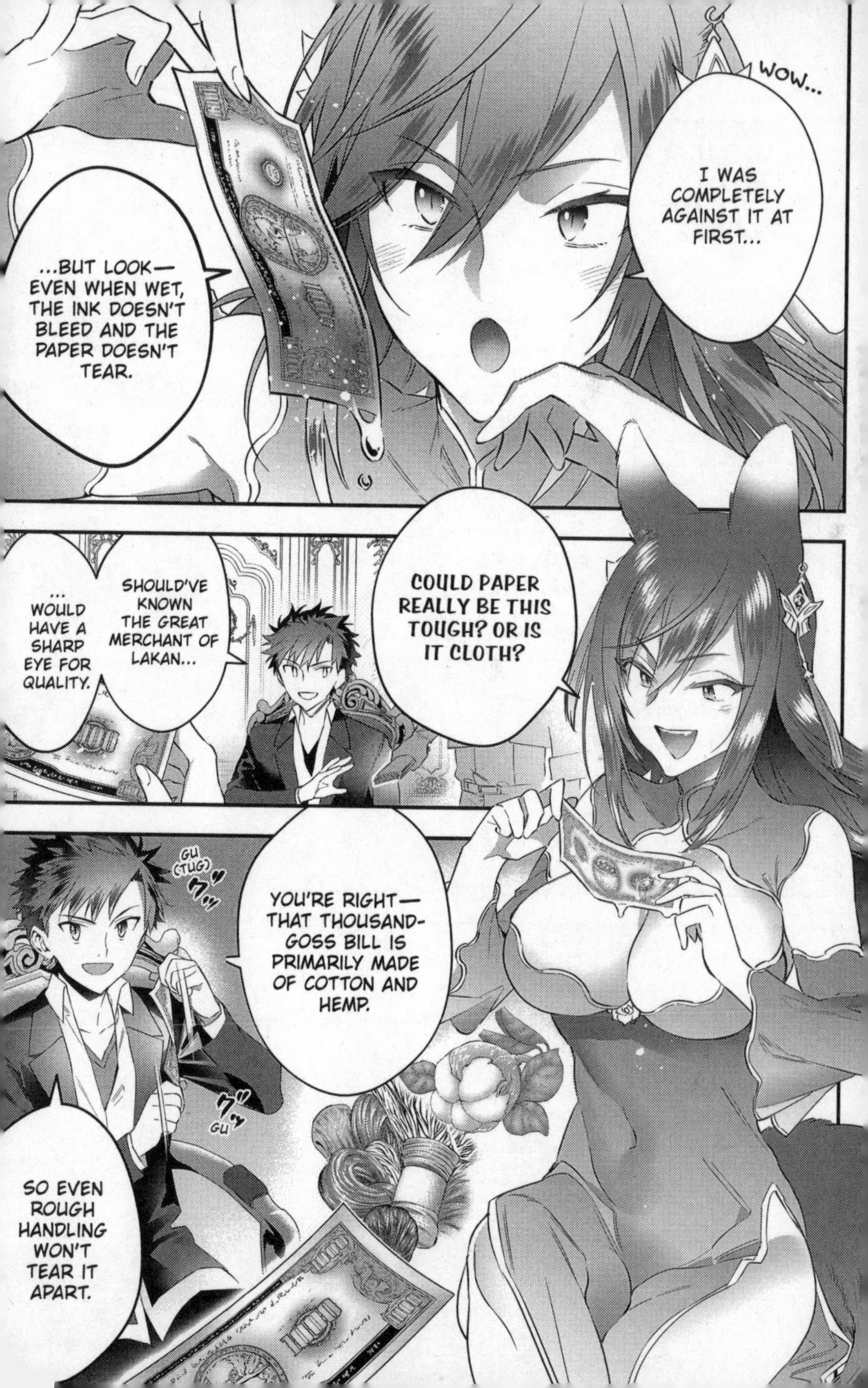
WOW...
I WAS COMPLETELY AGAINST IT AT FIRST...
...BUT LOOK—EVEN WHEN WET, THE INK DOESN'T BLEED AND THE PAPER DOESN'T TEAR.
COULD PAPER REALLY BE THIS TOUGH? OR IS IT CLOTH?
SHOULD'VE KNOWN THE GREAT MERCHANT OF LAKAN...
...WOULD HAVE A SHARP EYE FOR QUALITY.
YOU'RE RIGHT—THAT THOUSAND-GOSS BILL IS PRIMARILY MADE OF COTTON AND HEMP.
GU (TUG)
GU
SO EVEN ROUGH HANDLING WON'T TEAR IT APART.

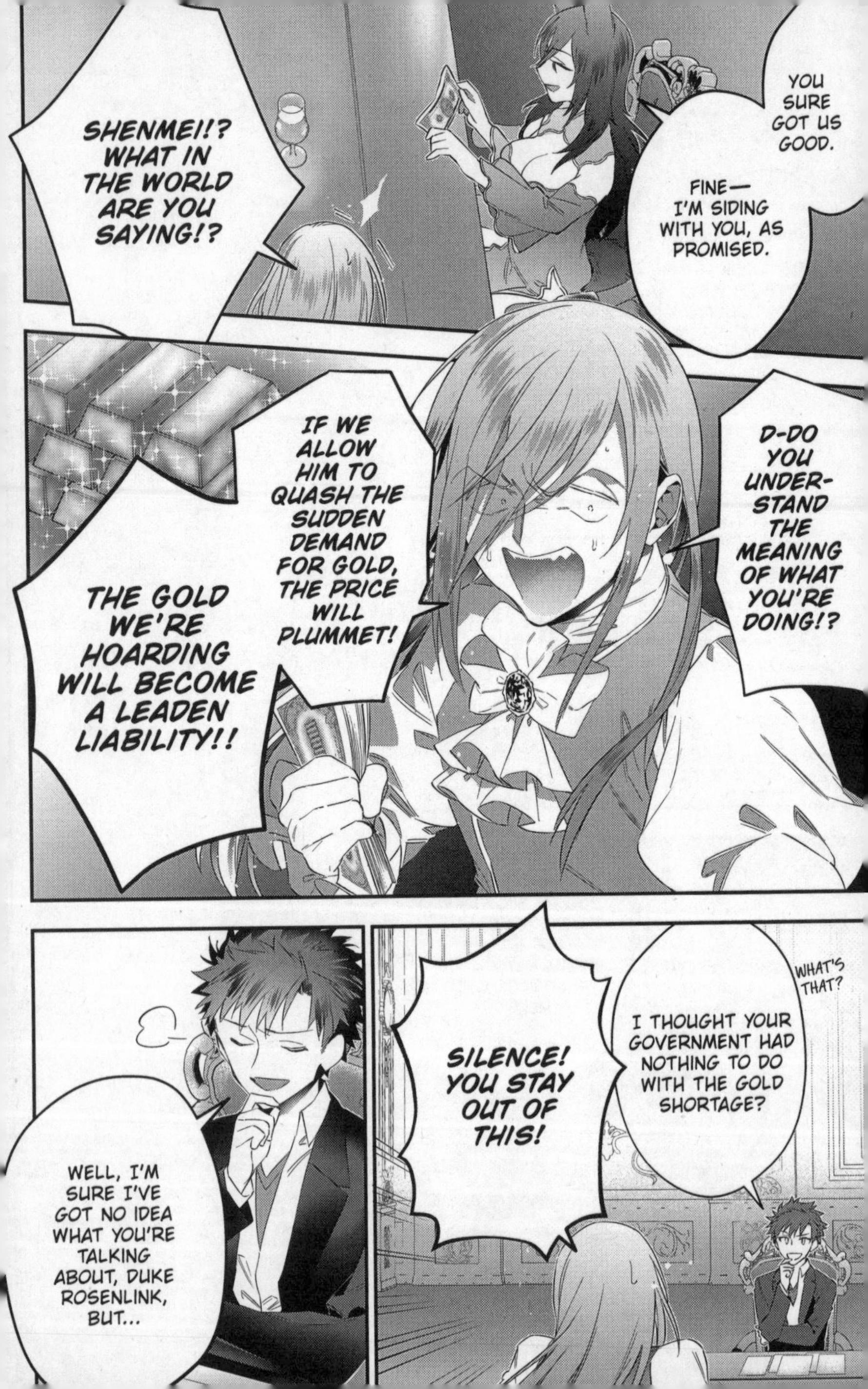
YOU SURE GOT US GOOD.
FINE— I'M SIDING WITH YOU, AS PROMISED.
SHENMEI!? WHAT IN THE WORLD ARE YOU SAYING!?
D-DO YOU UNDER-STAND THE MEANING OF WHAT YOU'RE DOING!?
IF WE ALLOW HIM TO QUASH THE SUDDEN DEMAND FOR GOLD, THE PRICE WILL PLUMMET!
THE GOLD WE'RE HOARDING WILL BECOME A LEADEN LIABILITY!!
WHAT'S THAT?
I THOUGHT YOUR GOVERNMENT HAD NOTHING TO DO WITH THE GOLD SHORTAGE?
SILENCE! YOU STAY OUT OF THIS!
WELL, I'M SURE I'VE GOT NO IDEA WHAT YOU'RE TALKING ABOUT, DUKE ROSENLINK, BUT...

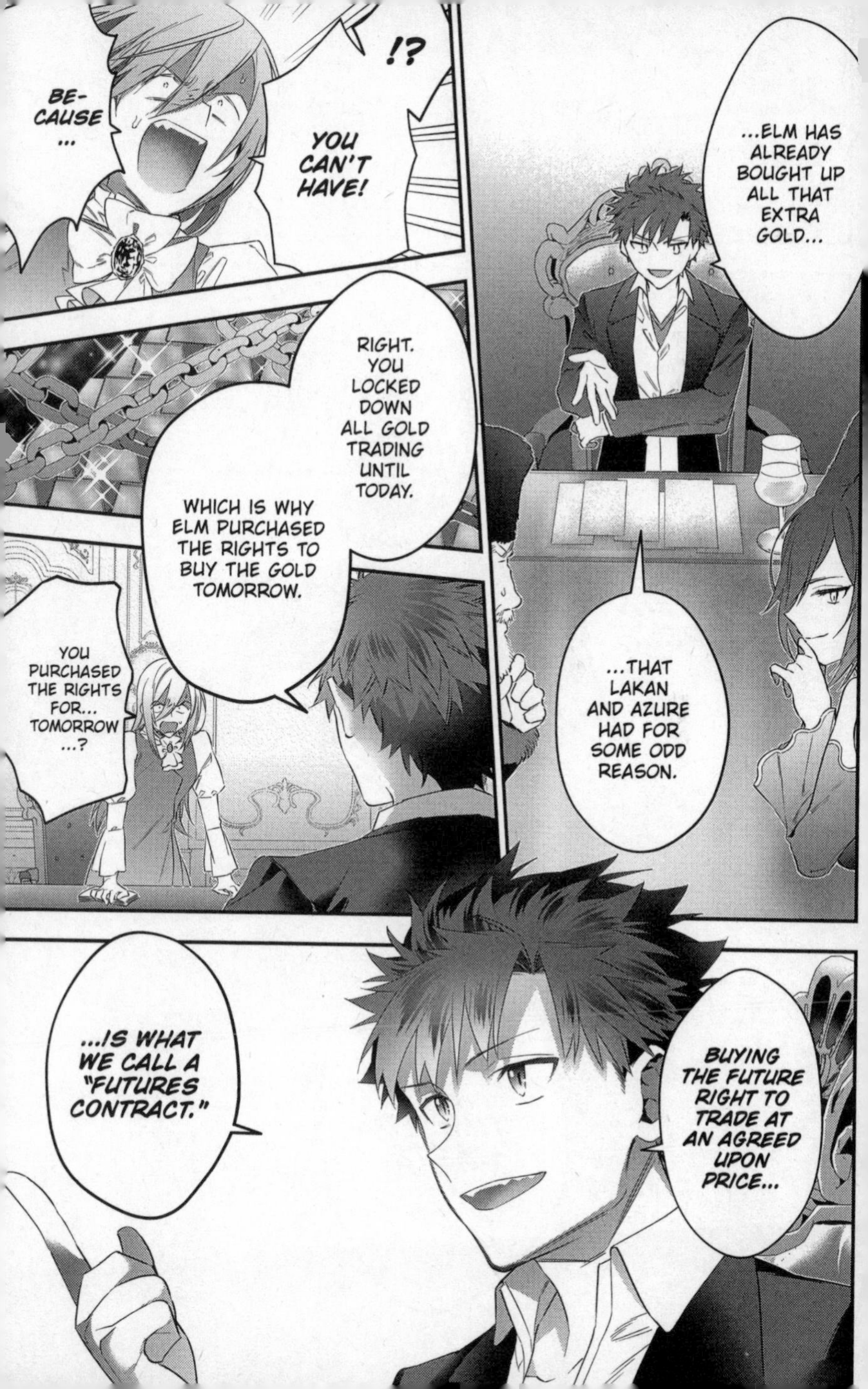
...ELM HAS ALREADY BOUGHT UP ALL THAT EXTRA GOLD...
...THAT LAKAN AND AZURE HAD FOR SOME ODD REASON.
!?
YOU CAN'T HAVE!
BE-CAUSE ...
RIGHT. YOU LOCKED DOWN ALL GOLD TRADING UNTIL TODAY.
WHICH IS WHY ELM PURCHASED THE RIGHTS TO BUY THE GOLD TOMORROW.
YOU PURCHASED THE RIGHTS FOR... TOMORROW ...?
BUYING THE FUTURE RIGHT TO TRADE AT AN AGREED UPON PRICE...
...IS WHAT WE CALL A "FUTURES CONTRACT."

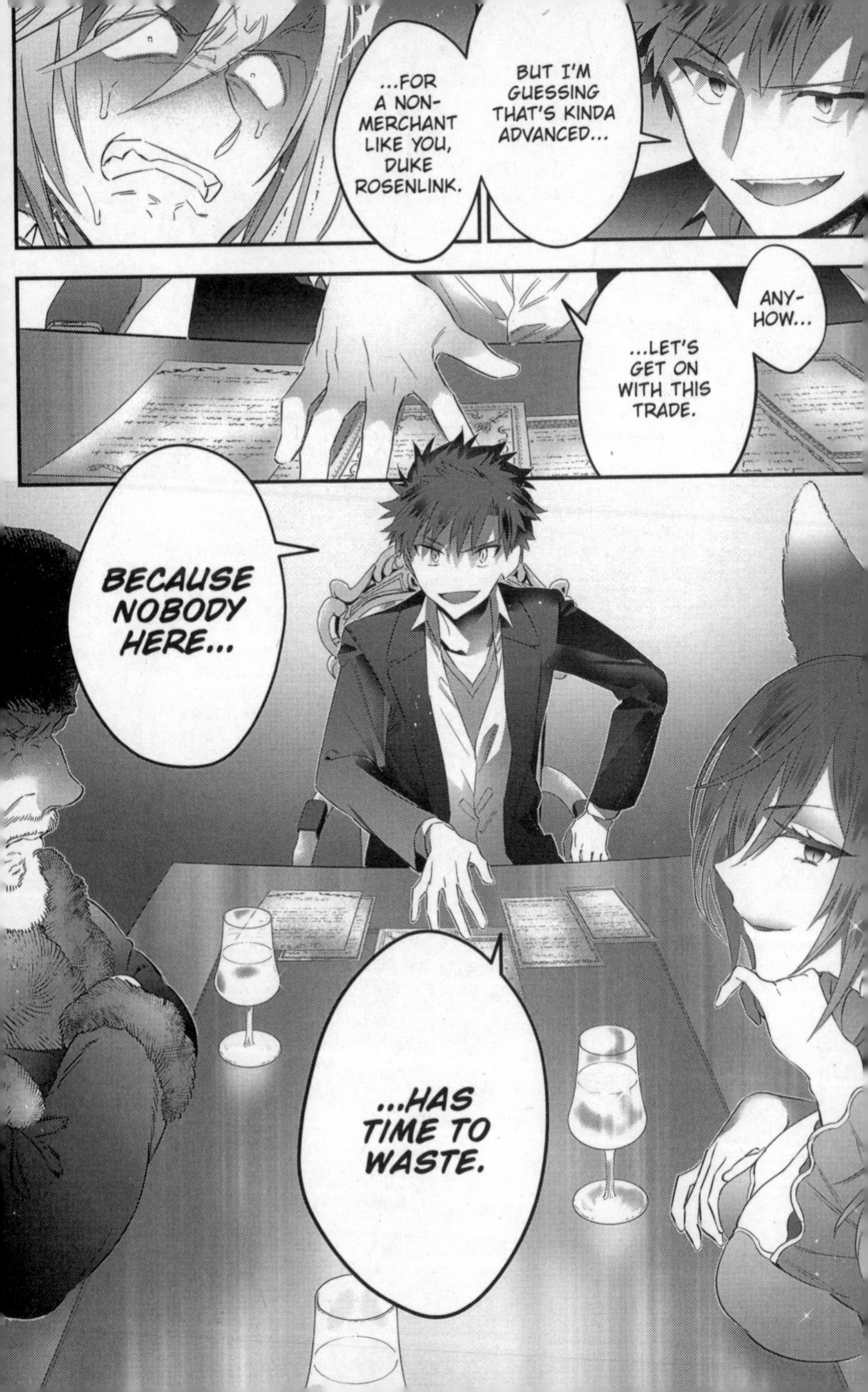
BUT I'M GUESSING THAT'S KINDA ADVANCED...
...FOR A NON-MERCHANT LIKE YOU, DUKE ROSENLINK.
ANY-HOW...
...LET'S GET ON WITH THIS TRADE.
BECAUSE NOBODY HERE...
...HAS TIME TO WASTE.

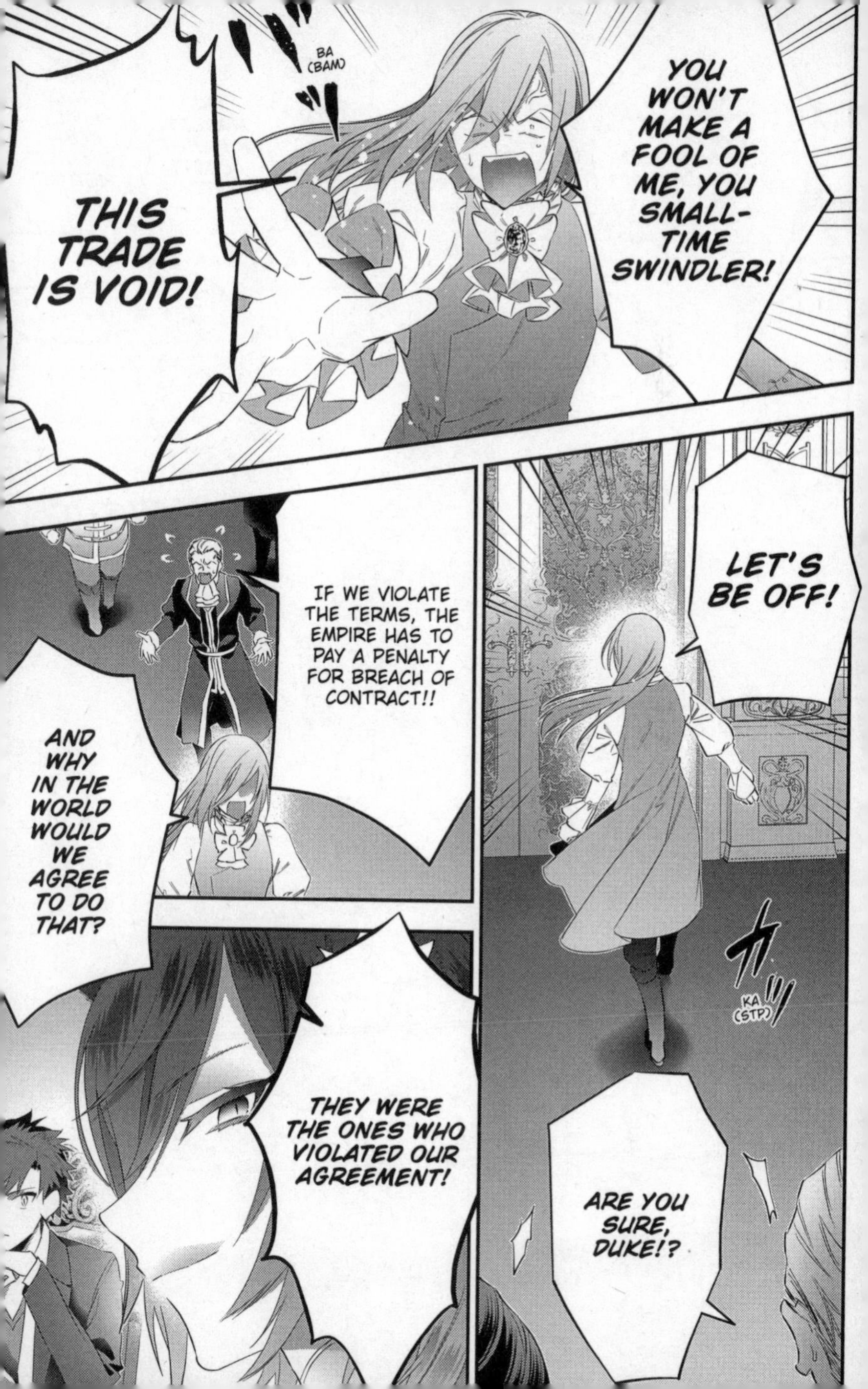
YOU WON'T MAKE A FOOL OF ME, YOU SMALL-TIME SWINDLER!
BA (BAM)
THIS TRADE IS VOID!
LET'S BE OFF!
KA (STP)
ARE YOU SURE, DUKE!?
IF WE VIOLATE THE TERMS, THE EMPIRE HAS TO PAY A PENALTY FOR BREACH OF CONTRACT!!
AND WHY IN THE WORLD WOULD WE AGREE TO DO THAT?
THEY WERE THE ONES WHO VIOLATED OUR AGREEMENT!

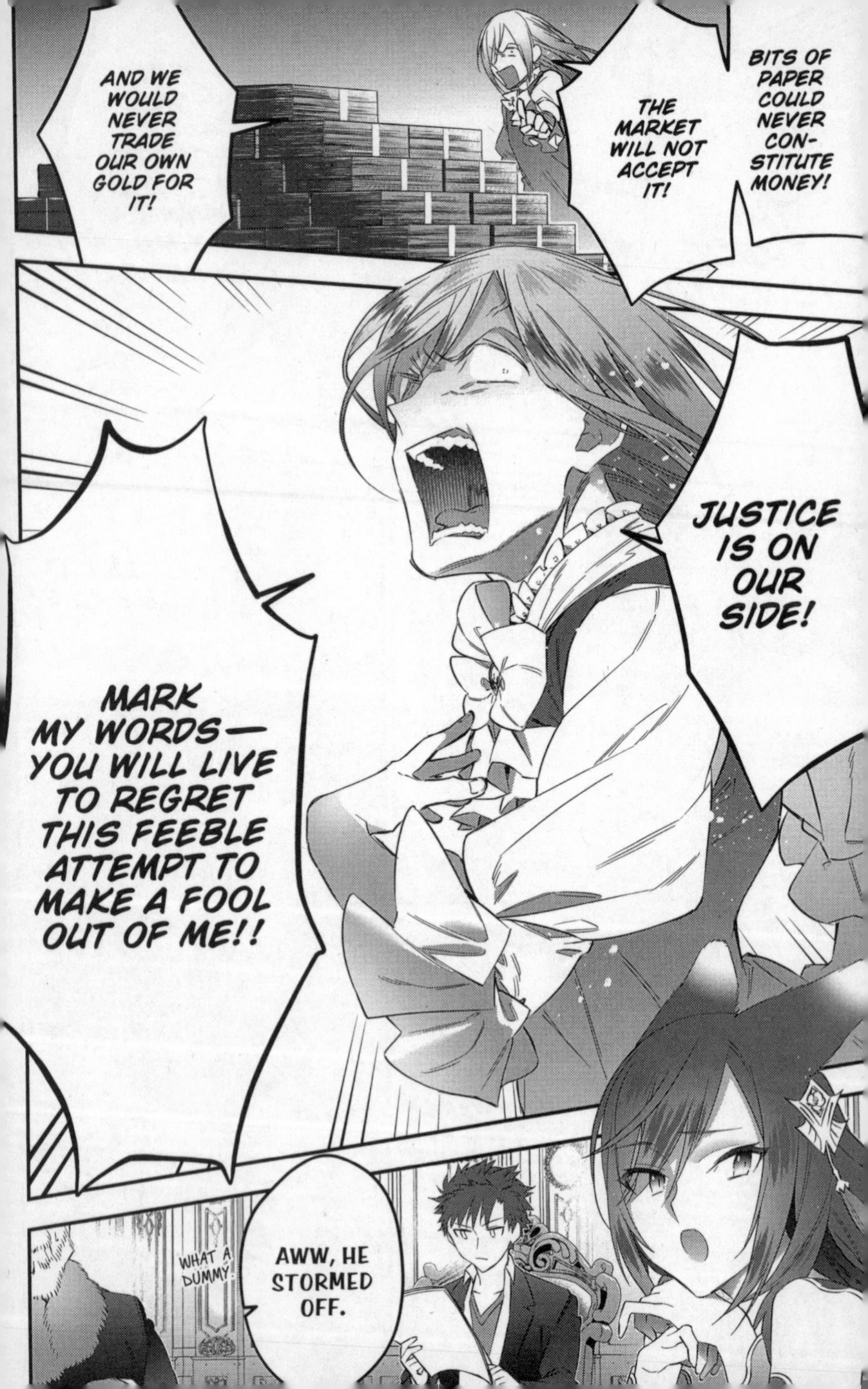
BITS OF PAPER COULD NEVER CON-STITUTE MONEY!
THE MARKET WILL NOT ACCEPT IT!
AND WE WOULD NEVER TRADE OUR OWN GOLD FOR IT!
JUSTICE IS ON OUR SIDE!
MARK MY WORDS—YOU WILL LIVE TO REGRET THIS FEEBLE ATTEMPT TO MAKE A FOOL OUT OF ME!!
AWW, HE STORMED OFF.
WHAT A DUMMY!

HIGH SCHOOL PRODIGIES HAVE IT EASY EVEN IN ANOTHER WORLD!

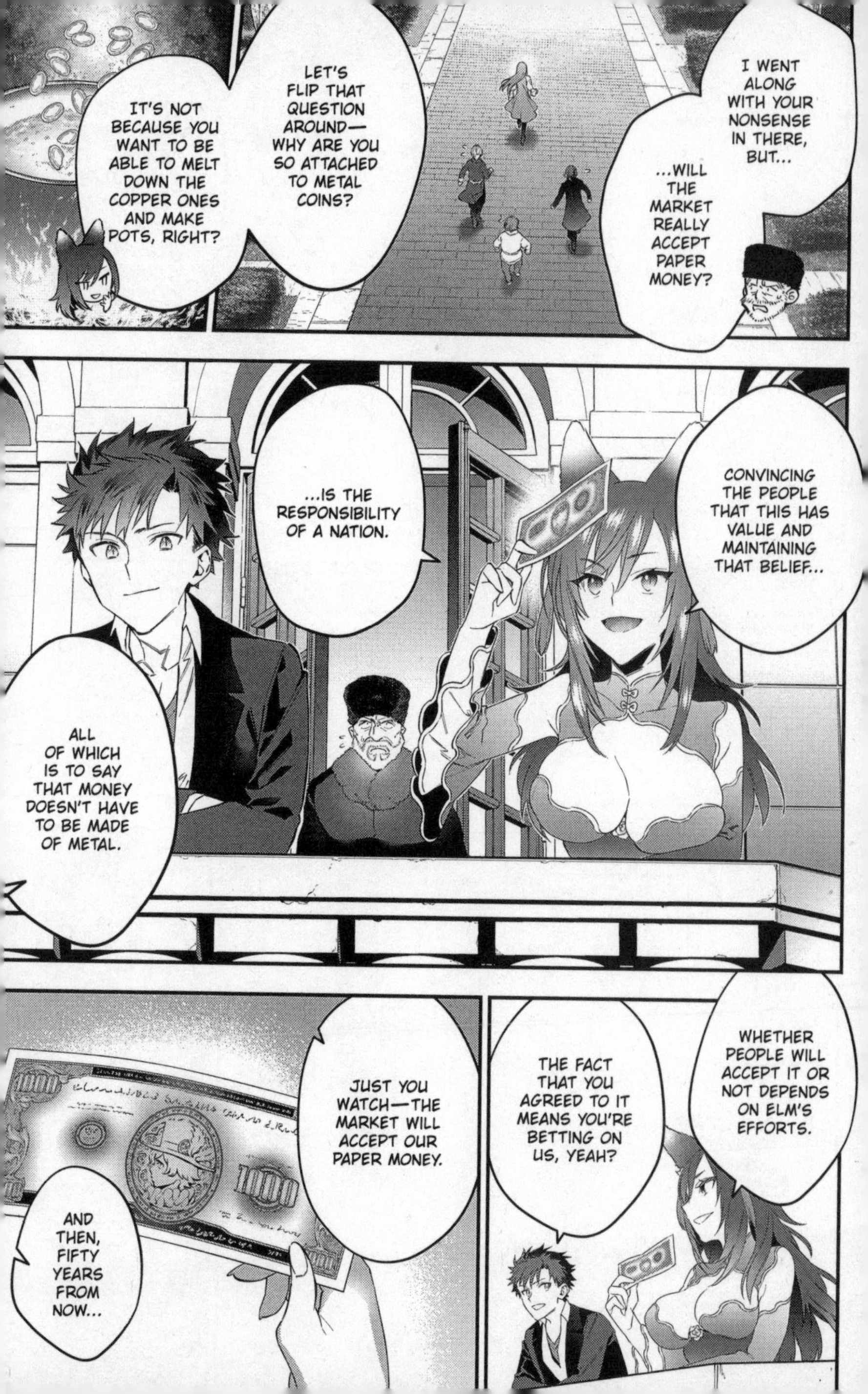

I WENT ALONG WITH YOUR NONSENSE IN THERE, BUT...
...WILL THE MARKET REALLY ACCEPT PAPER MONEY?
LET'S FLIP THAT QUESTION AROUND—WHY ARE YOU SO ATTACHED TO METAL COINS?
IT'S NOT BECAUSE YOU WANT TO BE ABLE TO MELT DOWN THE COPPER ONES AND MAKE POTS, RIGHT?
CONVINCING THE PEOPLE THAT THIS HAS VALUE AND MAINTAINING THAT BELIEF...
...IS THE RESPONSIBILITY OF A NATION.
ALL OF WHICH IS TO SAY THAT MONEY DOESN'T HAVE TO BE MADE OF METAL.
WHETHER PEOPLE WILL ACCEPT IT OR NOT DEPENDS ON ELM'S EFFORTS.
THE FACT THAT YOU AGREED TO IT MEANS YOU'RE BETTING ON US, YEAH?
JUST YOU WATCH—THE MARKET WILL ACCEPT OUR PAPER MONEY.
AND THEN, FIFTY YEARS FROM NOW...

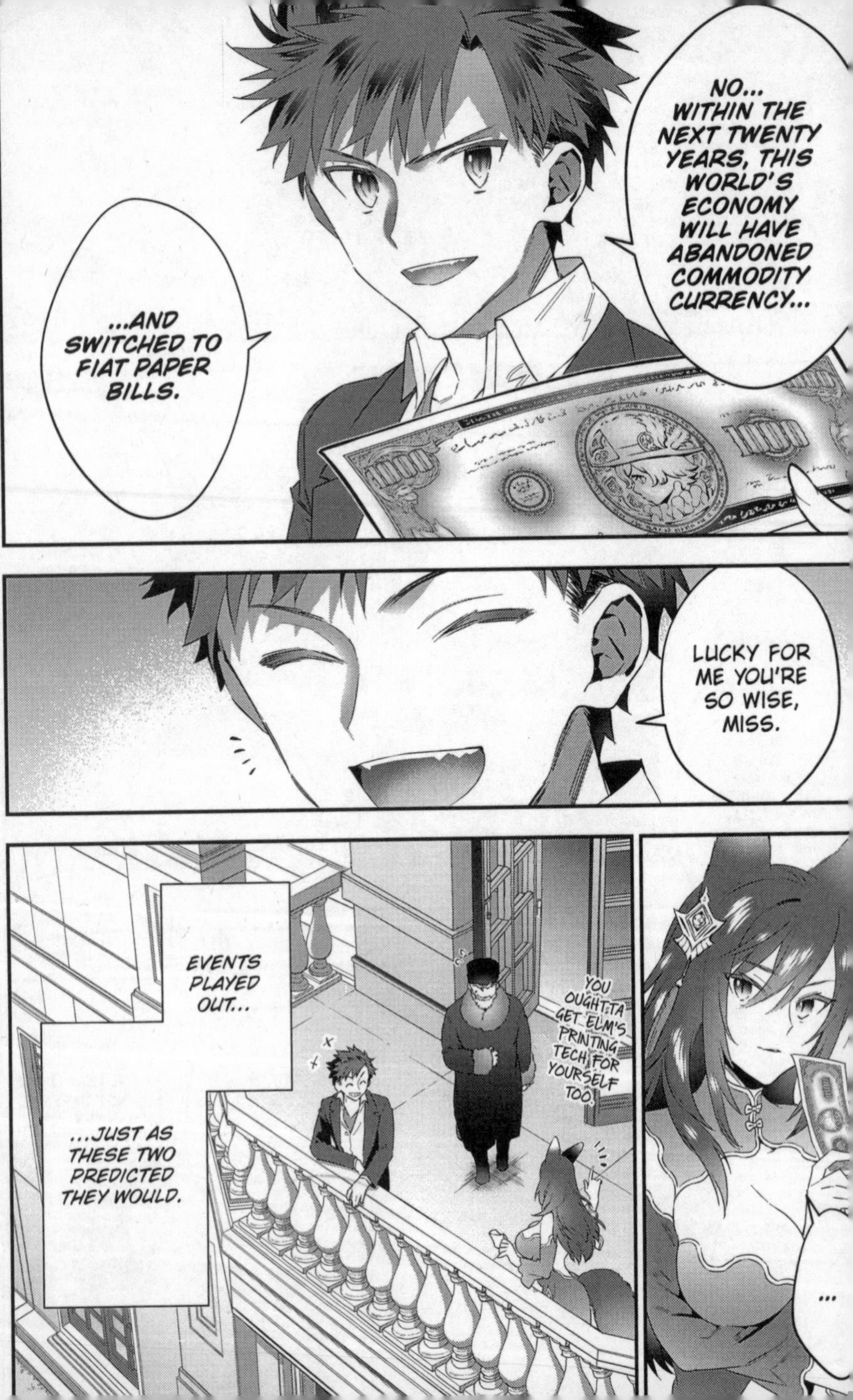
NO... WITHIN THE NEXT TWENTY YEARS, THIS WORLD'S ECONOMY WILL HAVE ABANDONED COMMODITY CURRENCY...
...AND SWITCHED TO FIAT PAPER BILLS.
LUCKY FOR ME YOU'RE SO WISE, MISS.
...
YOU OUGHTTA GET ELM'S PRINTING TECH FOR YOURSELF TOO.
EVENTS PLAYED OUT...
...JUST AS THESE TWO PREDICTED THEY WOULD.

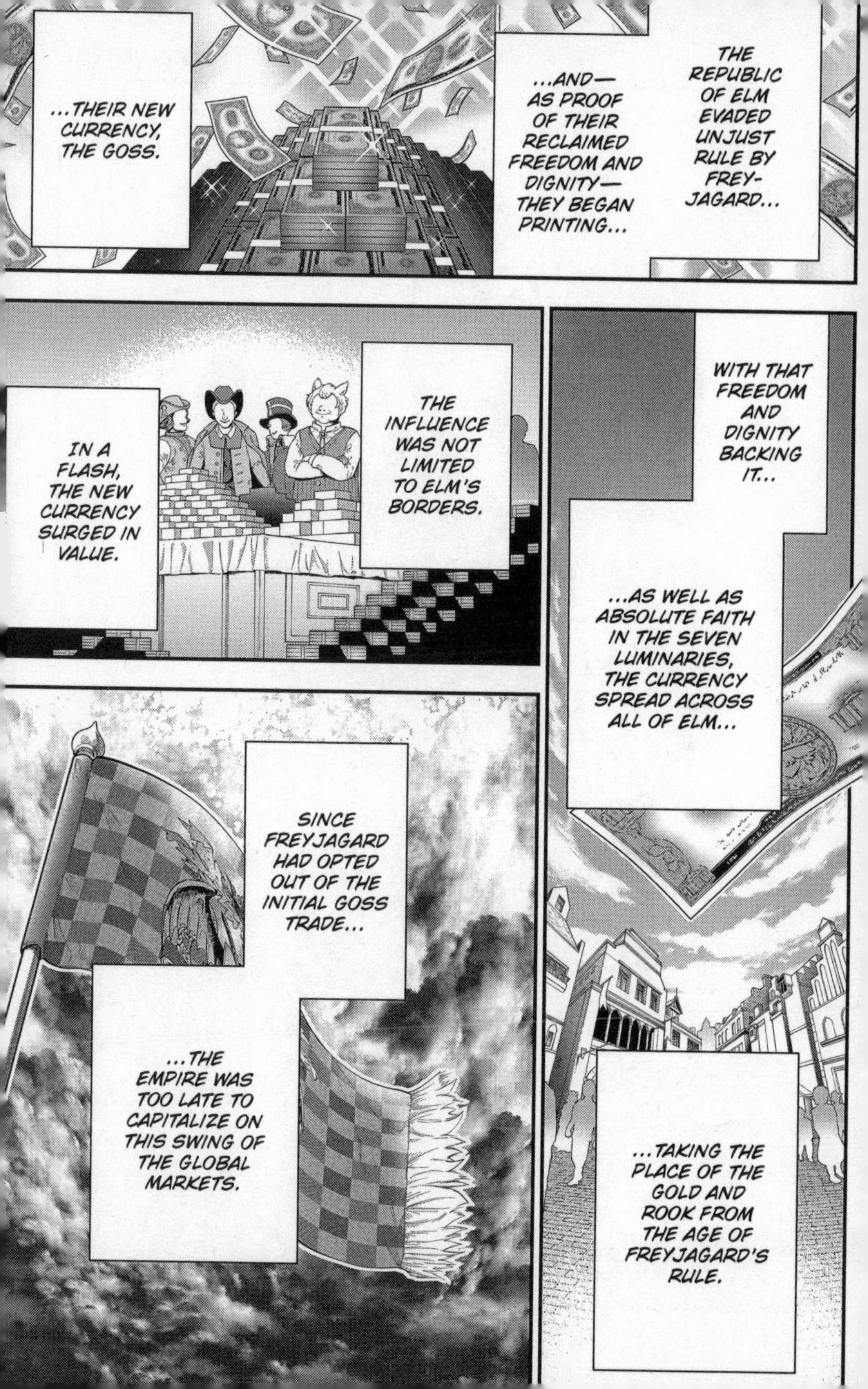
THE REPUBLIC OF ELM EVADED UNJUST RULE BY FREY-JAGARD...
...AND—AS PROOF OF THEIR RECLAIMED FREEDOM AND DIGNITY—THEY BEGAN PRINTING...
...THEIR NEW CURRENCY, THE GOSS.
WITH THAT FREEDOM AND DIGNITY BACKING IT...
...AS WELL AS ABSOLUTE FAITH IN THE SEVEN LUMINARIES, THE CURRENCY SPREAD ACROSS ALL OF ELM...
...TAKING THE PLACE OF THE GOLD AND ROOK FROM THE AGE OF FREYJAGARD'S RULE.
THE INFLUENCE WAS NOT LIMITED TO ELM'S BORDERS.
IN A FLASH, THE NEW CURRENCY SURGED IN VALUE.
SINCE FREYJAGARD HAD OPTED OUT OF THE INITIAL GOSS TRADE...
...THE EMPIRE WAS TOO LATE TO CAPITALIZE ON THIS SWING OF THE GLOBAL MARKETS.

CHAPTER 60: **FIXED NOTION**

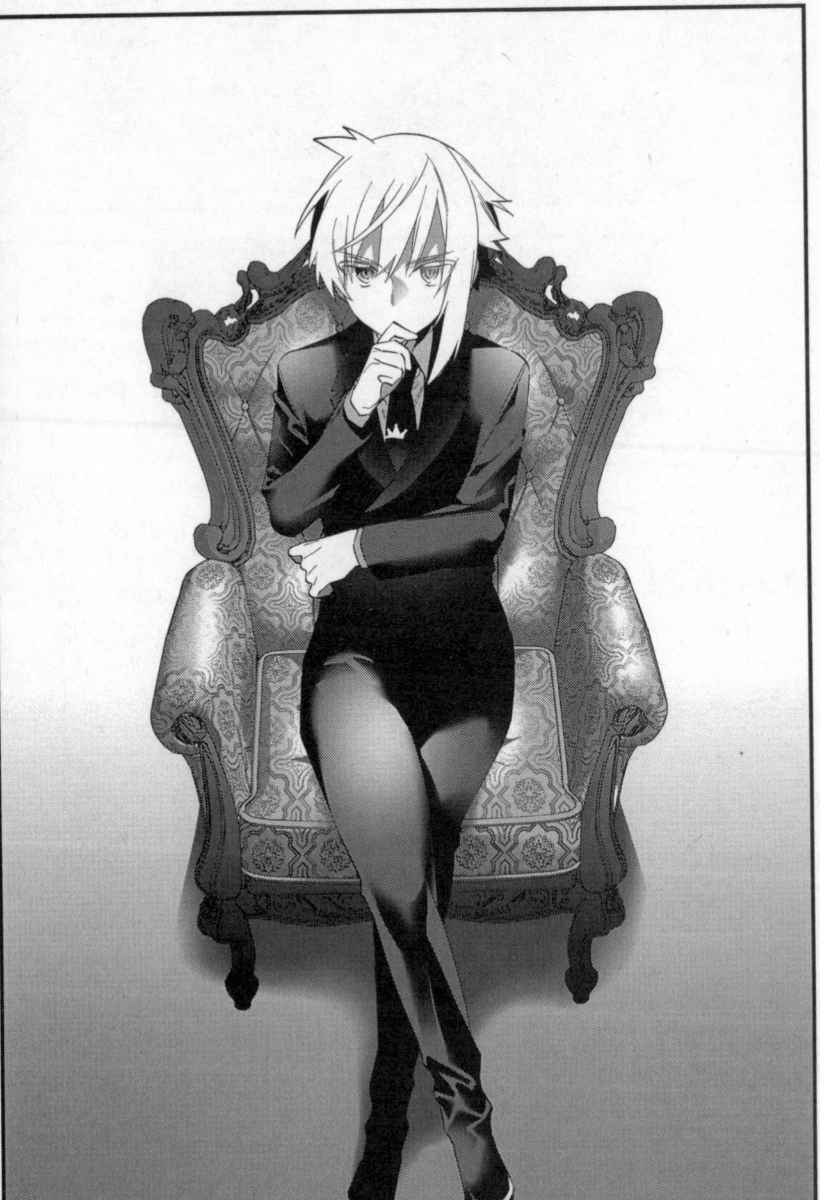

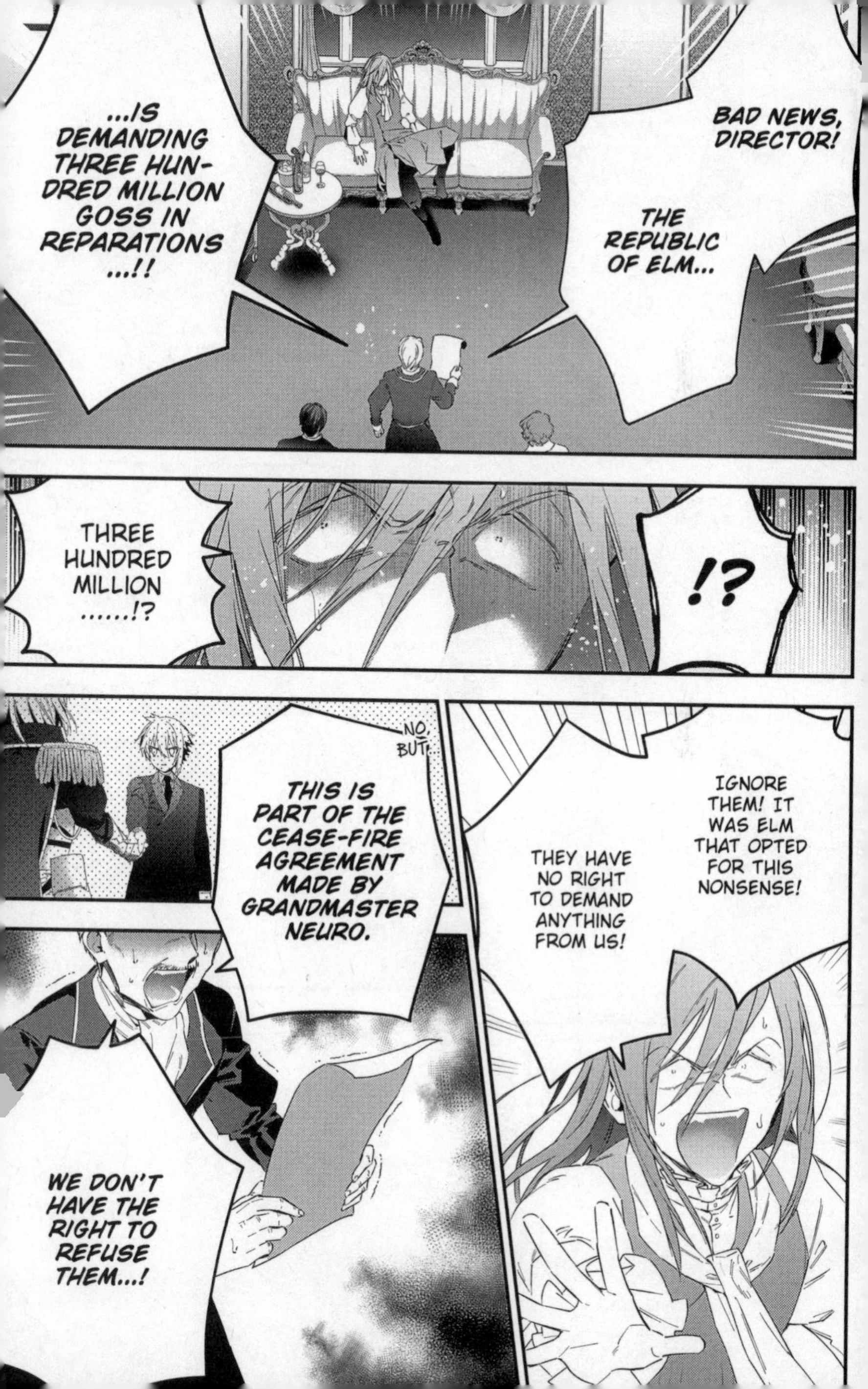
BAD NEWS, DIRECTOR!
THE REPUBLIC OF ELM...
...IS DEMANDING THREE HUNDRED MILLION GOSS IN REPARATIONS...!!
!?
THREE HUNDRED MILLION ......!?
IGNORE THEM! IT WAS ELM THAT OPTED FOR THIS NONSENSE!
THEY HAVE NO RIGHT TO DEMAND ANYTHING FROM US!
NO, BUT...
THIS IS PART OF THE CEASE-FIRE AGREEMENT MADE BY GRANDMASTER NEURO.
WE DON'T HAVE THE RIGHT TO REFUSE THEM...!

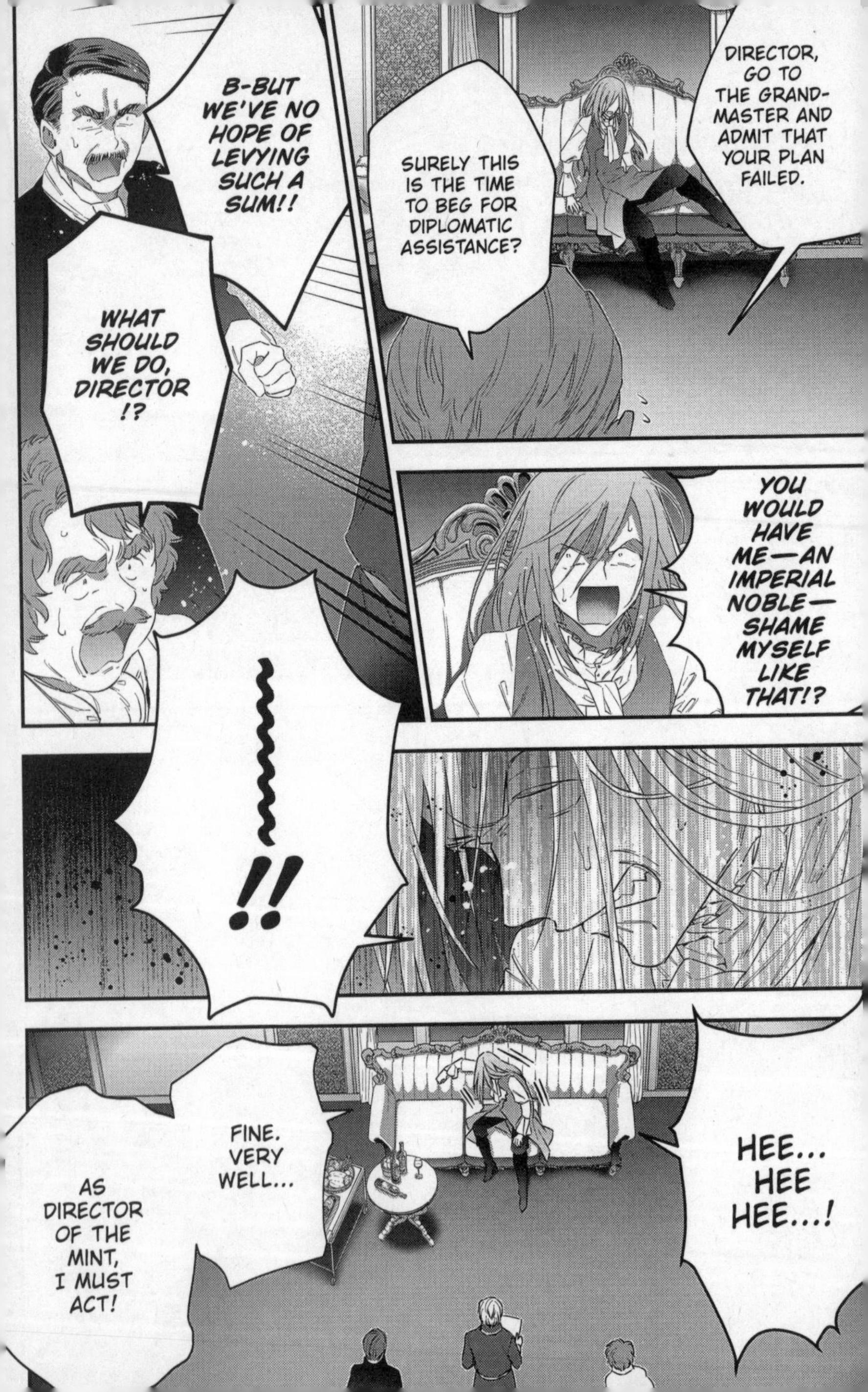
DIRECTOR, GO TO THE GRAND-MASTER AND ADMIT THAT YOUR PLAN FAILED.
SURELY THIS IS THE TIME TO BEG FOR DIPLOMATIC ASSISTANCE?
YOU WOULD HAVE ME—AN IMPERIAL NOBLE—SHAME MYSELF LIKE THAT!?
B-BUT WE'VE NO HOPE OF LEVYING SUCH A SUM!!
WHAT SHOULD WE DO, DIRECTOR!?
~~~~~~!!
HEE... HEE HEE...!
FINE. VERY WELL...
AS DIRECTOR OF THE MINT, I MUST ACT!
~~~~~~

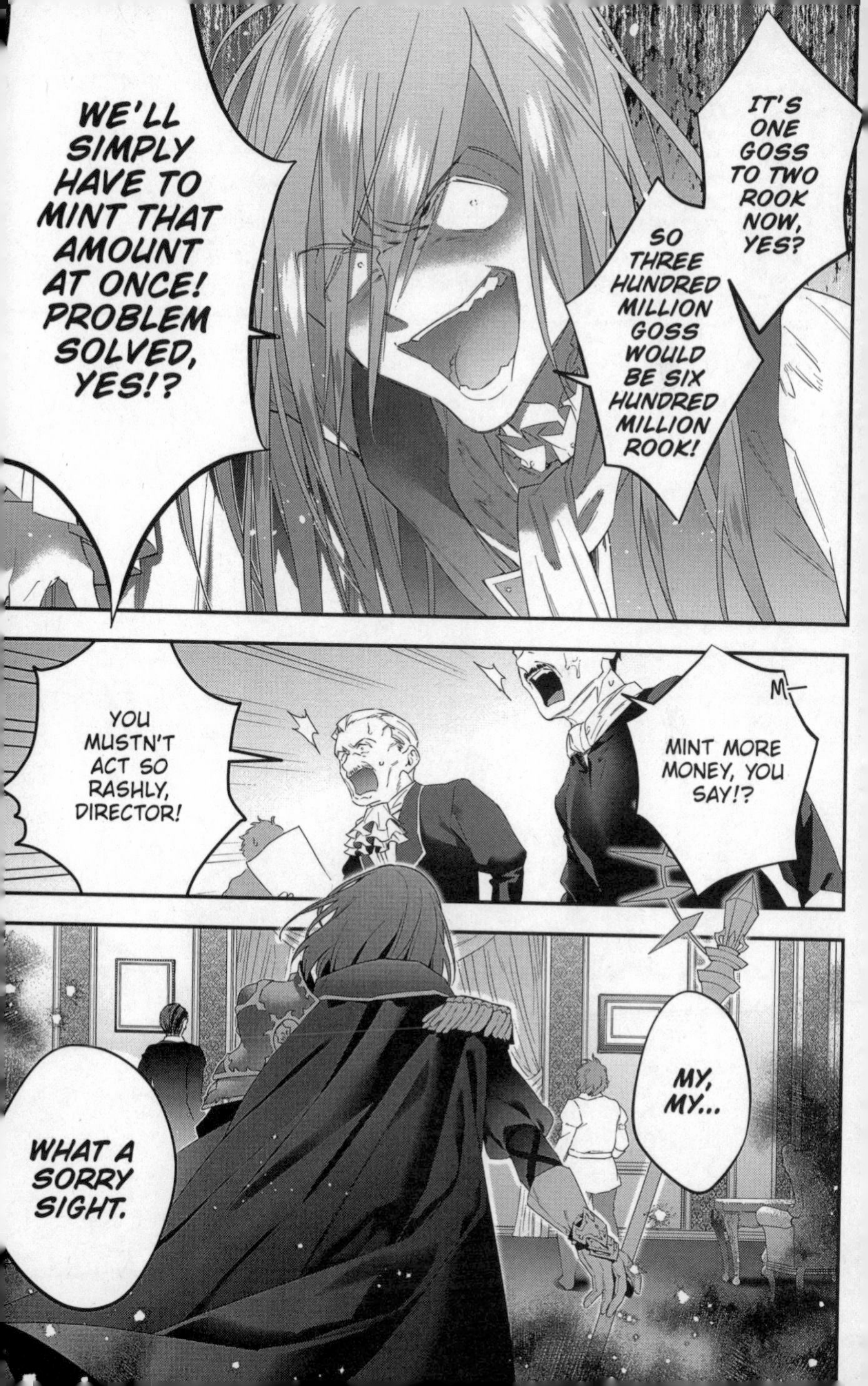
IT'S ONE GOSS TO TWO ROOK NOW, YES?
SO THREE HUNDRED MILLION GOSS WOULD BE SIX HUNDRED MILLION ROOK!
WE'LL SIMPLY HAVE TO MINT THAT AMOUNT AT ONCE! PROBLEM SOLVED, YES!?
M—
MINT MORE MONEY, YOU SAY!?
YOU MUSTN'T ACT SO RASHLY, DIRECTOR!
MY, MY...
WHAT A SORRY SIGHT.

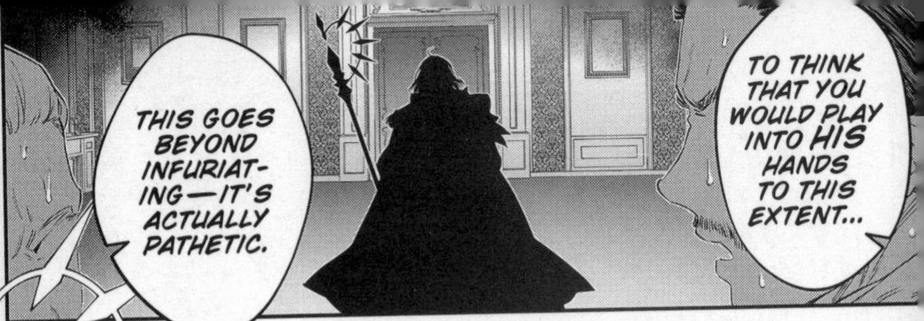
TO THINK THAT YOU WOULD PLAY INTO HIS HANDS TO THIS EXTENT...
THIS GOES BEYOND INFURIATING—IT'S ACTUALLY PATHETIC.
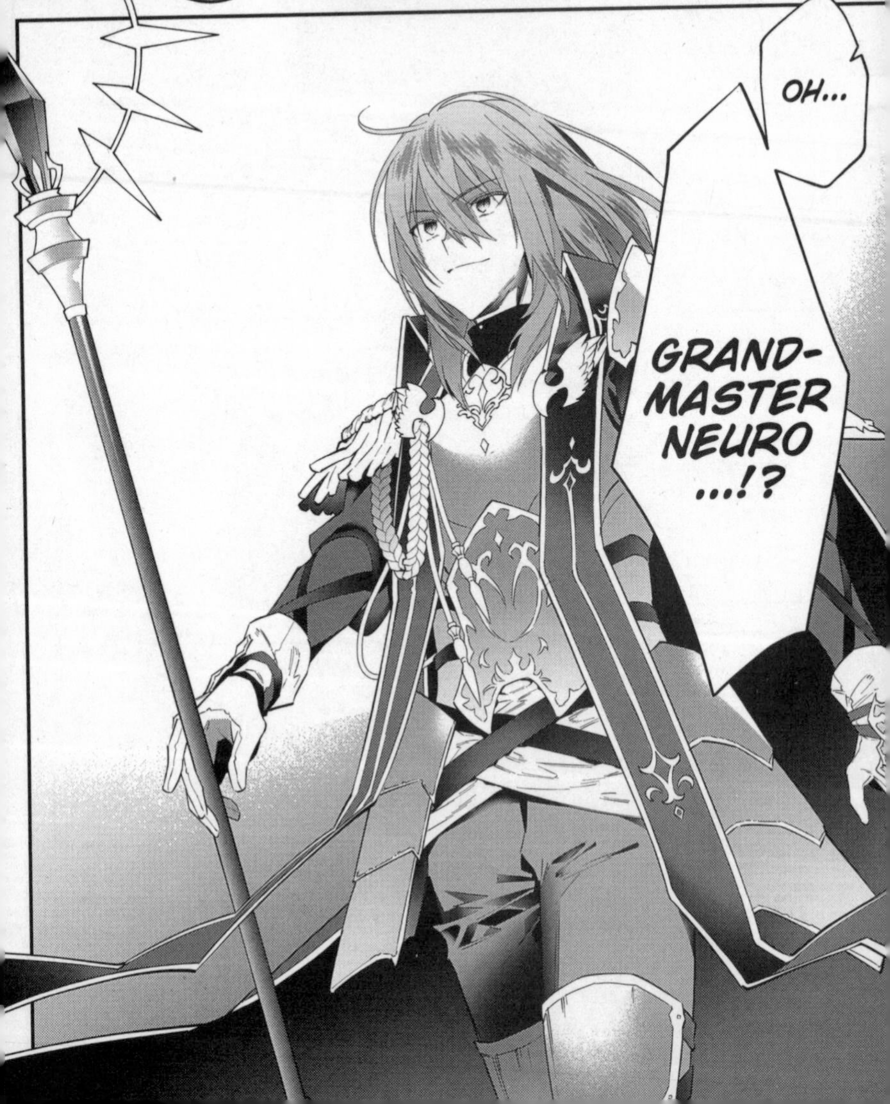
OH...
GRAND-MASTER NEURO ...!?

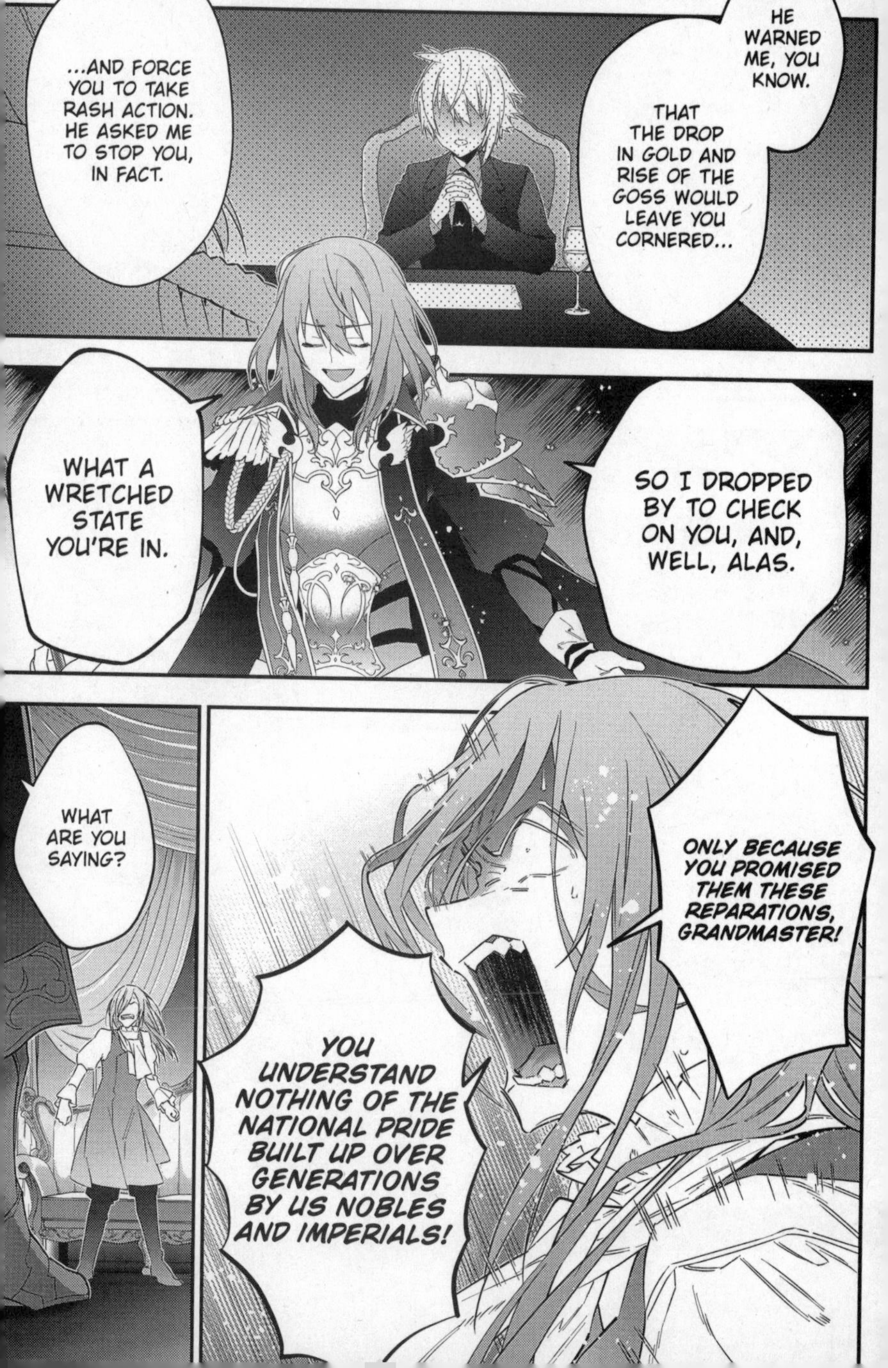
HE WARNED ME, YOU KNOW.
THAT THE DROP IN GOLD AND RISE OF THE GOSS WOULD LEAVE YOU CORNERED...
...AND FORCE YOU TO TAKE RASH ACTION. HE ASKED ME TO STOP YOU, IN FACT.
SO I DROPPED BY TO CHECK ON YOU, AND, WELL, ALAS.
WHAT A WRETCHED STATE YOU'RE IN.
ONLY BECAUSE YOU PROMISED THEM THESE REPARATIONS, GRANDMASTER!
YOU UNDERSTAND NOTHING OF THE NATIONAL PRIDE BUILT UP OVER GENERATIONS BY US NOBLES AND IMPERIALS!
WHAT ARE YOU SAYING?

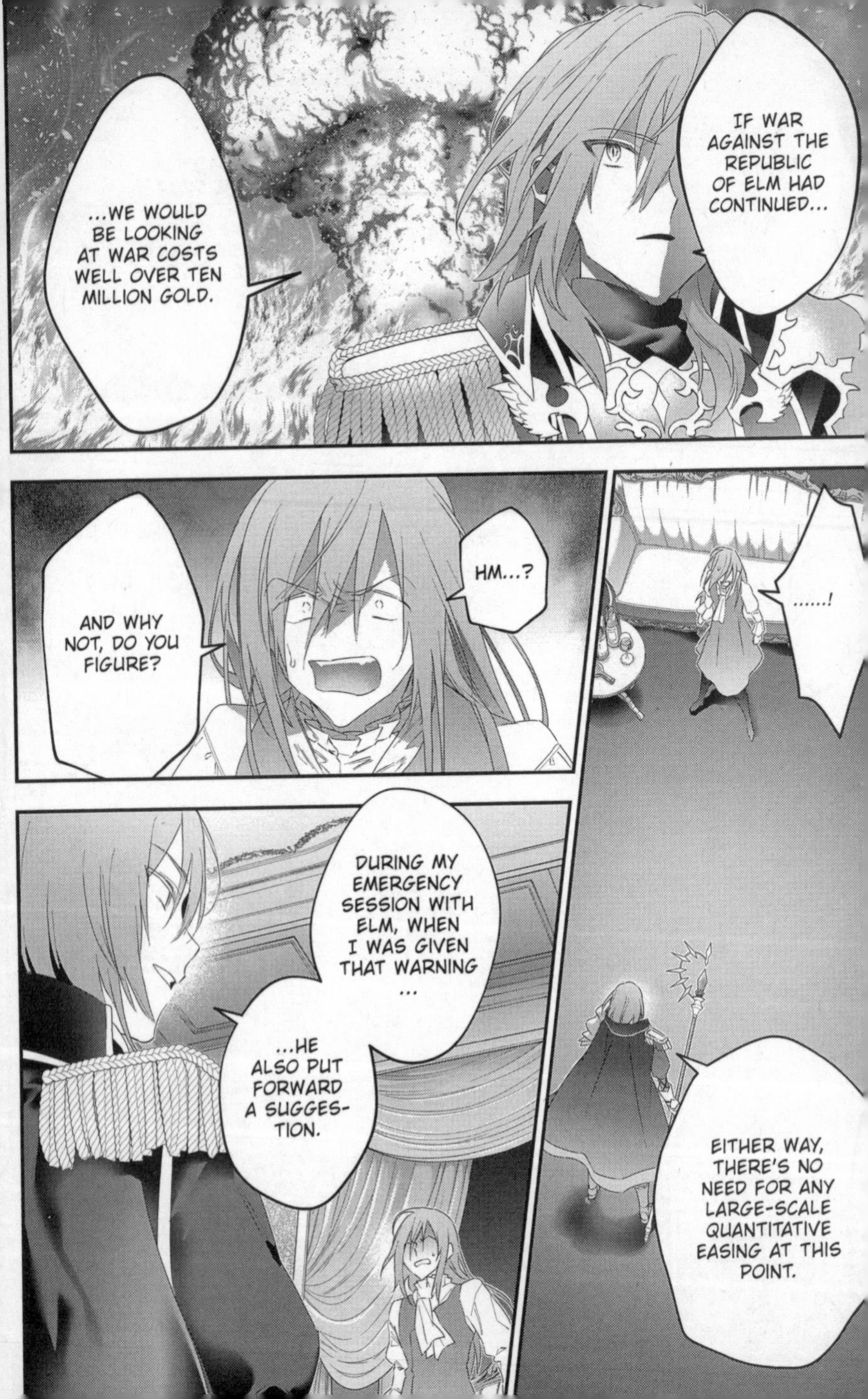
IF WAR AGAINST THE REPUBLIC OF ELM HAD CONTINUED...
...WE WOULD BE LOOKING AT WAR COSTS WELL OVER TEN MILLION GOLD.
......!
HM...?
AND WHY NOT, DO YOU FIGURE?
EITHER WAY, THERE'S NO NEED FOR ANY LARGE-SCALE QUANTITATIVE EASING AT THIS POINT.
DURING MY EMERGENCY SESSION WITH ELM, WHEN I WAS GIVEN THAT WARNING...
...HE ALSO PUT FORWARD A SUGGES-TION.

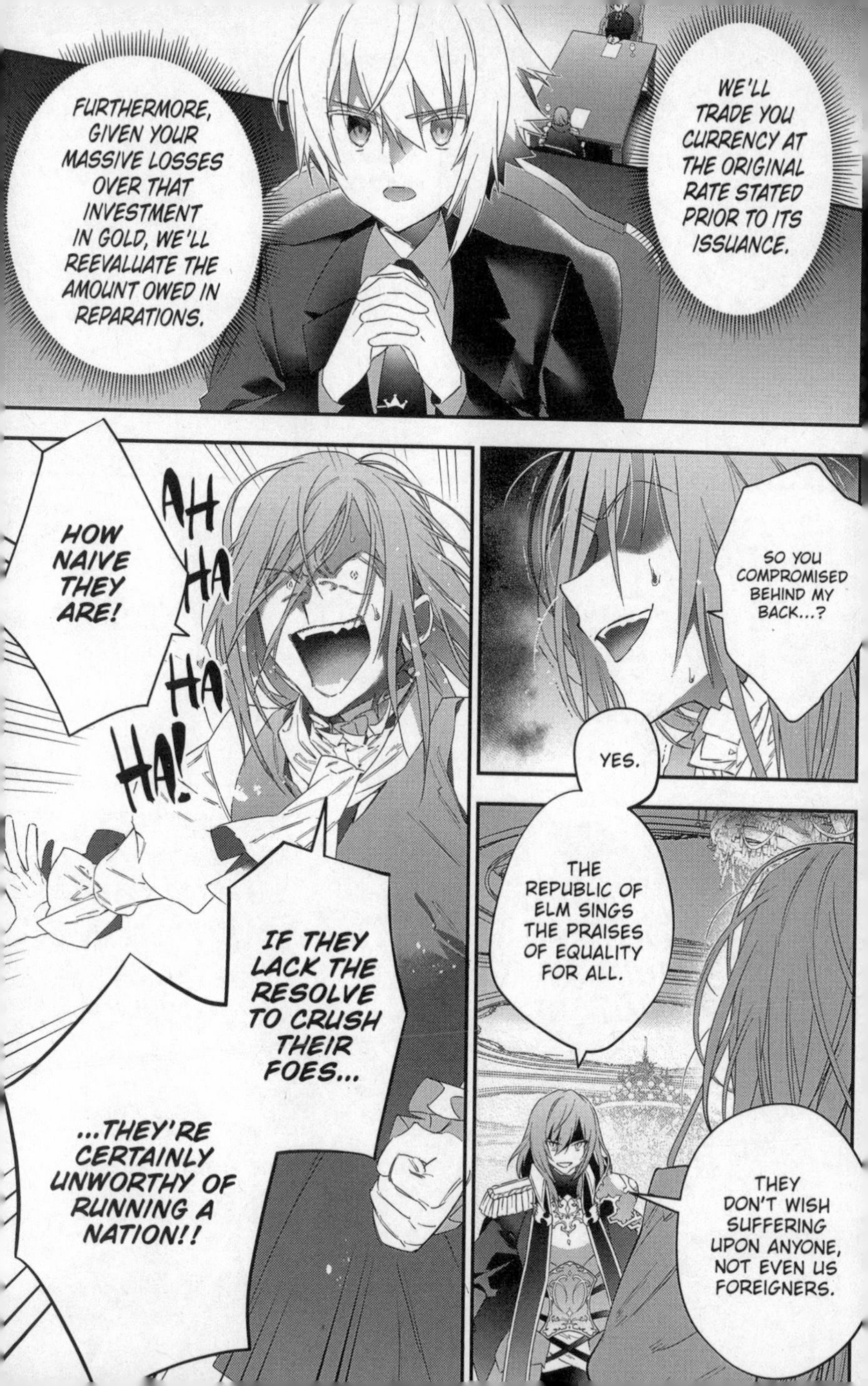
WE'LL TRADE YOU CURRENCY AT THE ORIGINAL RATE STATED PRIOR TO ITS ISSUANCE.
FURTHERMORE, GIVEN YOUR MASSIVE LOSSES OVER THAT INVESTMENT IN GOLD, WE'LL REEVALUATE THE AMOUNT OWED IN REPARATIONS.
SO YOU COMPROMISED BEHIND MY BACK...?
YES.
THE REPUBLIC OF ELM SINGS THE PRAISES OF EQUALITY FOR ALL.
THEY DON'T WISH SUFFERING UPON ANYONE, NOT EVEN US FOREIGNERS.
AH HA HA HA!
HOW NAIVE THEY ARE!
IF THEY LACK THE RESOLVE TO CRUSH THEIR FOES...
...THEY'RE CERTAINLY UNWORTHY OF RUNNING A NATION!!

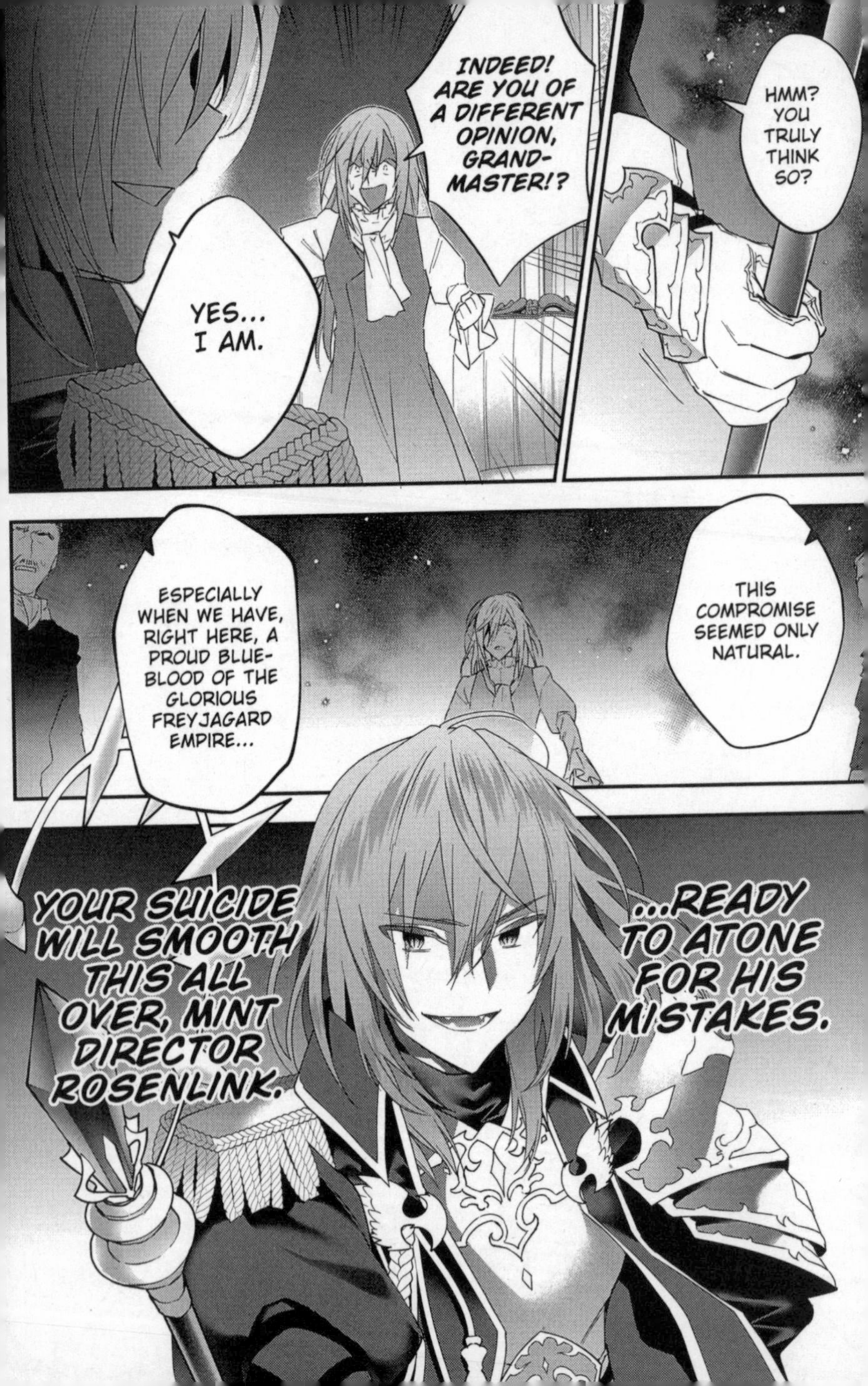
HMM? YOU TRULY THINK SO?
INDEED! ARE YOU OF A DIFFERENT OPINION, GRAND-MASTER!?
YES... I AM.
THIS COMPROMISE SEEMED ONLY NATURAL.
ESPECIALLY WHEN WE HAVE, RIGHT HERE, A PROUD BLUE-BLOOD OF THE GLORIOUS FREYJAGARD EMPIRE...
...READY TO ATONE FOR HIS MISTAKES.
YOUR SUICIDE WILL SMOOTH THIS ALL OVER, MINT DIRECTOR ROSENLINK.

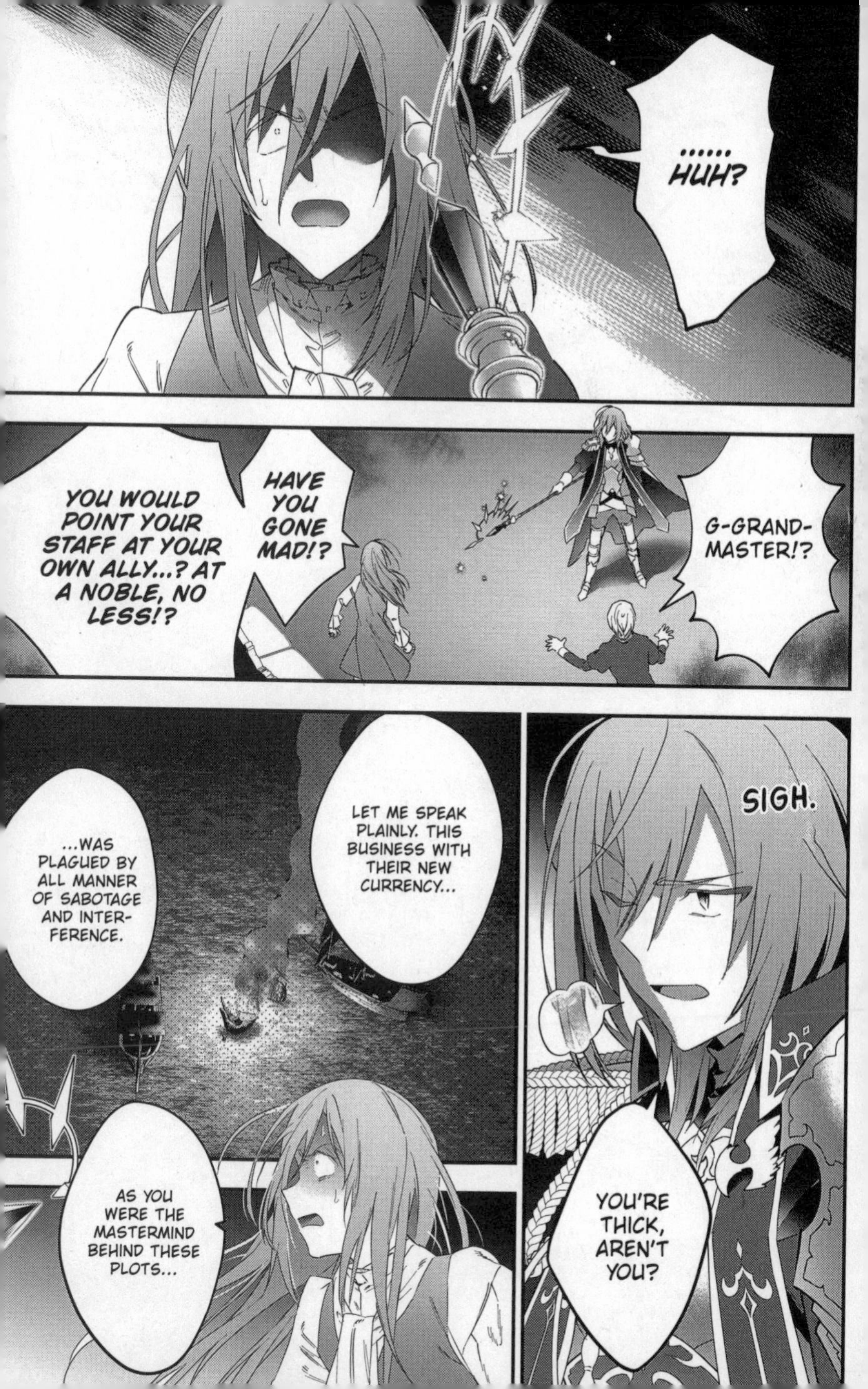

......HUH?
G-GRAND-MASTER!?
HAVE YOU GONE MAD!?
YOU WOULD POINT YOUR STAFF AT YOUR OWN ALLY...? AT A NOBLE, NO LESS!?
SIGH.
YOU'RE THICK, AREN'T YOU?
LET ME SPEAK PLAINLY. THIS BUSINESS WITH THEIR NEW CURRENCY...
...WAS PLAGUED BY ALL MANNER OF SABOTAGE AND INTER-FERENCE.
AS YOU WERE THE MASTERMIND BEHIND THESE PLOTS...

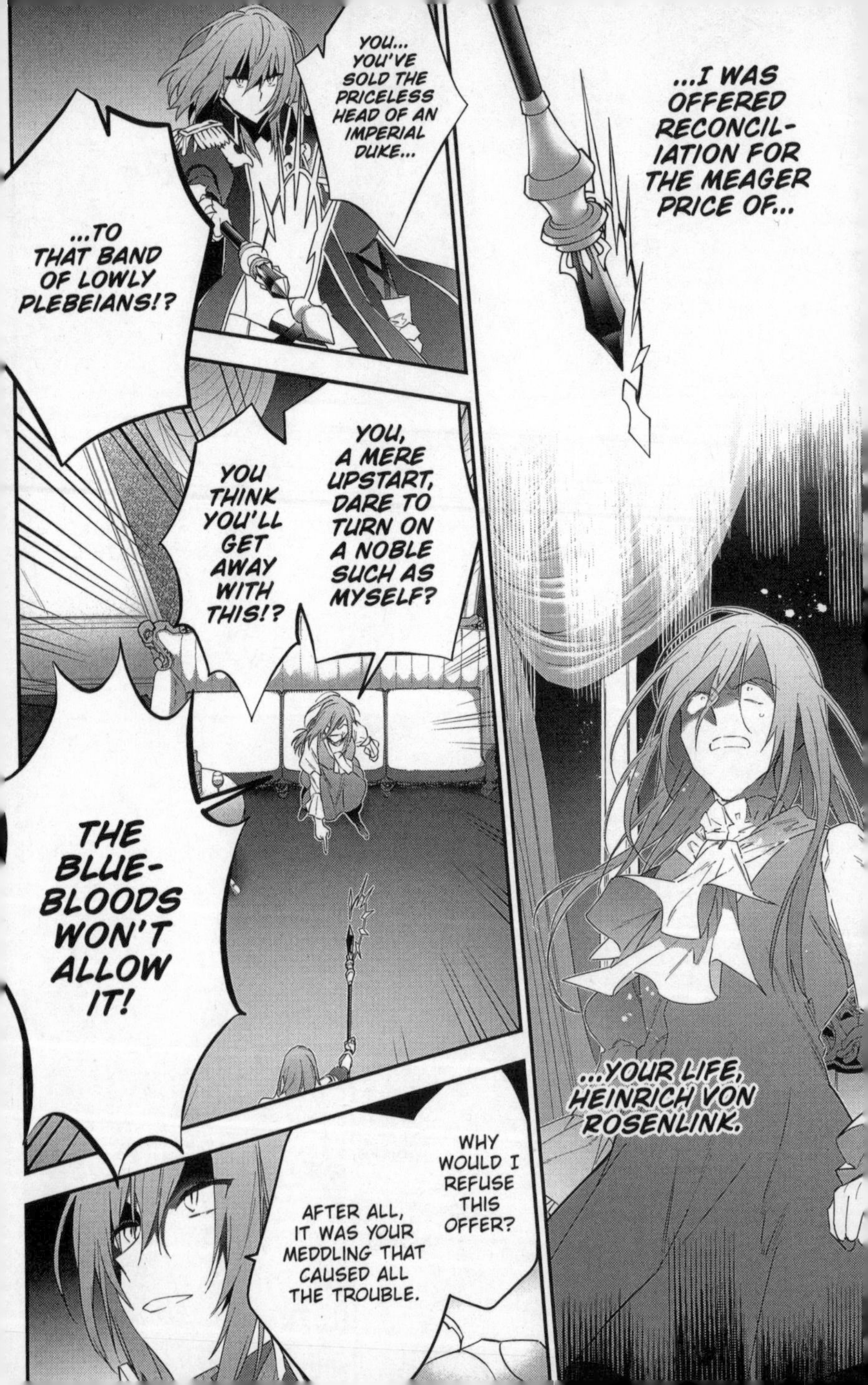
...I WAS OFFERED RECONCIL-IATION FOR THE MEAGER PRICE OF...
...YOUR LIFE, HEINRICH VON ROSENLINK.
YOU... YOU'VE SOLD THE PRICELESS HEAD OF AN IMPERIAL DUKE...
...TO THAT BAND OF LOWLY PLEBEIANS!?
YOU, A MERE UPSTART, DARE TO TURN ON A NOBLE SUCH AS MYSELF?
YOU THINK YOU'LL GET AWAY WITH THIS!?
THE BLUE-BLOODS WON'T ALLOW IT!
WHY WOULD I REFUSE THIS OFFER?
AFTER ALL, IT WAS YOUR MEDDLING THAT CAUSED ALL THE TROUBLE.

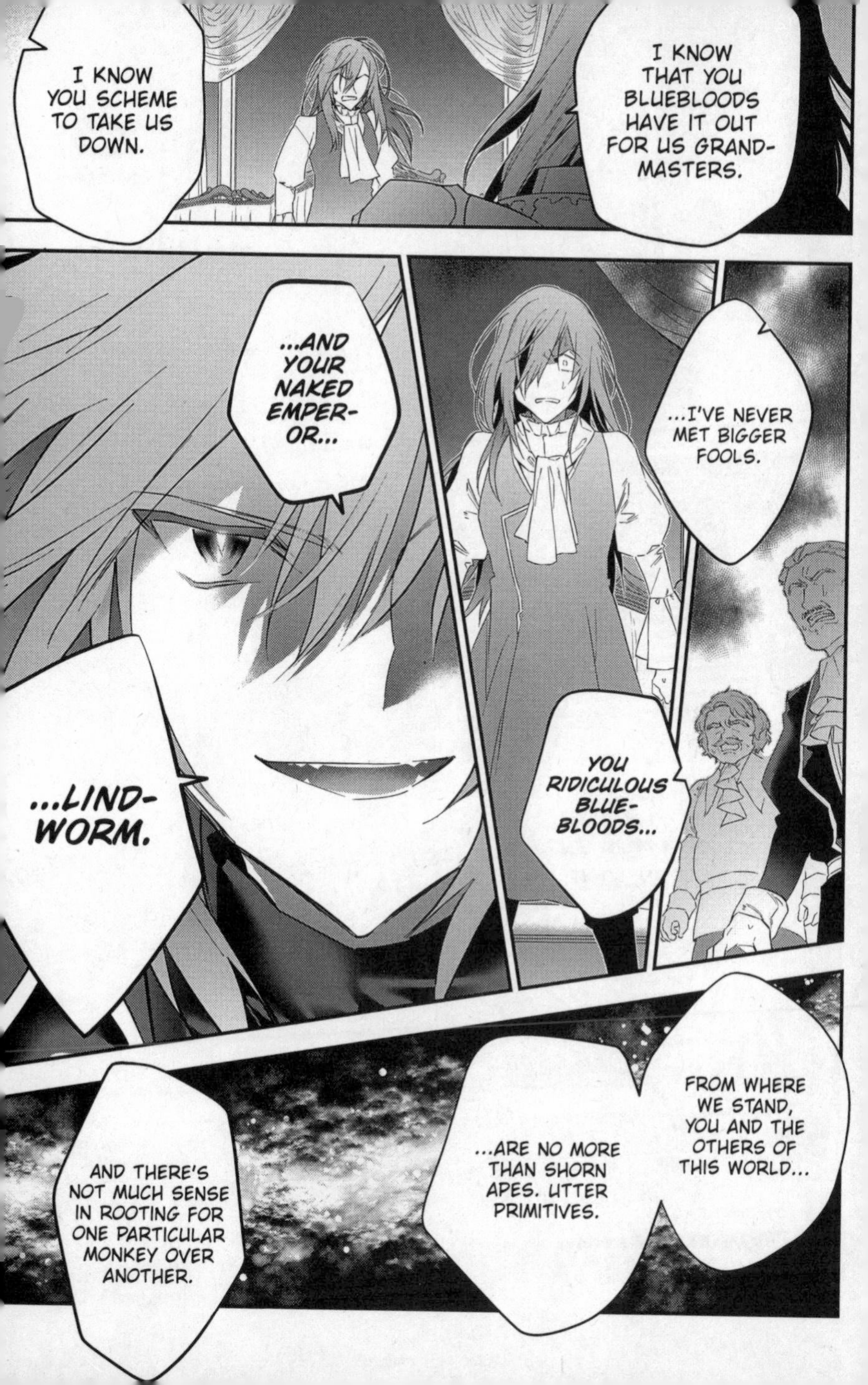
I KNOW THAT YOU BLUEBLOODS HAVE IT OUT FOR US GRAND-MASTERS.
I KNOW YOU SCHEME TO TAKE US DOWN.
...I'VE NEVER MET BIGGER FOOLS.
YOU RIDICULOUS BLUE-BLOODS...
...AND YOUR NAKED EMPEROR...
...LIND-WORM.
FROM WHERE WE STAND, YOU AND THE OTHERS OF THIS WORLD...
...ARE NO MORE THAN SHORN APES. UTTER PRIMITIVES.
AND THERE'S NOT MUCH SENSE IN ROOTING FOR ONE PARTICULAR MONKEY OVER ANOTHER.

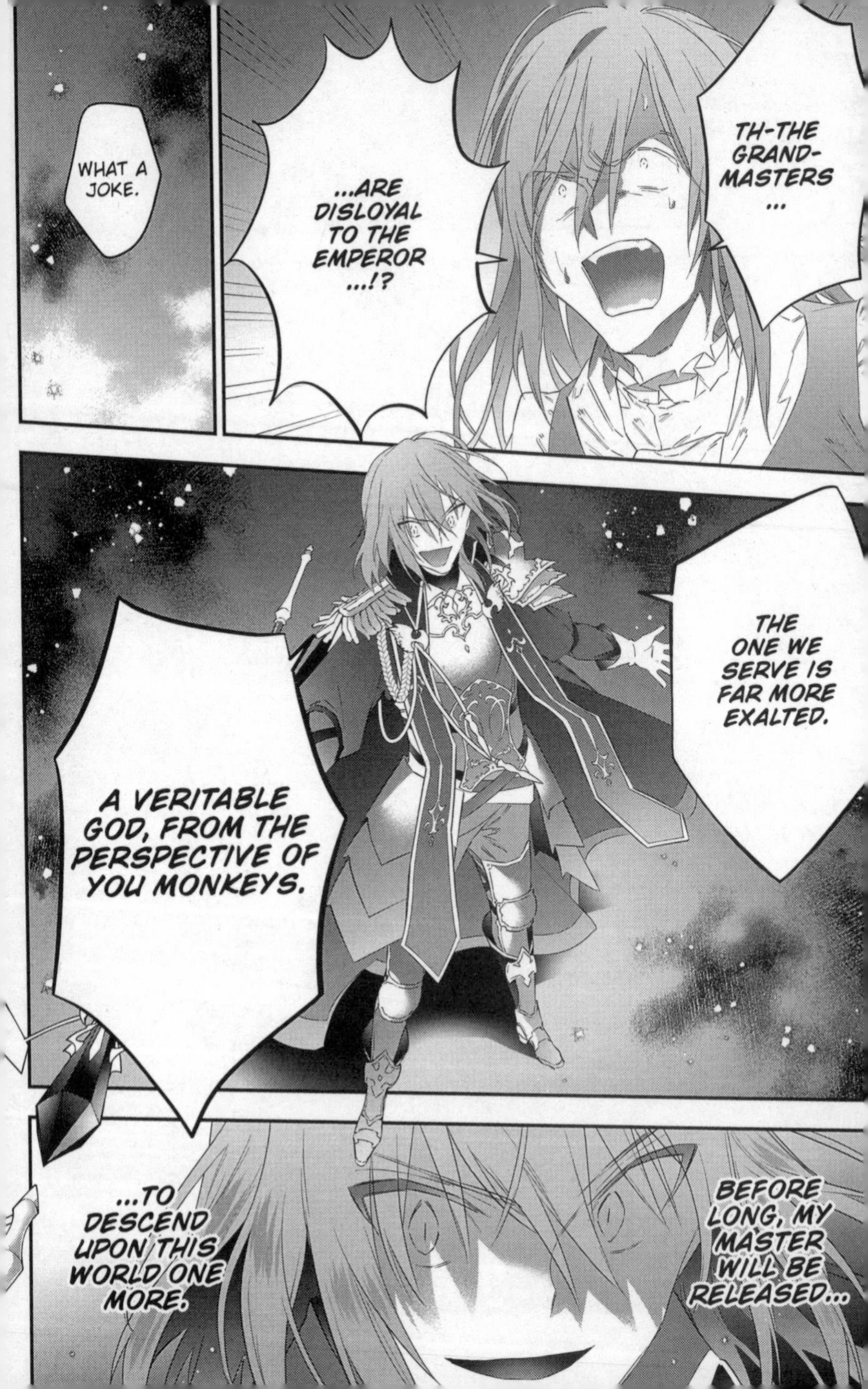
TH-THE GRANDMASTERS...
...ARE DISLOYAL TO THE EMPEROR...!?
WHAT A JOKE.
THE ONE WE SERVE IS FAR MORE EXALTED.
A VERITABLE GOD, FROM THE PERSPECTIVE OF YOU MONKEYS.
BEFORE LONG, MY MASTER WILL BE RELEASED...
...TO DESCEND UPON THIS WORLD ONE MORE.

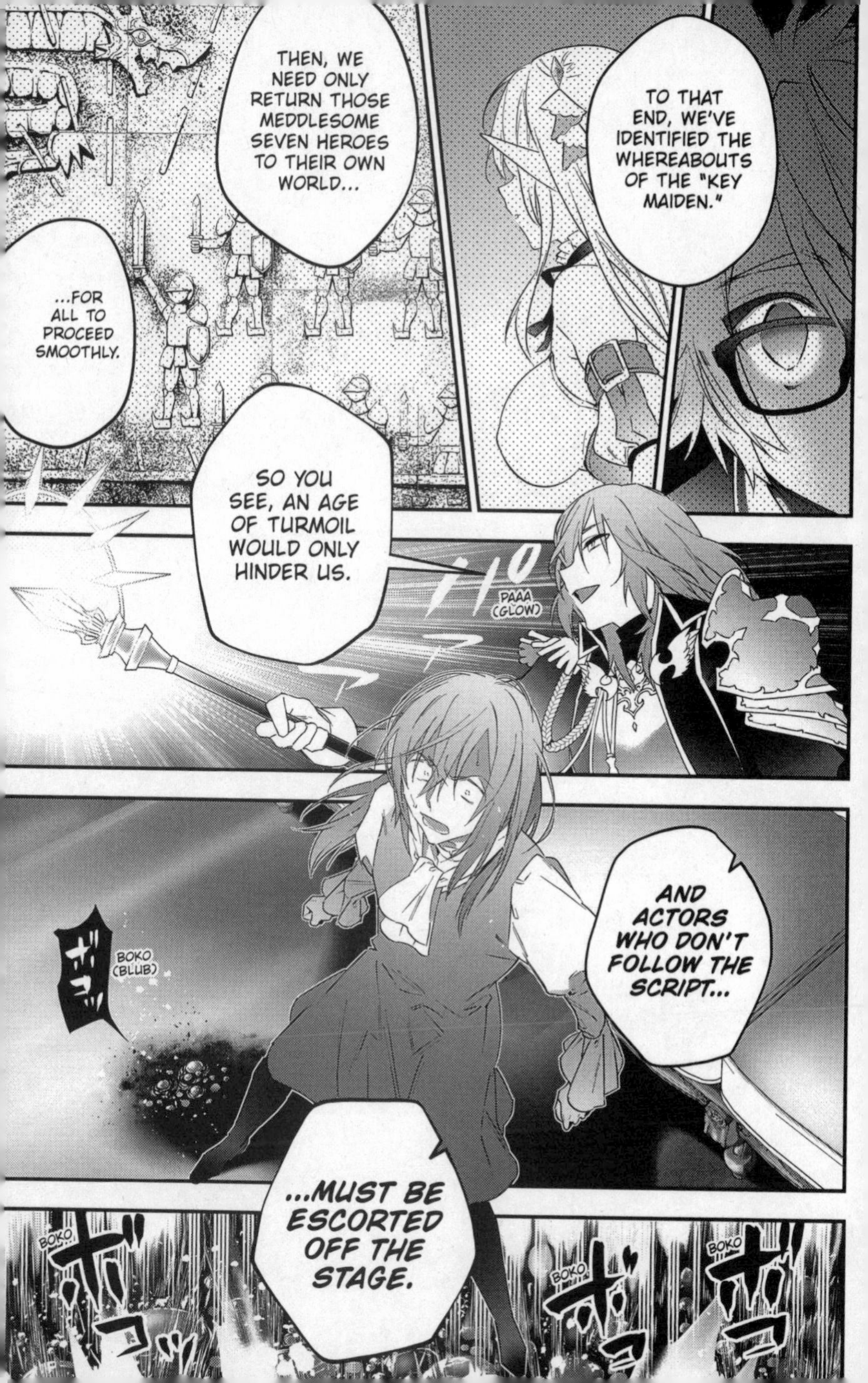
TO THAT END, WE'VE IDENTIFIED THE WHEREABOUTS OF THE "KEY MAIDEN."
THEN, WE NEED ONLY RETURN THOSE MEDDLESOME SEVEN HEROES TO THEIR OWN WORLD...
...FOR ALL TO PROCEED SMOOTHLY.
SO YOU SEE, AN AGE OF TURMOIL WOULD ONLY HINDER US.
PAAA (GLOW)
AND ACTORS WHO DON'T FOLLOW THE SCRIPT...
BOKO (BLUB)
...MUST BE ESCORTED OFF THE STAGE.
BOKO
BOKO
BOKO

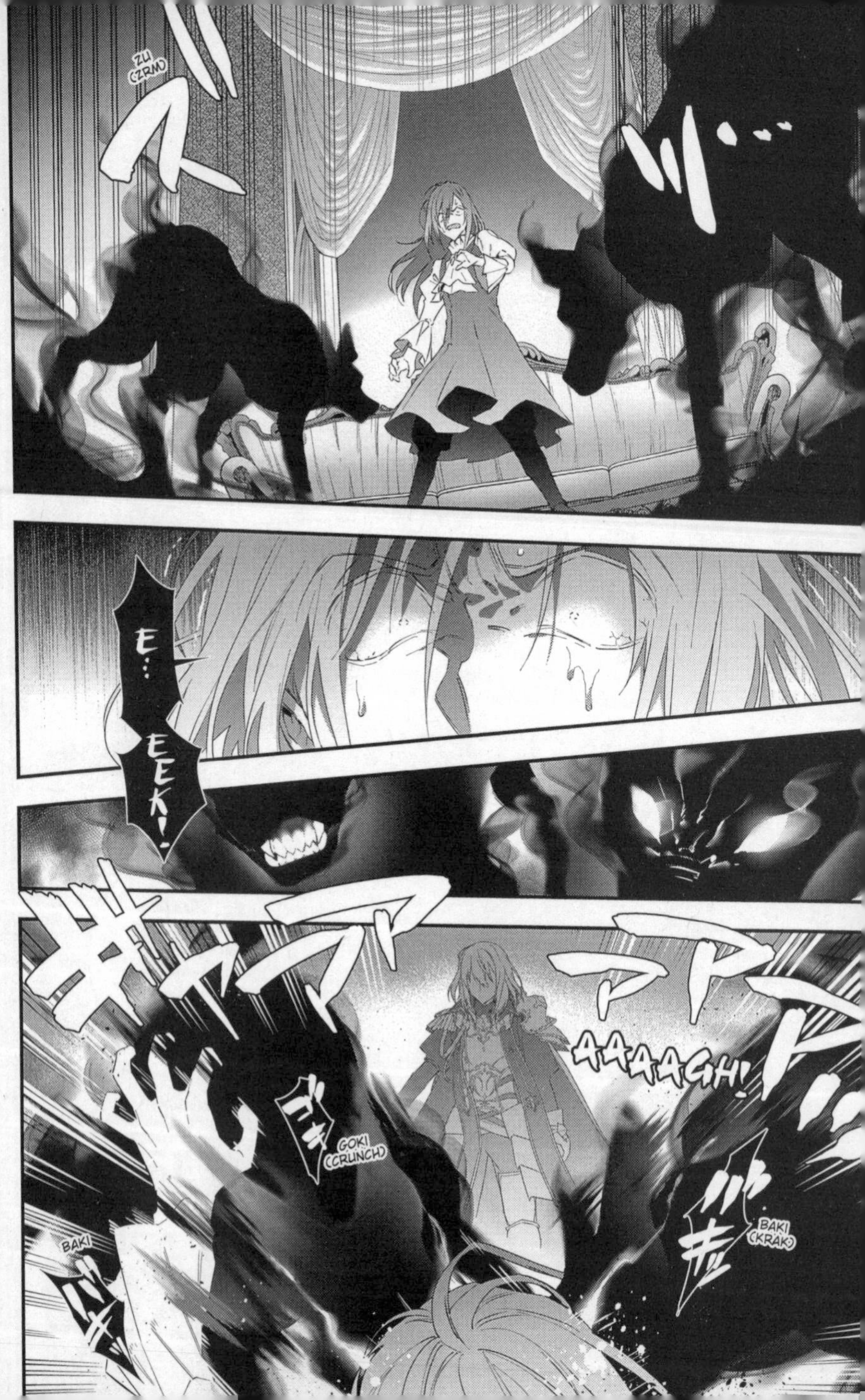
ZU (ZRM)
E... EEK!
BAKI (KRAK)
AAAAAGH!
GOKI (CRUNCH)
BAKI

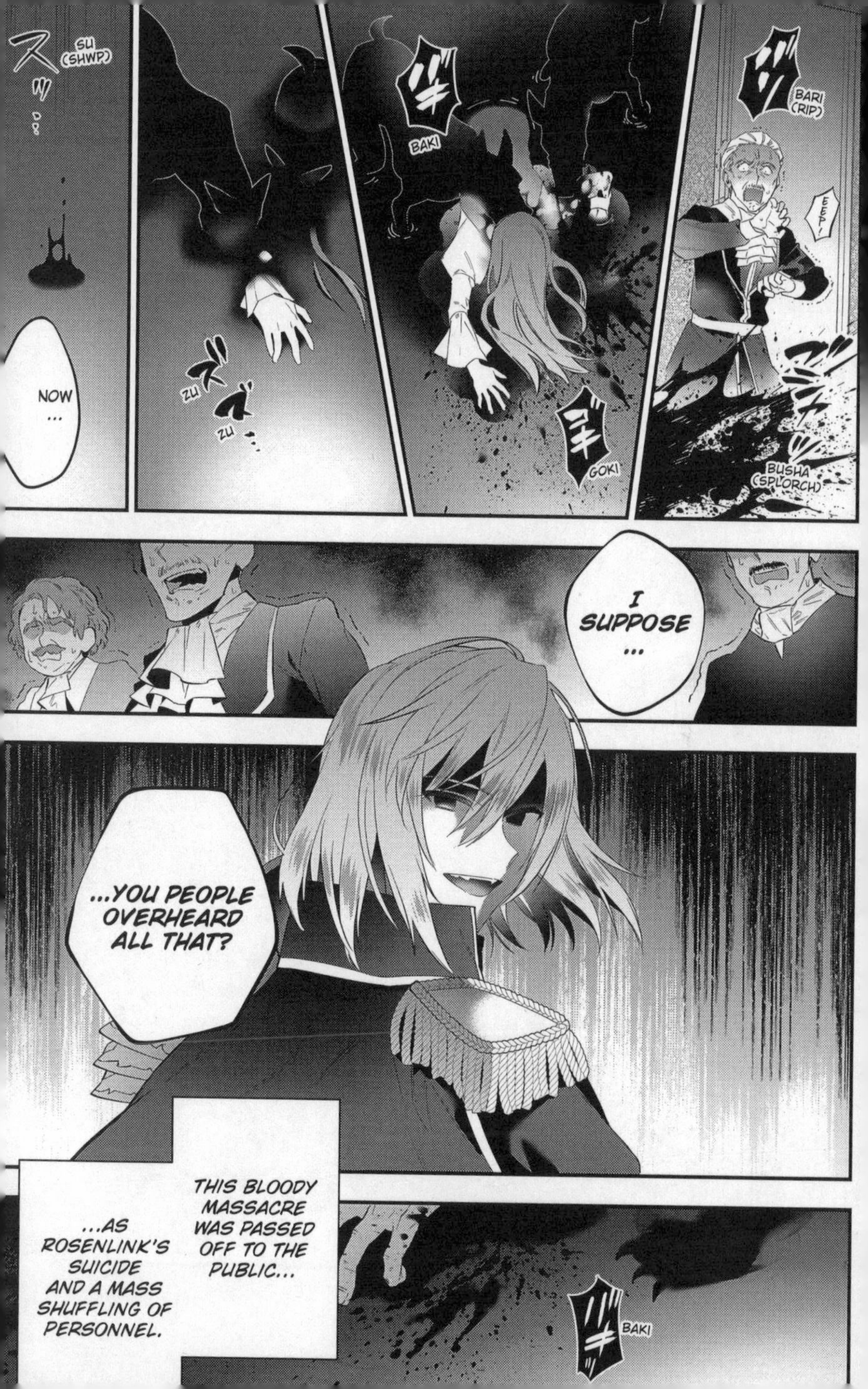
BARI (RIP)
EEEP!
BUSHA (SPLORCH)
BAKI
GOKI
ZU
ZU
SU (SHWP)
NOW...
I SUPPOSE...
...YOU PEOPLE OVERHEARD ALL THAT?
THIS BLOODY MASSACRE WAS PASSED OFF TO THE PUBLIC...
...AS ROSENLINK'S SUICIDE AND A MASS SHUFFLING OF PERSONNEL.
BAKI

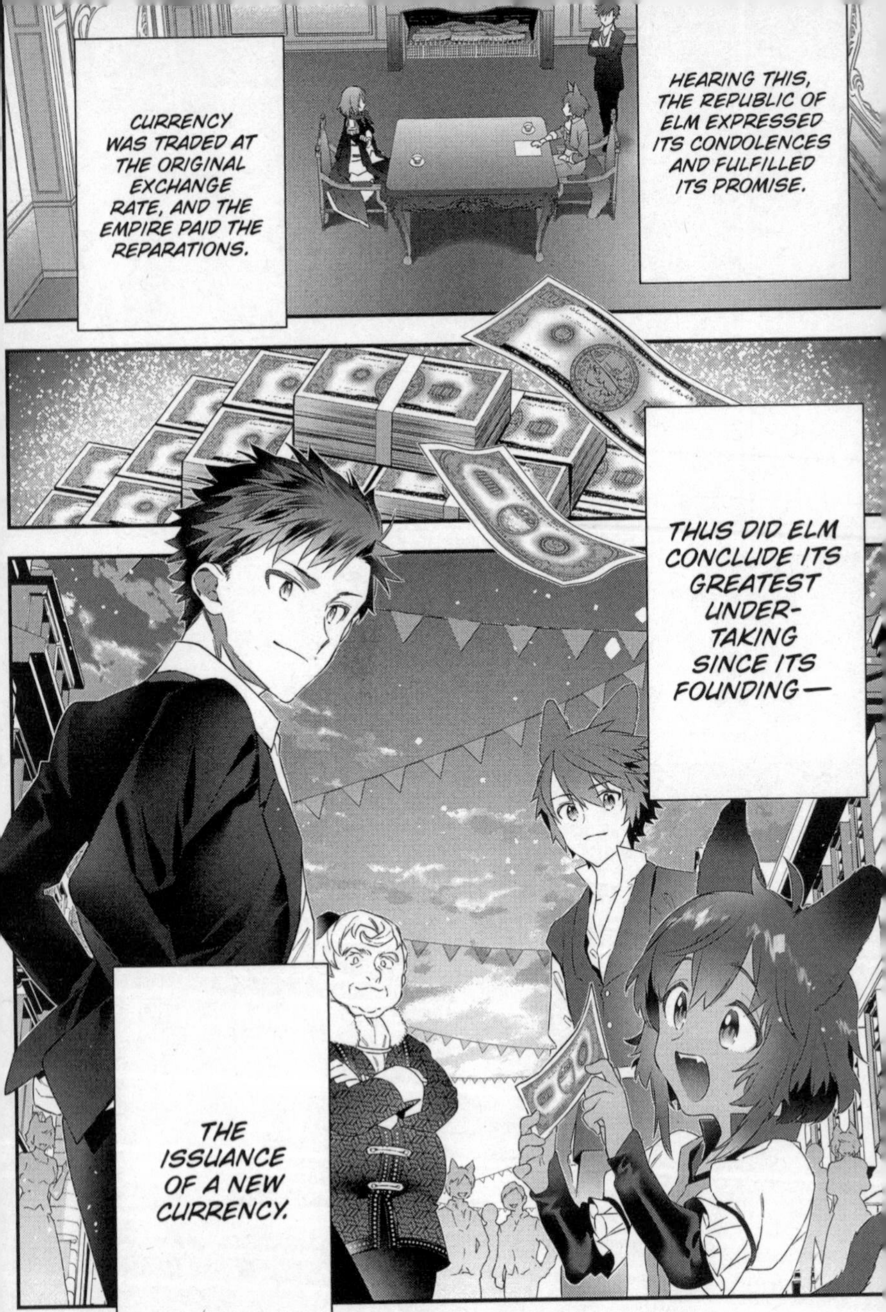
HEARING THIS, THE REPUBLIC OF ELM EXPRESSED ITS CONDOLENCES AND FULFILLED ITS PROMISE.
CURRENCY WAS TRADED AT THE ORIGINAL EXCHANGE RATE, AND THE EMPIRE PAID THE REPARATIONS.
THUS DID ELM CONCLUDE ITS GREATEST UNDER-TAKING SINCE ITS FOUNDING—
THE ISSUANCE OF A NEW CURRENCY.

HIGH SCHOOL PRODIGIES HAVE IT EASY EVEN IN ANOTHER WORLD!

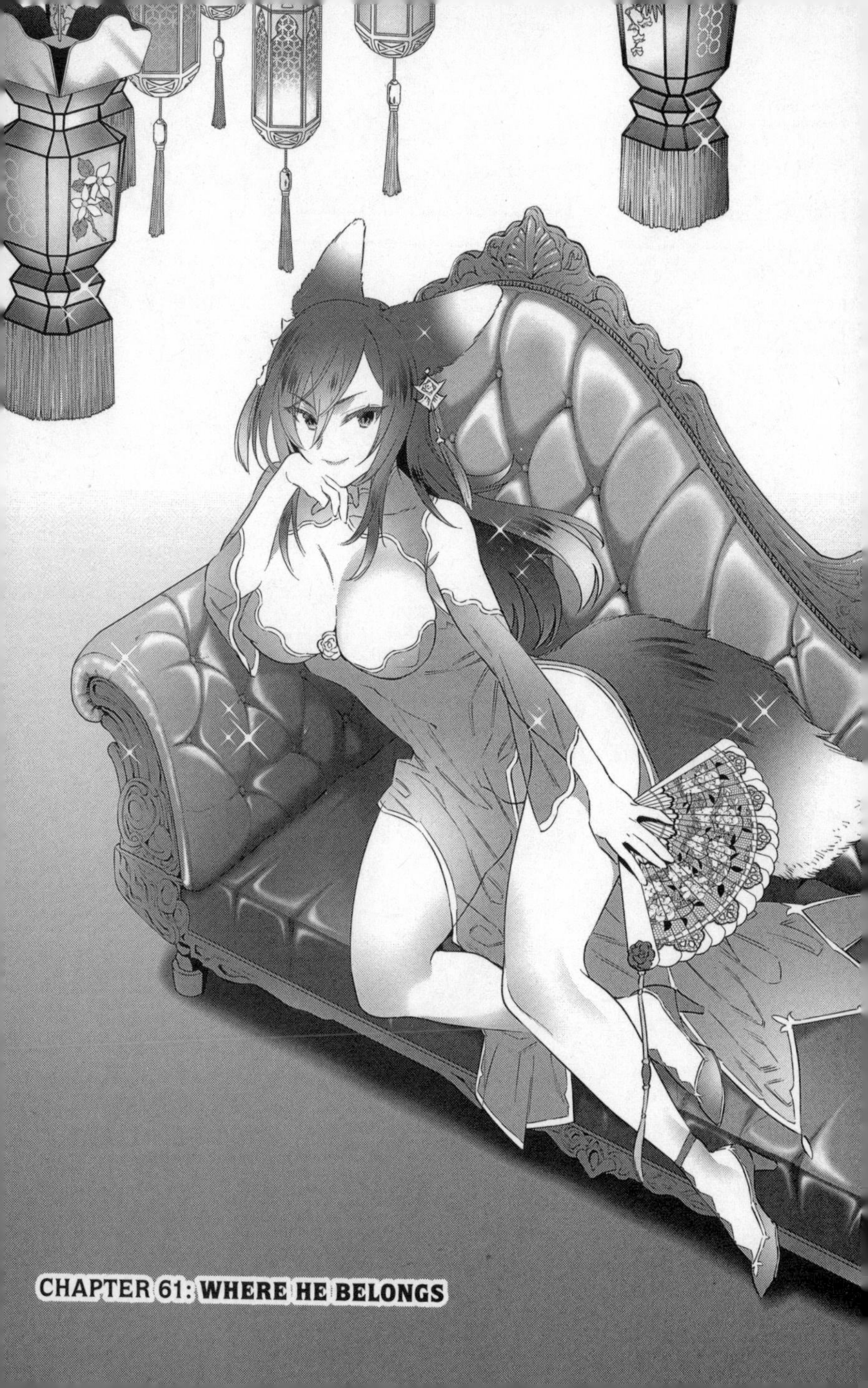

CHAPTER 61: WHERE HE BELONGS

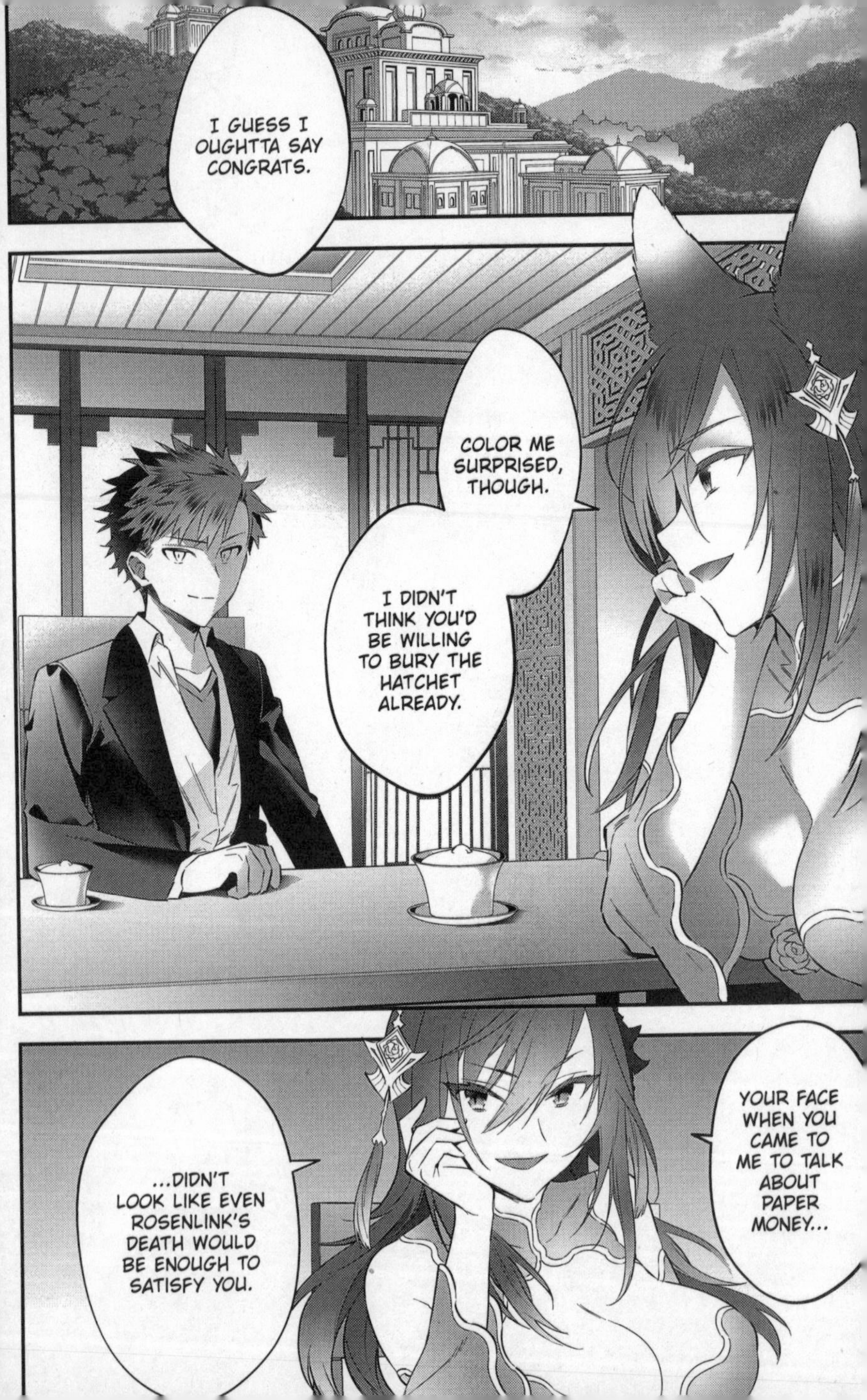
I GUESS I OUGHTTA SAY CONGRATS.
COLOR ME SURPRISED, THOUGH.
I DIDN'T THINK YOU'D BE WILLING TO BURY THE HATCHET ALREADY.
YOUR FACE WHEN YOU CAME TO ME TO TALK ABOUT PAPER MONEY...
...DIDN'T LOOK LIKE EVEN ROSENLINK'S DEATH WOULD BE ENOUGH TO SATISFY YOU.

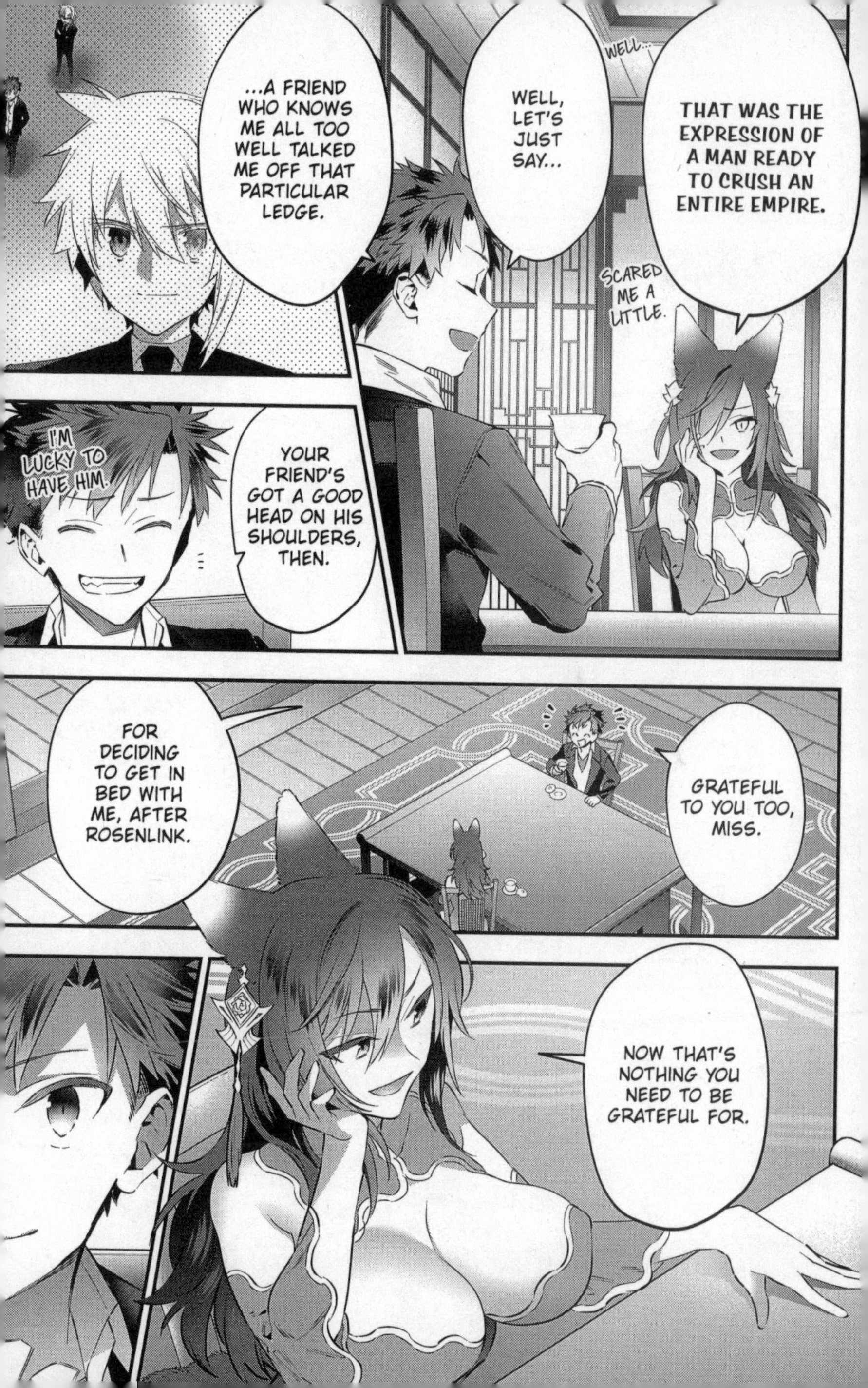
THAT WAS THE EXPRESSION OF A MAN READY TO CRUSH AN ENTIRE EMPIRE.
SCARED ME A LITTLE.
WELL...
WELL, LET'S JUST SAY...
...A FRIEND WHO KNOWS ME ALL TOO WELL TALKED ME OFF THAT PARTICULAR LEDGE.
YOUR FRIEND'S GOT A GOOD HEAD ON HIS SHOULDERS, THEN.
I'M LUCKY TO HAVE HIM.
GRATEFUL TO YOU TOO, MISS.
FOR DECIDING TO GET IN BED WITH ME, AFTER ROSENLINK.
NOW THAT'S NOTHING YOU NEED TO BE GRATEFUL FOR.

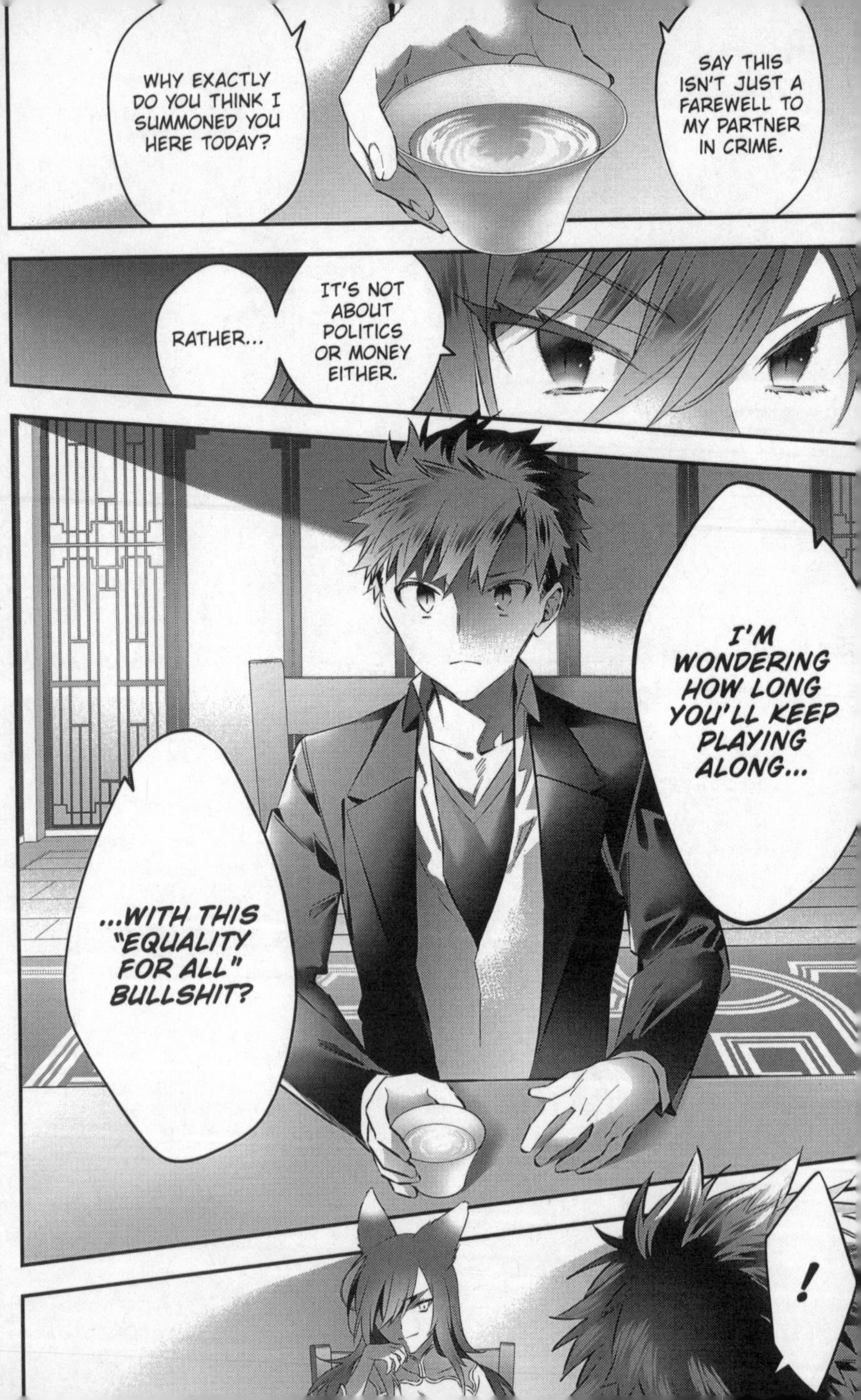
SAY THIS ISN'T JUST A FAREWELL TO MY PARTNER IN CRIME.
WHY EXACTLY DO YOU THINK I SUMMONED YOU HERE TODAY?
IT'S NOT ABOUT POLITICS OR MONEY EITHER.
RATHER...
I'M WONDERING HOW LONG YOU'LL KEEP PLAYING ALONG...
...WITH THIS "EQUALITY FOR ALL" BULLSHIT?
!

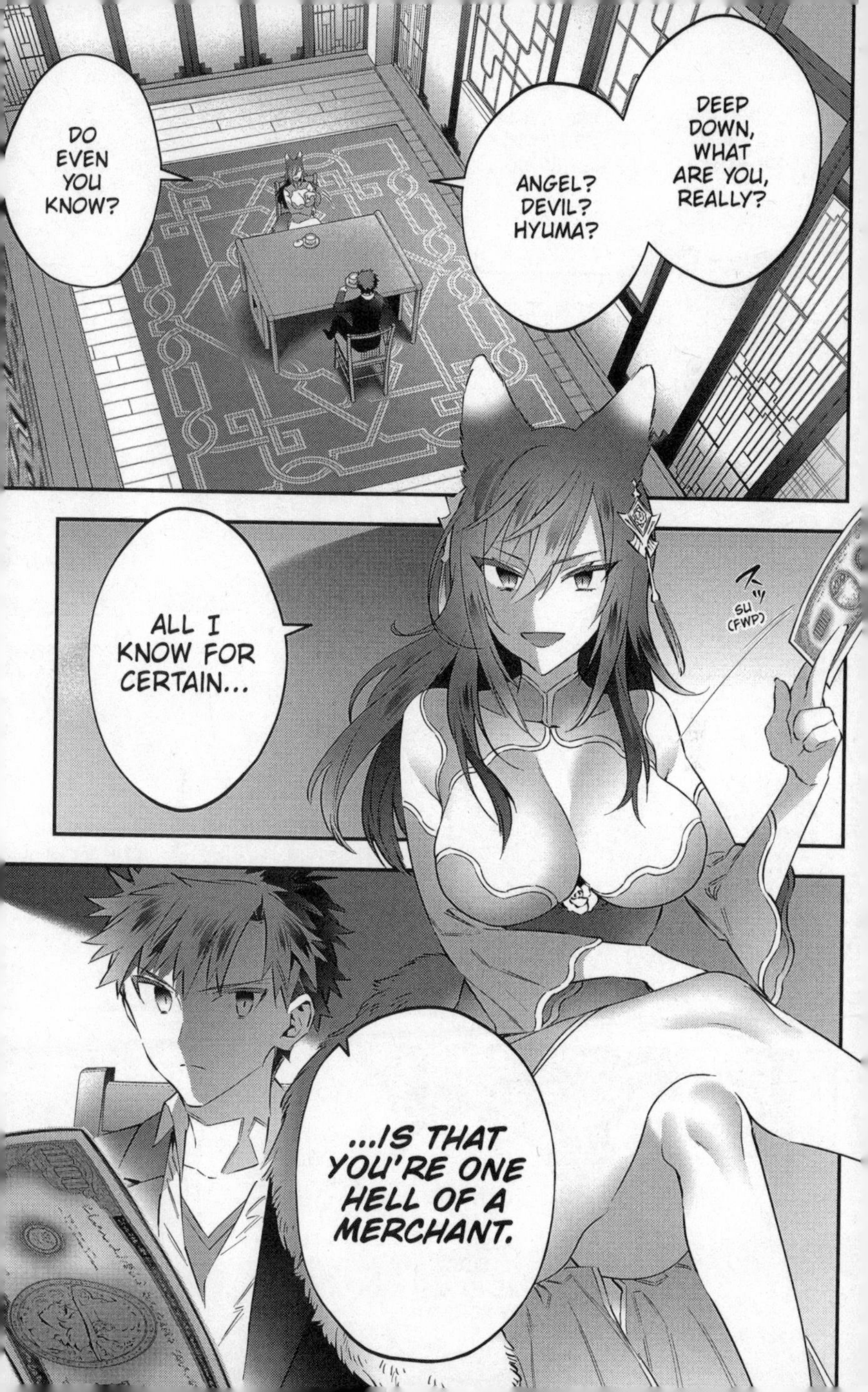
DEEP DOWN, WHAT ARE YOU, REALLY? ANGEL? DEVIL? HYUMA?
DO EVEN YOU KNOW?
スッ
SU (FWP)
ALL I KNOW FOR CERTAIN...
...IS THAT YOU'RE ONE HELL OF A MERCHANT.

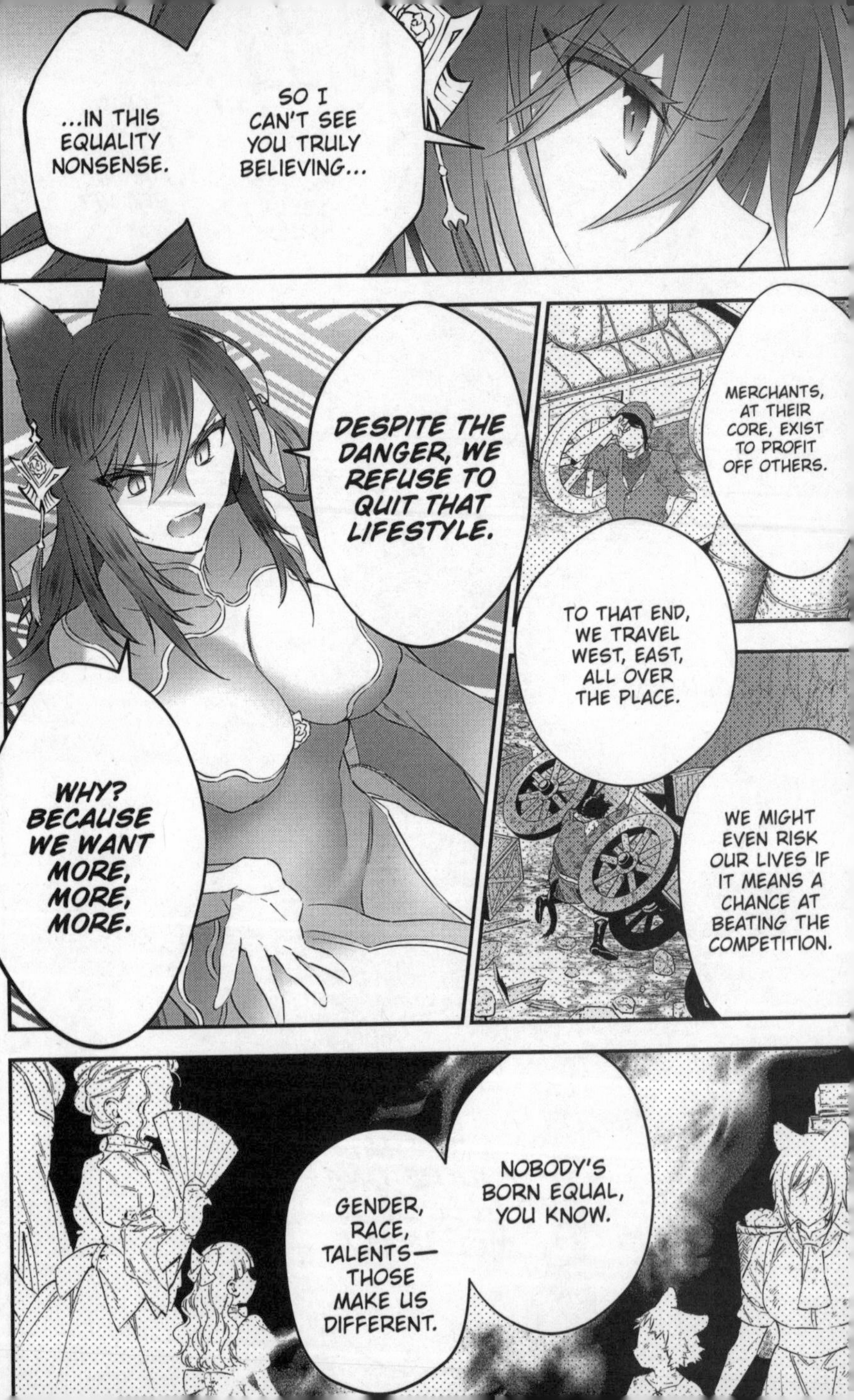
SO I CAN'T SEE YOU TRULY BELIEVING...
...IN THIS EQUALITY NONSENSE.
MERCHANTS, AT THEIR CORE, EXIST TO PROFIT OFF OTHERS.
TO THAT END, WE TRAVEL WEST, EAST, ALL OVER THE PLACE.
WE MIGHT EVEN RISK OUR LIVES IF IT MEANS A CHANCE AT BEATING THE COMPETITION.
DESPITE THE DANGER, WE REFUSE TO QUIT THAT LIFESTYLE.
WHY? BECAUSE WE WANT MORE, MORE, MORE.
NOBODY'S BORN EQUAL, YOU KNOW.
GENDER, RACE, TALENTS—THOSE MAKE US DIFFERENT.

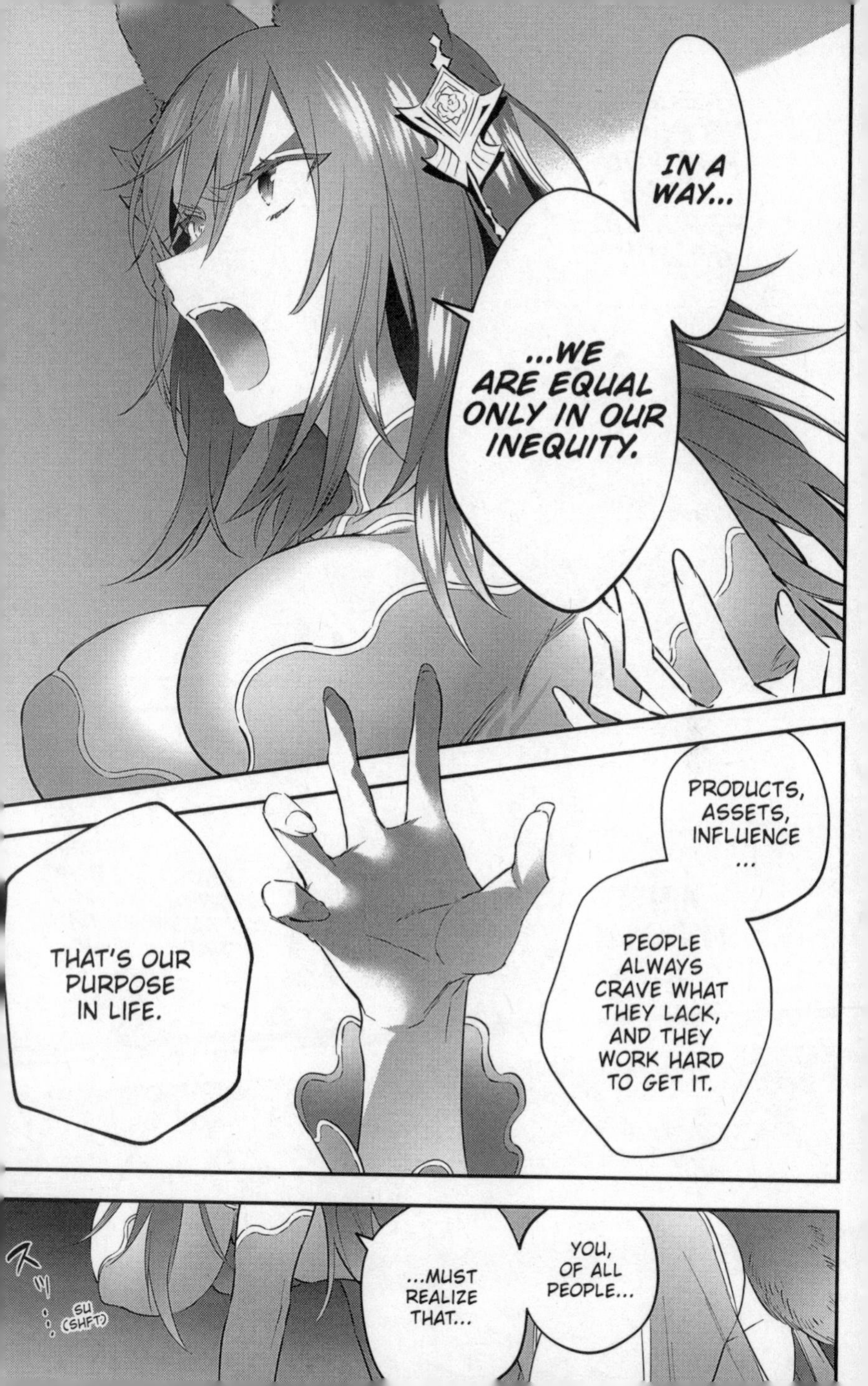
IN A WAY...
...WE ARE EQUAL ONLY IN OUR INEQUITY.
PRODUCTS, ASSETS, INFLUENCE ...
PEOPLE ALWAYS CRAVE WHAT THEY LACK, AND THEY WORK HARD TO GET IT.
THAT'S OUR PURPOSE IN LIFE.
YOU, OF ALL PEOPLE...
...MUST REALIZE THAT...
SU (SHFT)

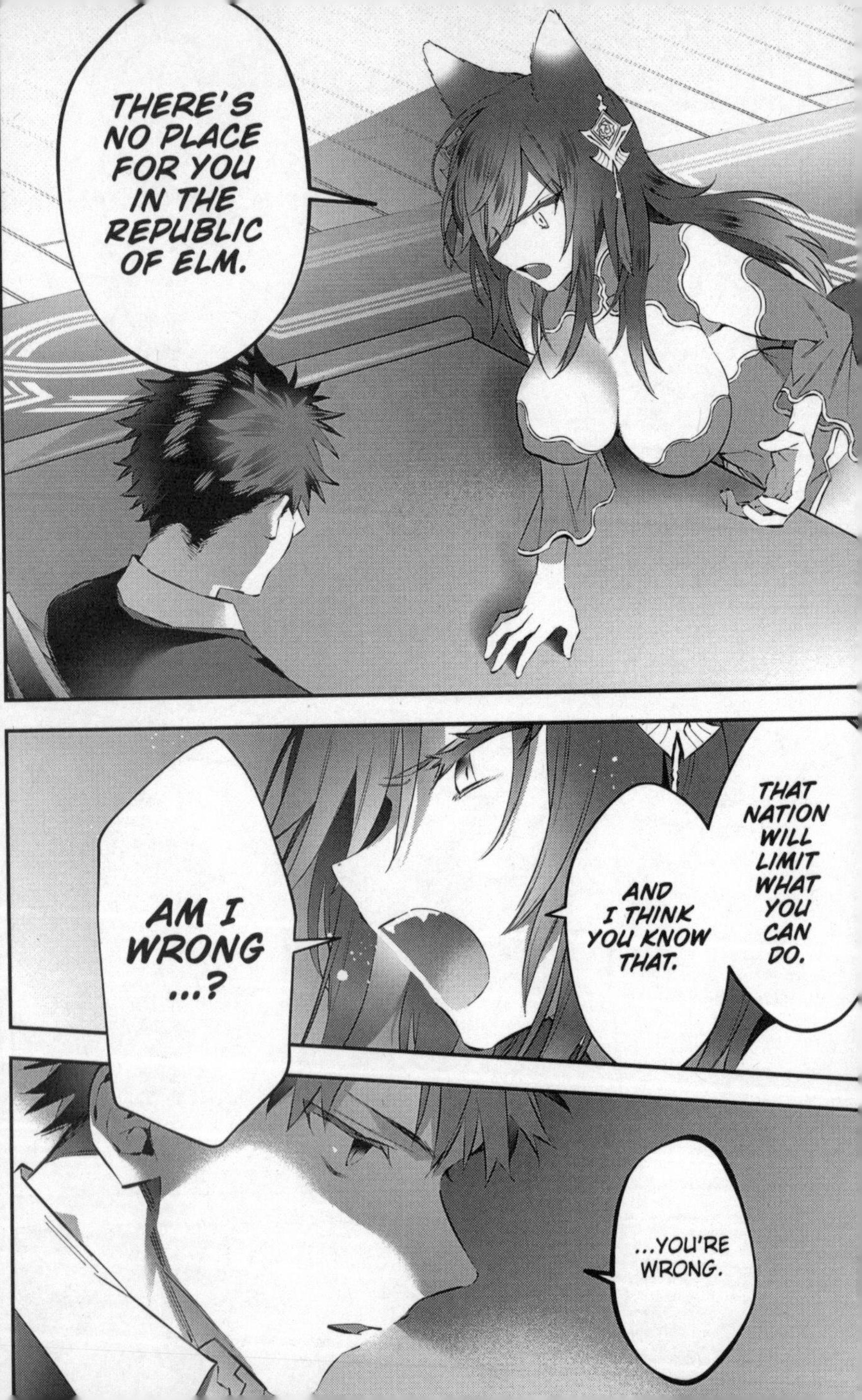
THERE'S NO PLACE FOR YOU IN THE REPUBLIC OF ELM.
THAT NATION WILL LIMIT WHAT YOU CAN DO.
AND I THINK YOU KNOW THAT.
AM I WRONG ...?
...YOU'RE WRONG.

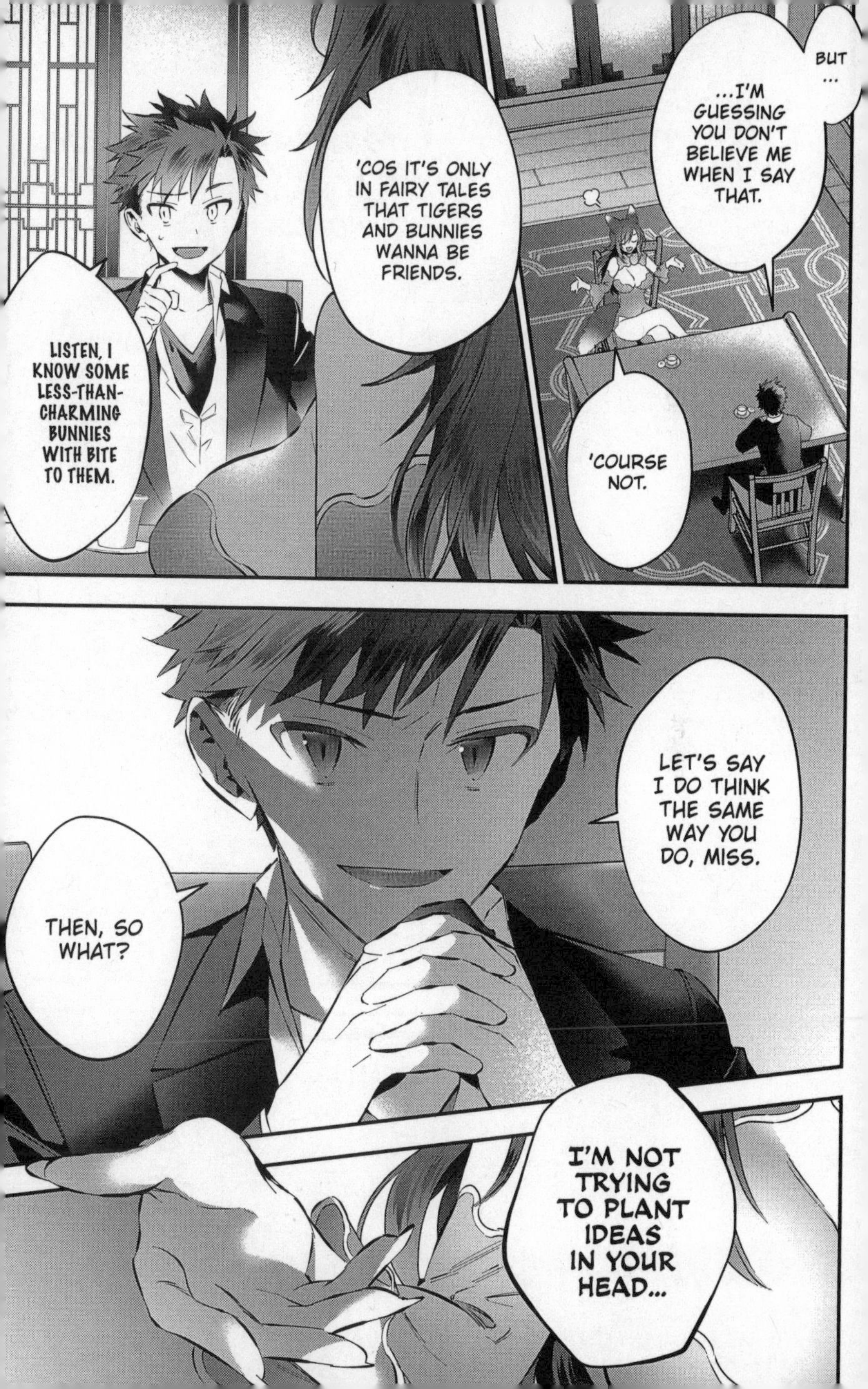
BUT ...
...I'M GUESSING YOU DON'T BELIEVE ME WHEN I SAY THAT.
'COURSE NOT.
'COS IT'S ONLY IN FAIRY TALES THAT TIGERS AND BUNNIES WANNA BE FRIENDS.
LISTEN, I KNOW SOME LESS-THAN-CHARMING BUNNIES WITH BITE TO THEM.
LET'S SAY I DO THINK THE SAME WAY YOU DO, MISS.
THEN, SO WHAT?
I'M NOT TRYING TO PLANT IDEAS IN YOUR HEAD...

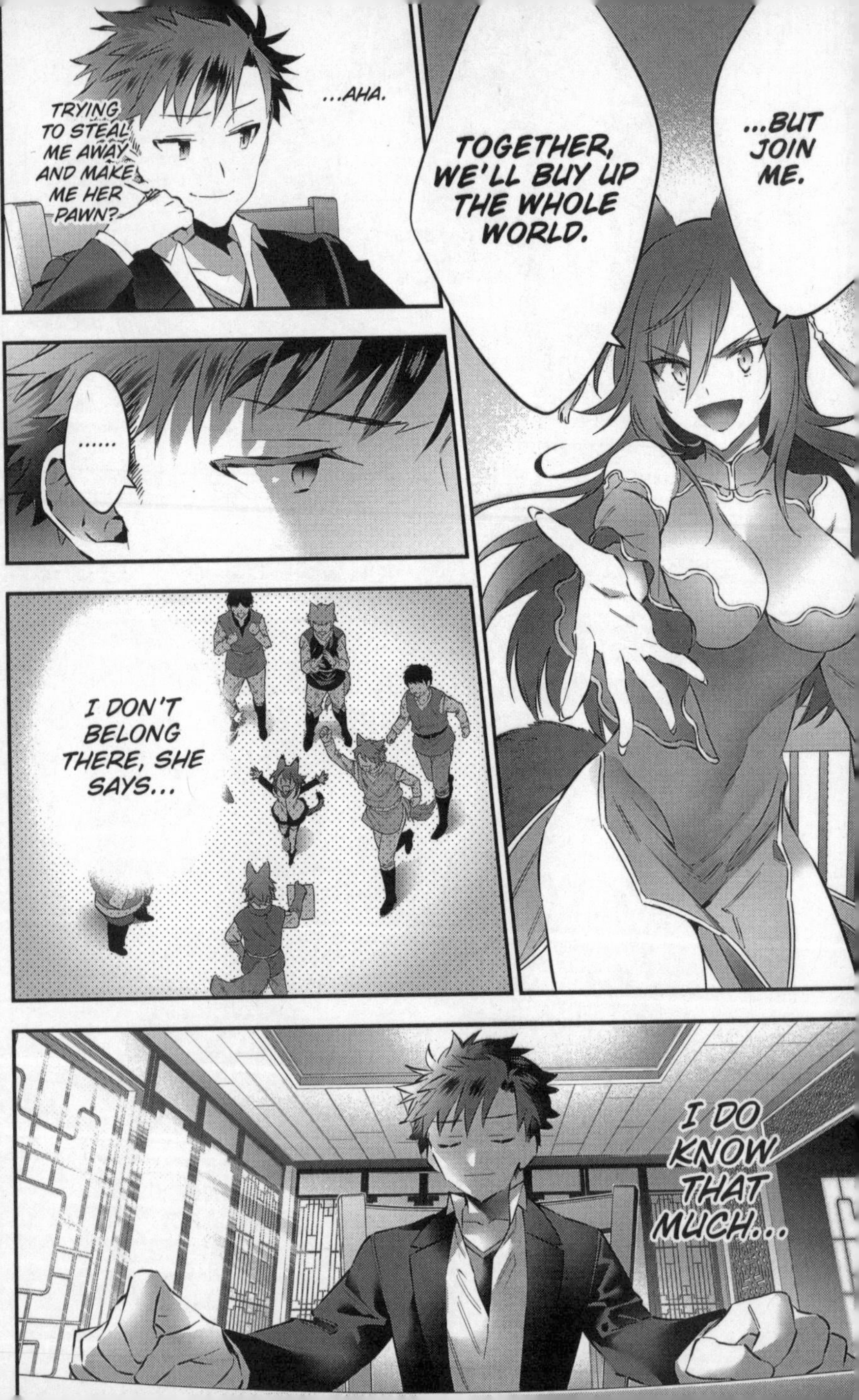
...BUT JOIN ME.
TOGETHER, WE'LL BUY UP THE WHOLE WORLD.
...AHA.
TRYING TO STEAL ME AWAY AND MAKE ME HER PAWN?
......
I DON'T BELONG THERE, SHE SAYS...
I DO KNOW THAT MUCH...

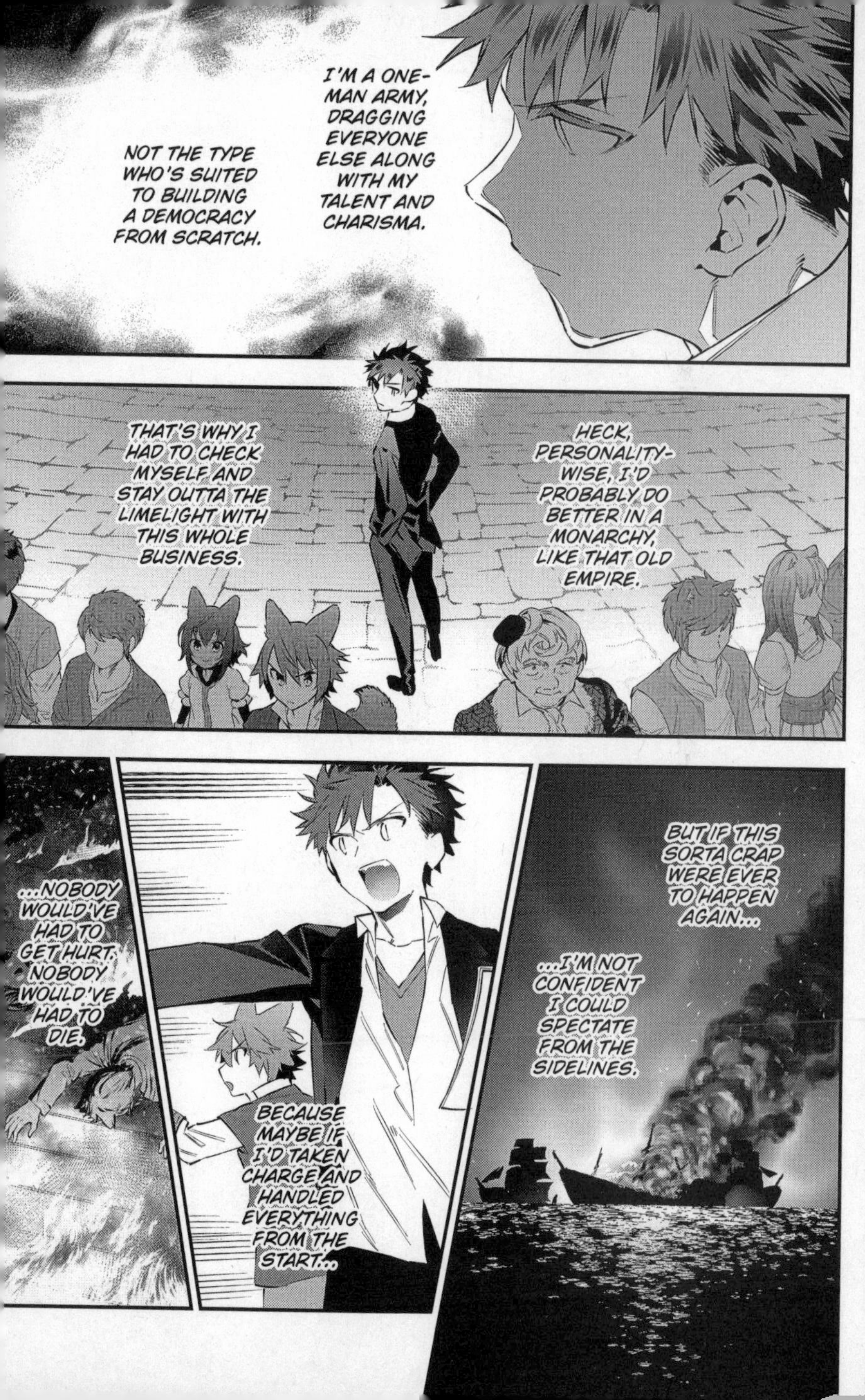
I'M A ONE-MAN ARMY, DRAGGING EVERYONE ELSE ALONG WITH MY TALENT AND CHARISMA.
NOT THE TYPE WHO'S SUITED TO BUILDING A DEMOCRACY FROM SCRATCH.
HECK, PERSONALITY-WISE, I'D PROBABLY DO BETTER IN A MONARCHY, LIKE THAT OLD EMPIRE.
THAT'S WHY I HAD TO CHECK MYSELF AND STAY OUTTA THE LIMELIGHT WITH THIS WHOLE BUSINESS.
BUT IF THIS SORTA CRAP WERE EVER TO HAPPEN AGAIN...
...I'M NOT CONFIDENT I COULD SPECTATE FROM THE SIDELINES.
BECAUSE MAYBE IF I'D TAKEN CHARGE AND HANDLED EVERYTHING FROM THE START...
...NOBODY WOULD'VE HAD TO GET HURT. NOBODY WOULD'VE HAD TO DIE.

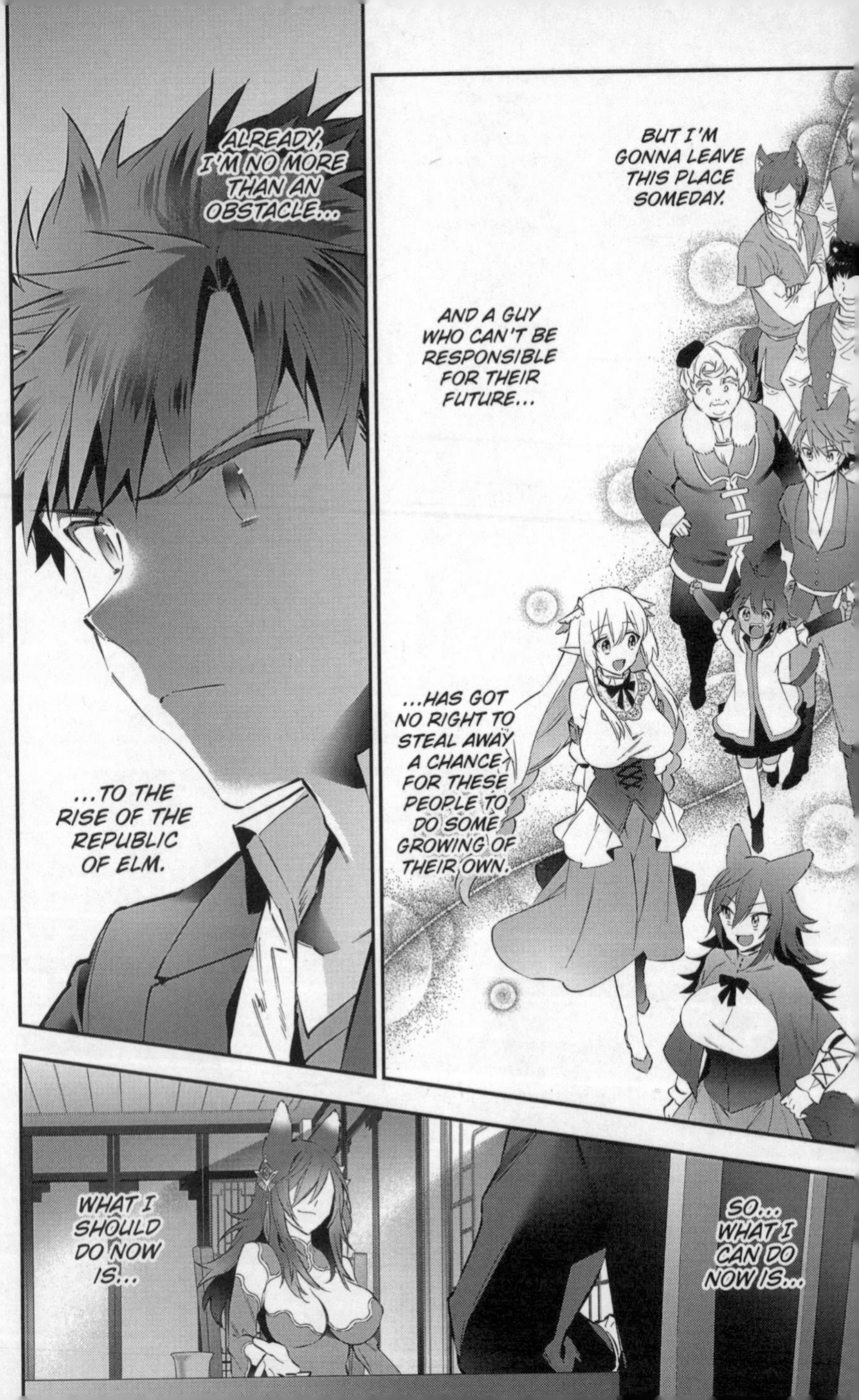
BUT I'M GONNA LEAVE THIS PLACE SOMEDAY.
AND A GUY WHO CAN'T BE RESPONSIBLE FOR THEIR FUTURE...
...HAS GOT NO RIGHT TO STEAL AWAY A CHANCE FOR THESE PEOPLE TO DO SOME GROWING OF THEIR OWN.
ALREADY, I'M NO MORE THAN AN OBSTACLE...
...TO THE RISE OF THE REPUBLIC OF ELM.
SO... WHAT I CAN DO NOW IS...
WHAT I SHOULD DO NOW IS...

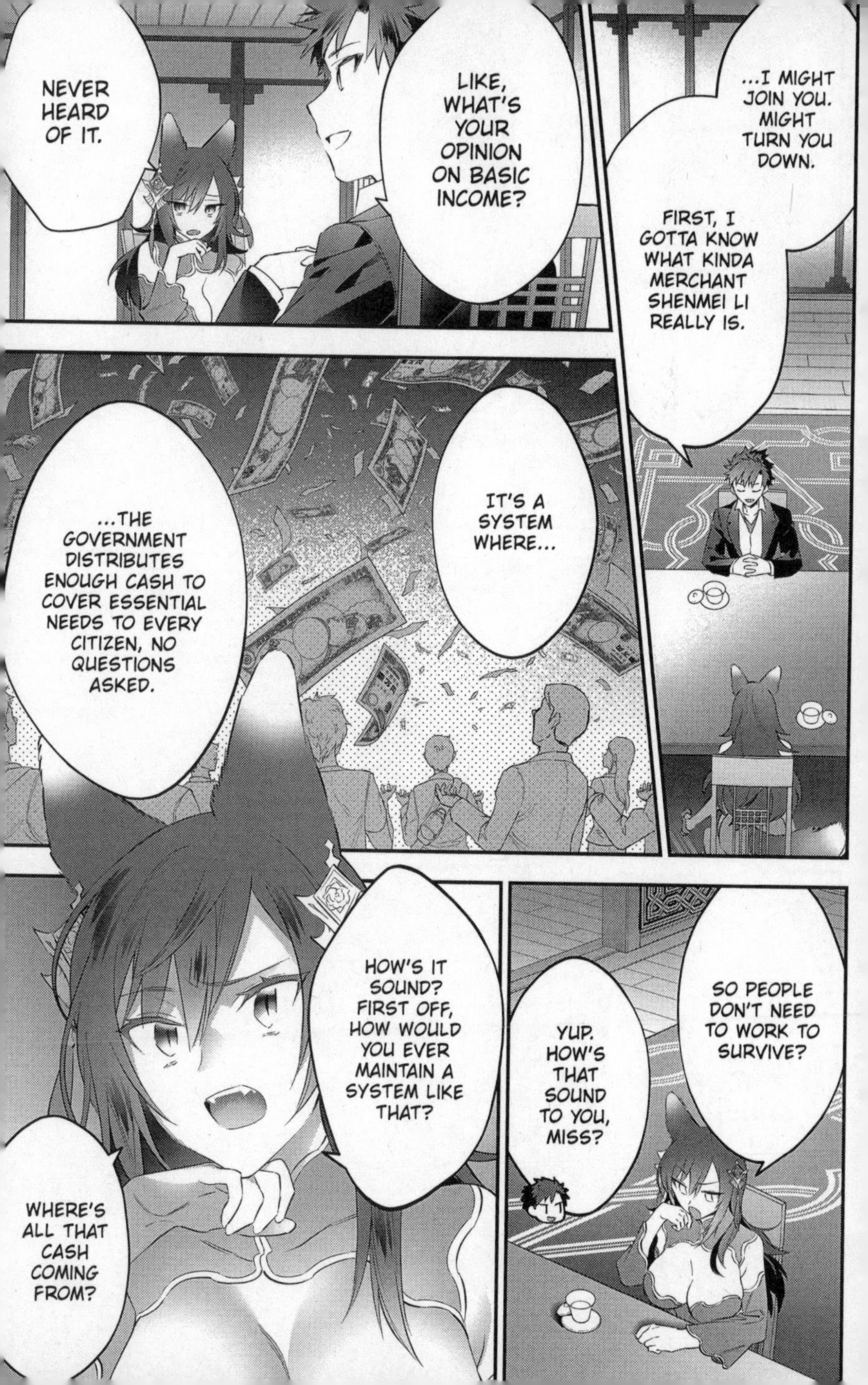
...I MIGHT JOIN YOU. MIGHT TURN YOU DOWN.
FIRST, I GOTTA KNOW WHAT KINDA MERCHANT SHENMEI LI REALLY IS.
LIKE, WHAT'S YOUR OPINION ON BASIC INCOME?
NEVER HEARD OF IT.
IT'S A SYSTEM WHERE...
...THE GOVERNMENT DISTRIBUTES ENOUGH CASH TO COVER ESSENTIAL NEEDS TO EVERY CITIZEN, NO QUESTIONS ASKED.
SO PEOPLE DON'T NEED TO WORK TO SURVIVE?
YUP. HOW'S THAT SOUND TO YOU, MISS?
HOW'S IT SOUND? FIRST OFF, HOW WOULD YOU EVER MAINTAIN A SYSTEM LIKE THAT?
WHERE'S ALL THAT CASH COMING FROM?

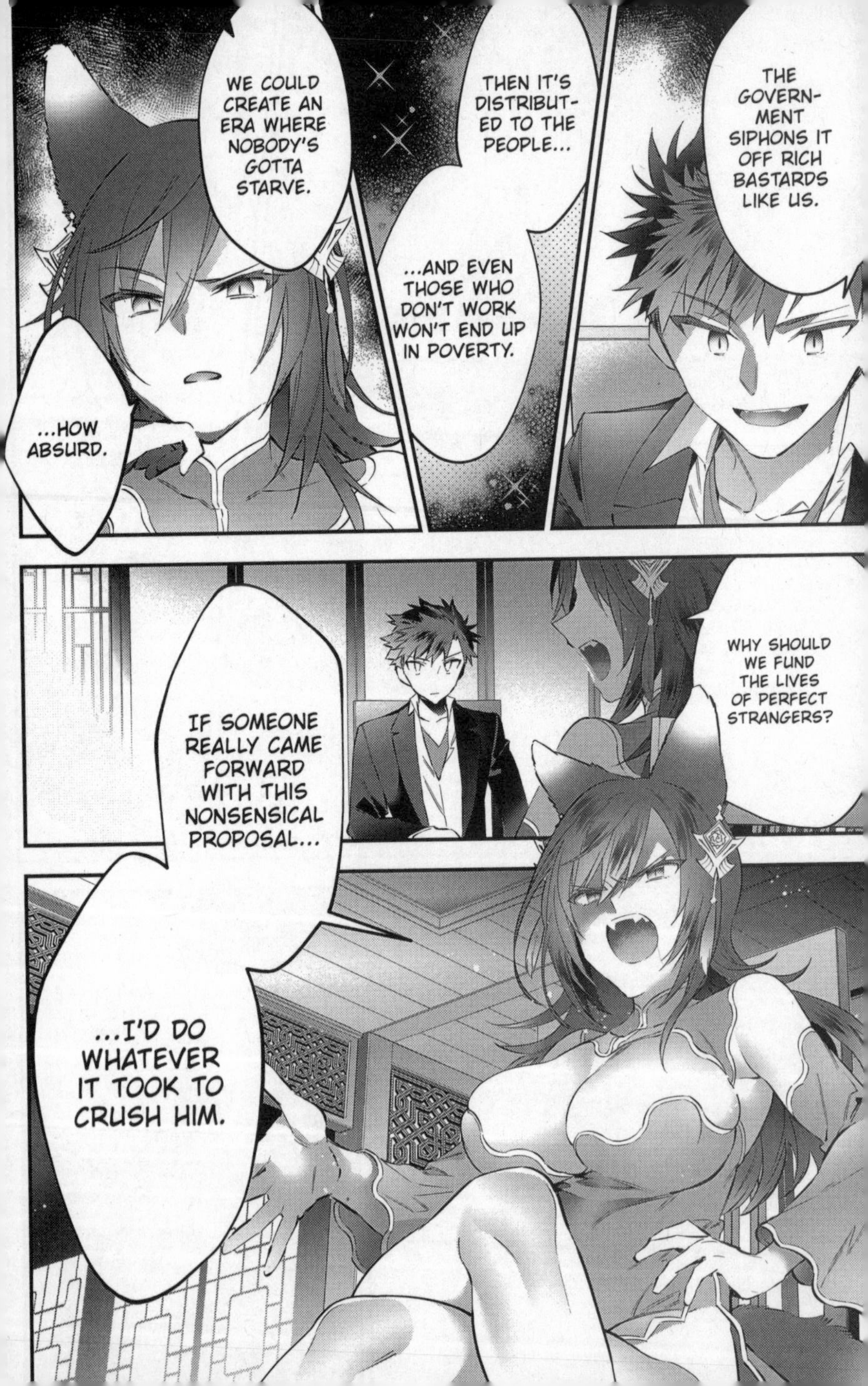
THE GOVERNMENT SIPHONS IT OFF RICH BASTARDS LIKE US.
THEN IT'S DISTRIBUTED TO THE PEOPLE...
...AND EVEN THOSE WHO DON'T WORK WON'T END UP IN POVERTY.
WE COULD CREATE AN ERA WHERE NOBODY'S GOTTA STARVE.
...HOW ABSURD.
WHY SHOULD WE FUND THE LIVES OF PERFECT STRANGERS?
IF SOMEONE REALLY CAME FORWARD WITH THIS NONSENSICAL PROPOSAL...
...I'D DO WHATEVER IT TOOK TO CRUSH HIM.

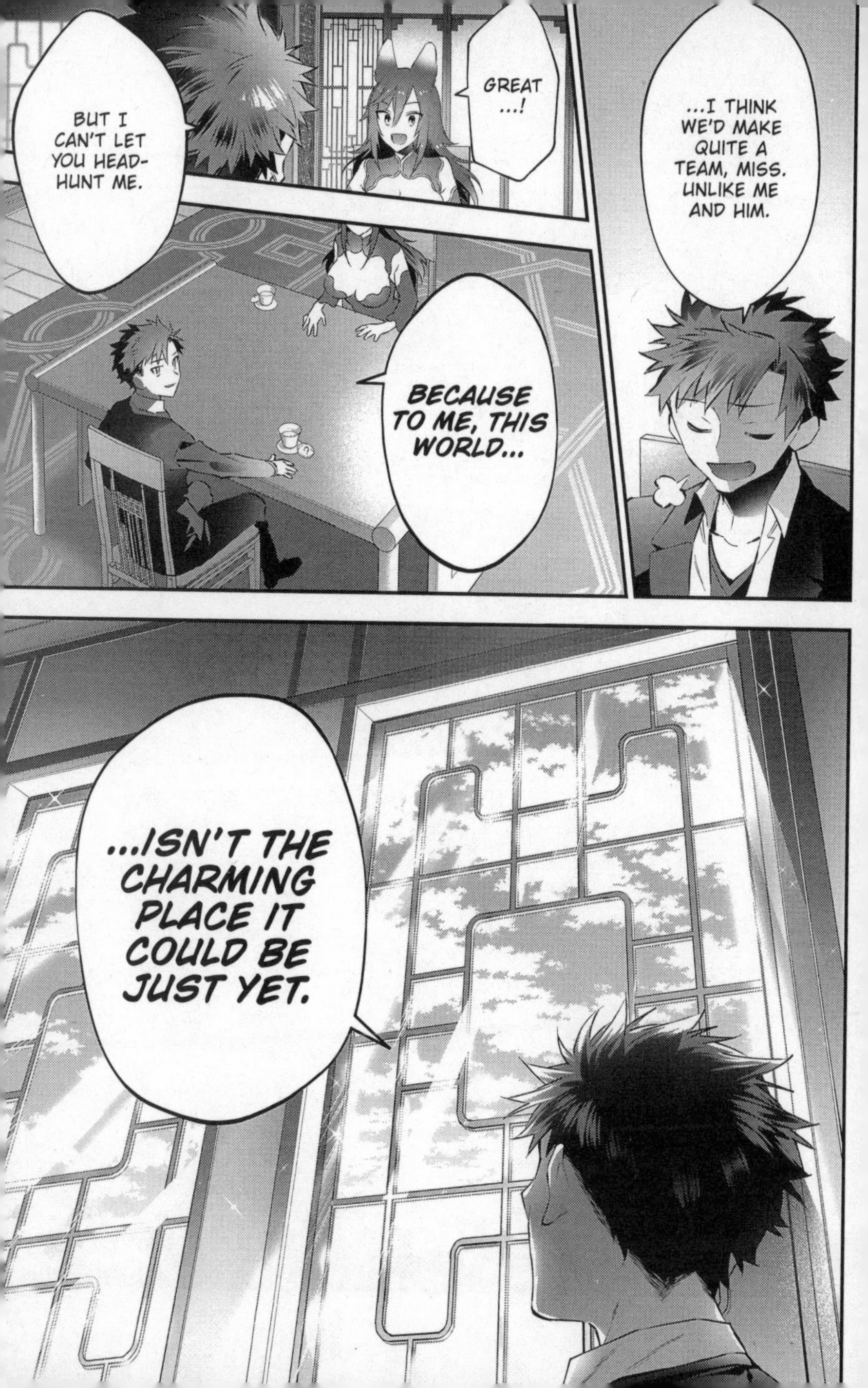
...I THINK WE'D MAKE QUITE A TEAM, MISS. UNLIKE ME AND HIM.
GREAT ...!
BUT I CAN'T LET YOU HEAD-HUNT ME.
BECAUSE TO ME, THIS WORLD...
...ISN'T THE CHARMING PLACE IT COULD BE JUST YET.

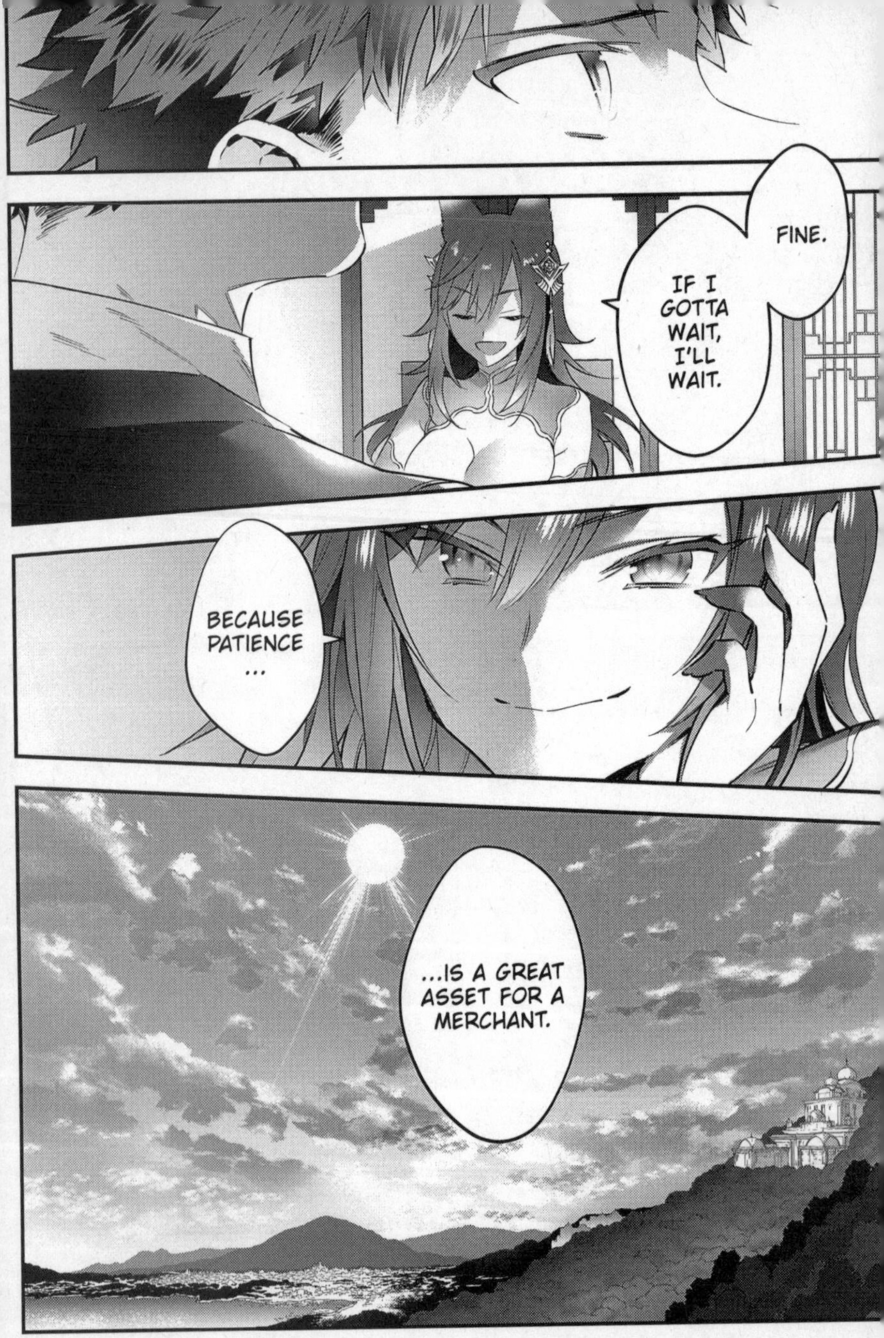
FINE.
IF I GOTTA WAIT, I'LL WAIT.
BECAUSE PATIENCE...
...IS A GREAT ASSET FOR A MERCHANT.

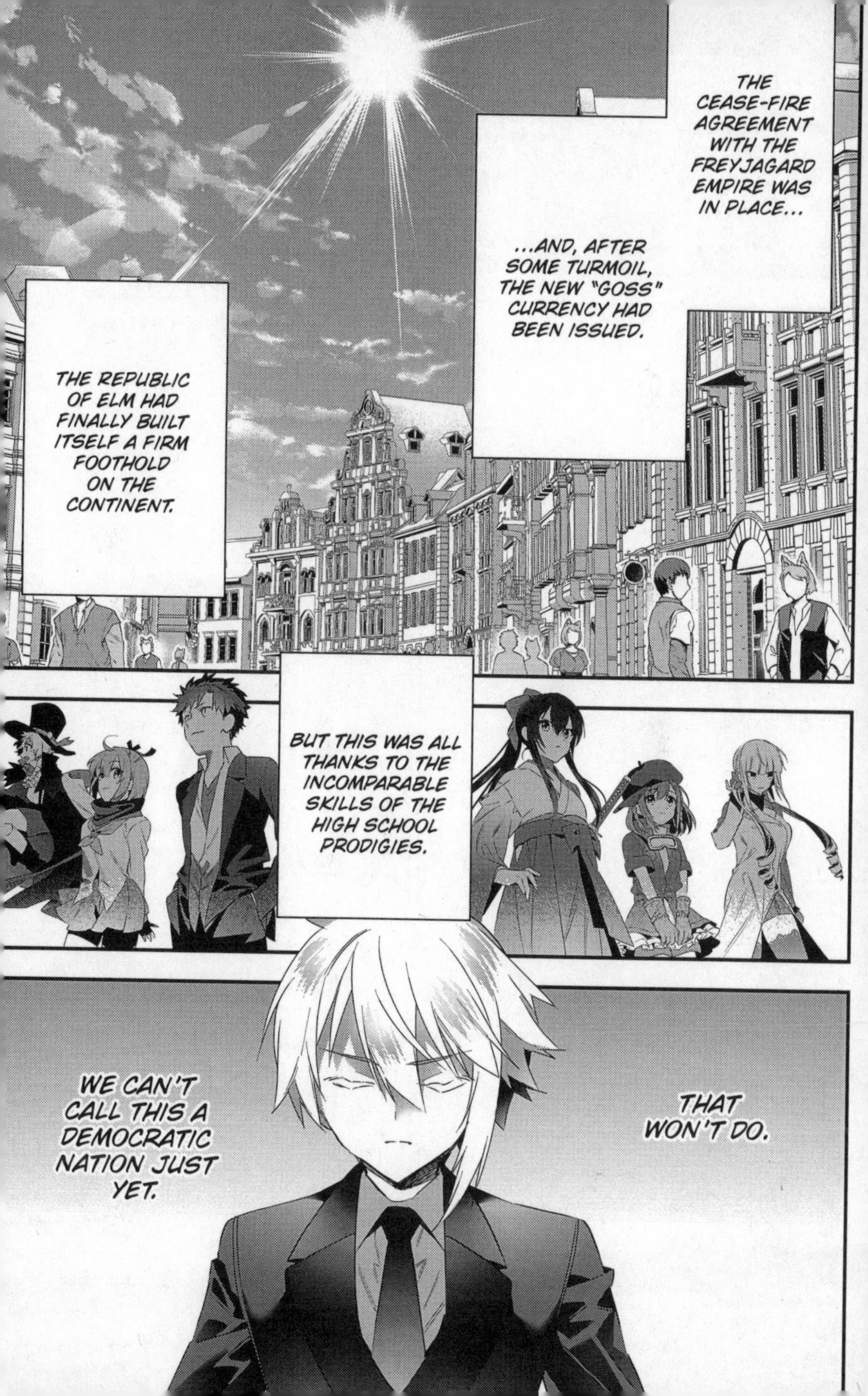
THE CEASE-FIRE AGREEMENT WITH THE FREYJAGARD EMPIRE WAS IN PLACE...
...AND, AFTER SOME TURMOIL, THE NEW "GOSS" CURRENCY HAD BEEN ISSUED.
THE REPUBLIC OF ELM HAD FINALLY BUILT ITSELF A FIRM FOOTHOLD ON THE CONTINENT.
BUT THIS WAS ALL THANKS TO THE INCOMPARABLE SKILLS OF THE HIGH SCHOOL PRODIGIES.
THAT WON'T DO.
WE CAN'T CALL THIS A DEMOCRATIC NATION JUST YET.

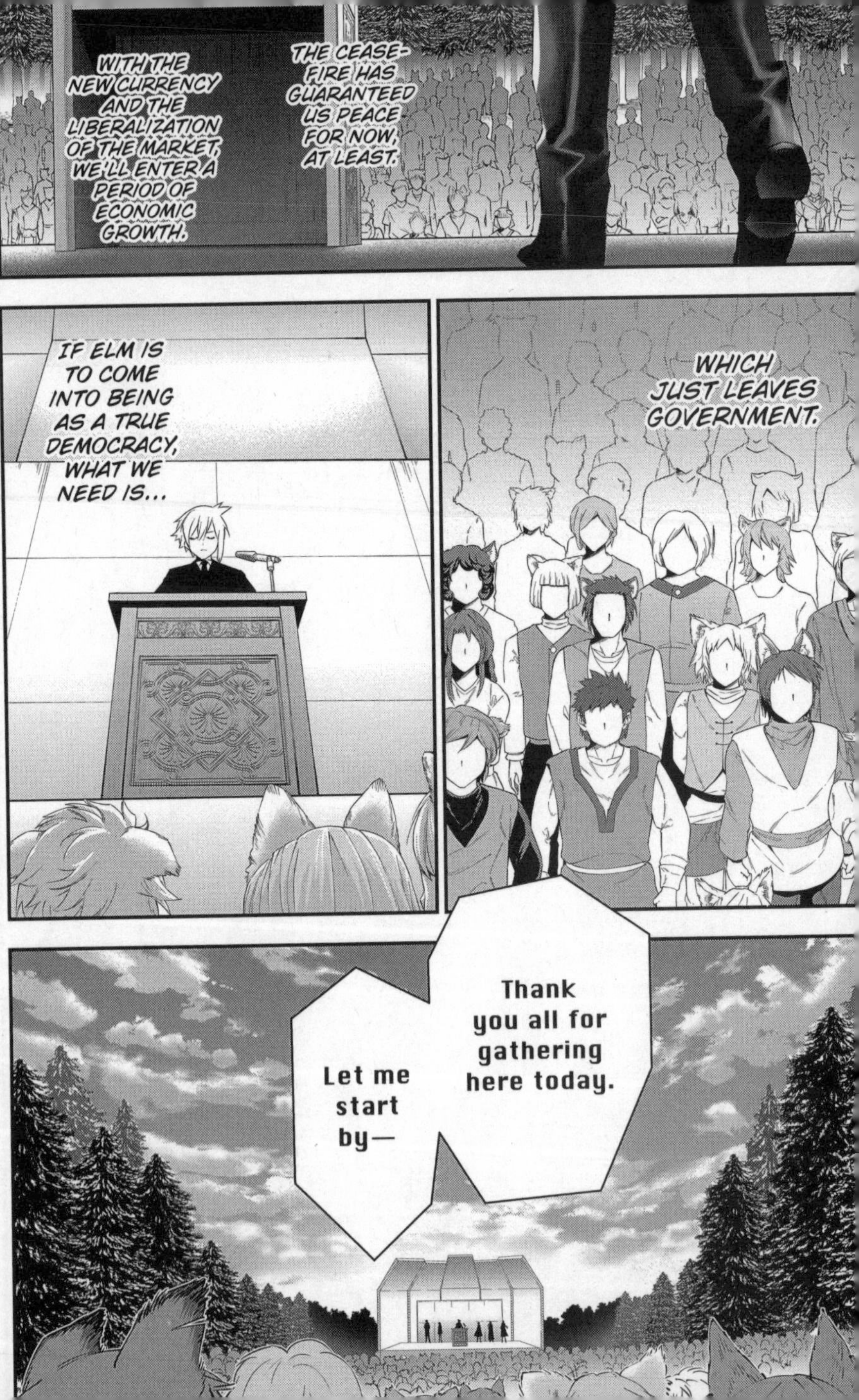
THE CEASE-FIRE HAS GUARANTEED US PEACE FOR NOW, AT LEAST.
WITH THE NEW CURRENCY AND THE LIBERALIZATION OF THE MARKET, WE'LL ENTER A PERIOD OF ECONOMIC GROWTH.
WHICH JUST LEAVES GOVERNMENT.
IF ELM IS TO COME INTO BEING AS A TRUE DEMOCRACY, WHAT WE NEED IS...
Thank you all for gathering here today.
Let me start by—

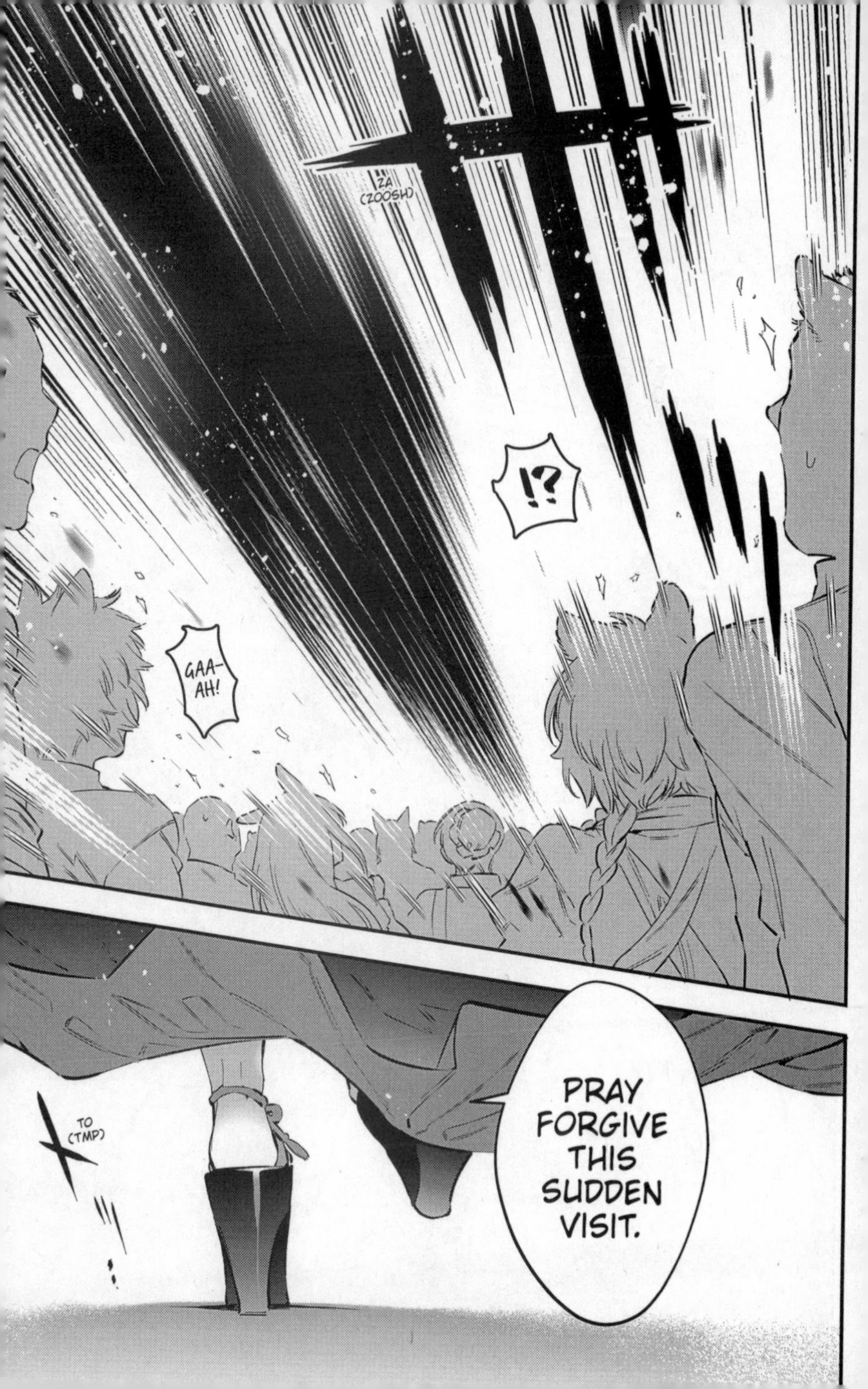
ZA (ZOOSH)
!?
GAA-AH!
PRAY FORGIVE THIS SUDDEN VISIT.
TO (TMP)

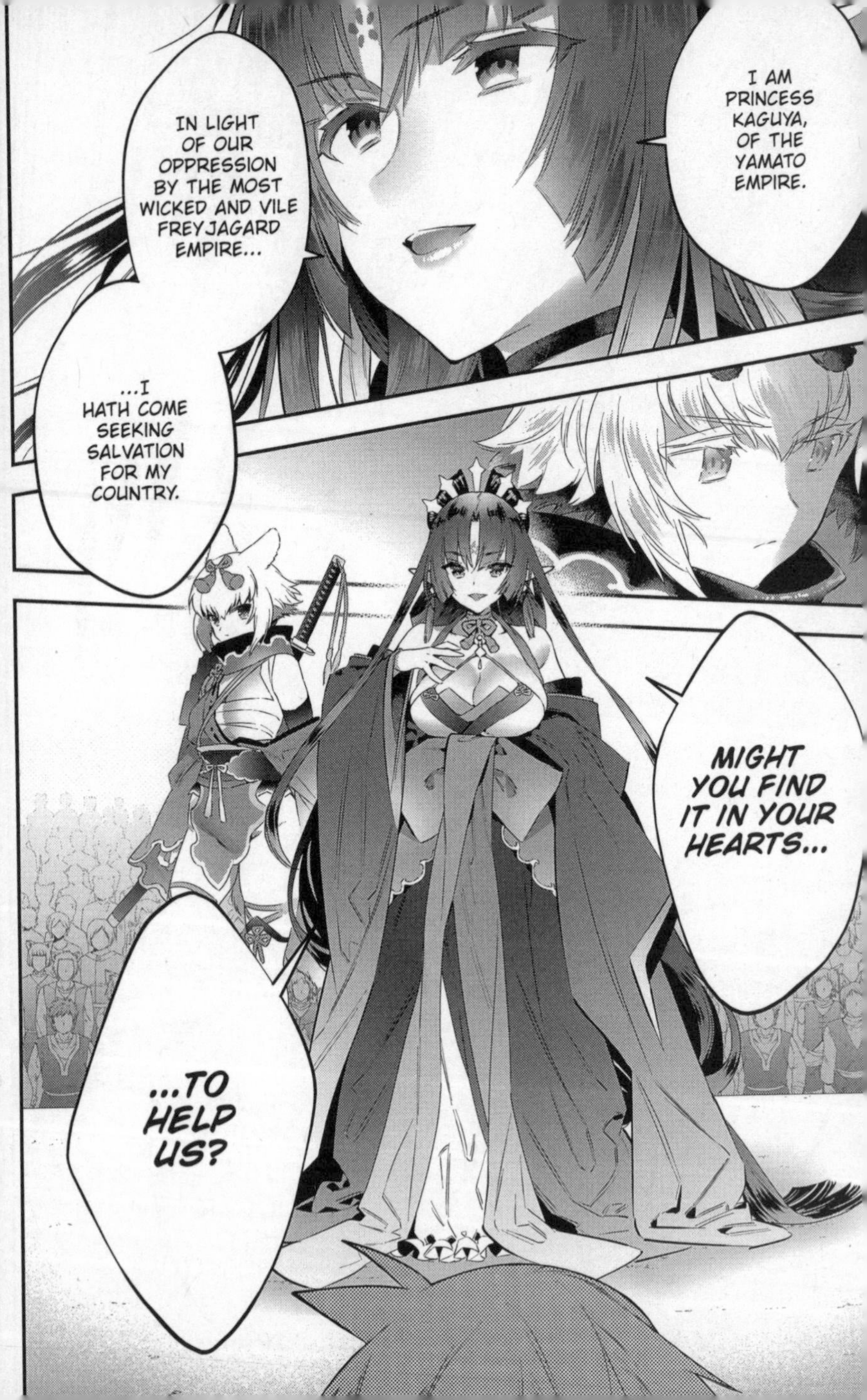
I AM PRINCESS KAGUYA, OF THE YAMATO EMPIRE.
IN LIGHT OF OUR OPPRESSION BY THE MOST WICKED AND VILE FREYJAGARD EMPIRE...
...I HATH COME SEEKING SALVATION FOR MY COUNTRY.
MIGHT YOU FIND IT IN YOUR HEARTS...
...TO HELP US?

HIGH SCHOOL PRODIGIES HAVE IT EASY EVEN IN ANOTHER WORLD!

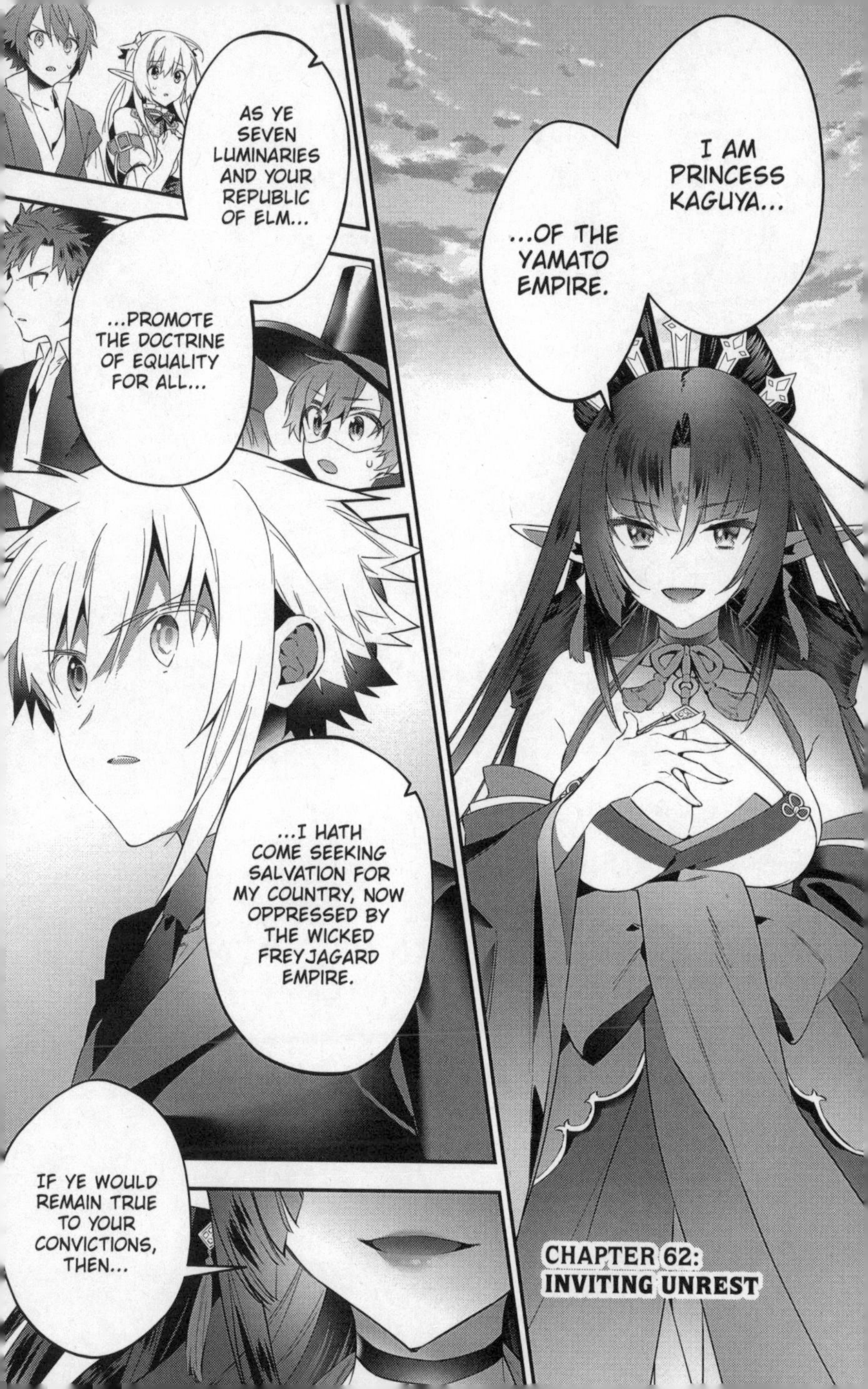
I AM PRINCESS KAGUYA...
...OF THE YAMATO EMPIRE.
CHAPTER 62: INVITING UNREST
AS YE SEVEN LUMINARIES AND YOUR REPUBLIC OF ELM...
...PROMOTE THE DOCTRINE OF EQUALITY FOR ALL...
...I HATH COME SEEKING SALVATION FOR MY COUNTRY, NOW OPPRESSED BY THE WICKED FREYJAGARD EMPIRE.
IF YE WOULD REMAIN TRUE TO YOUR CONVICTIONS, THEN...

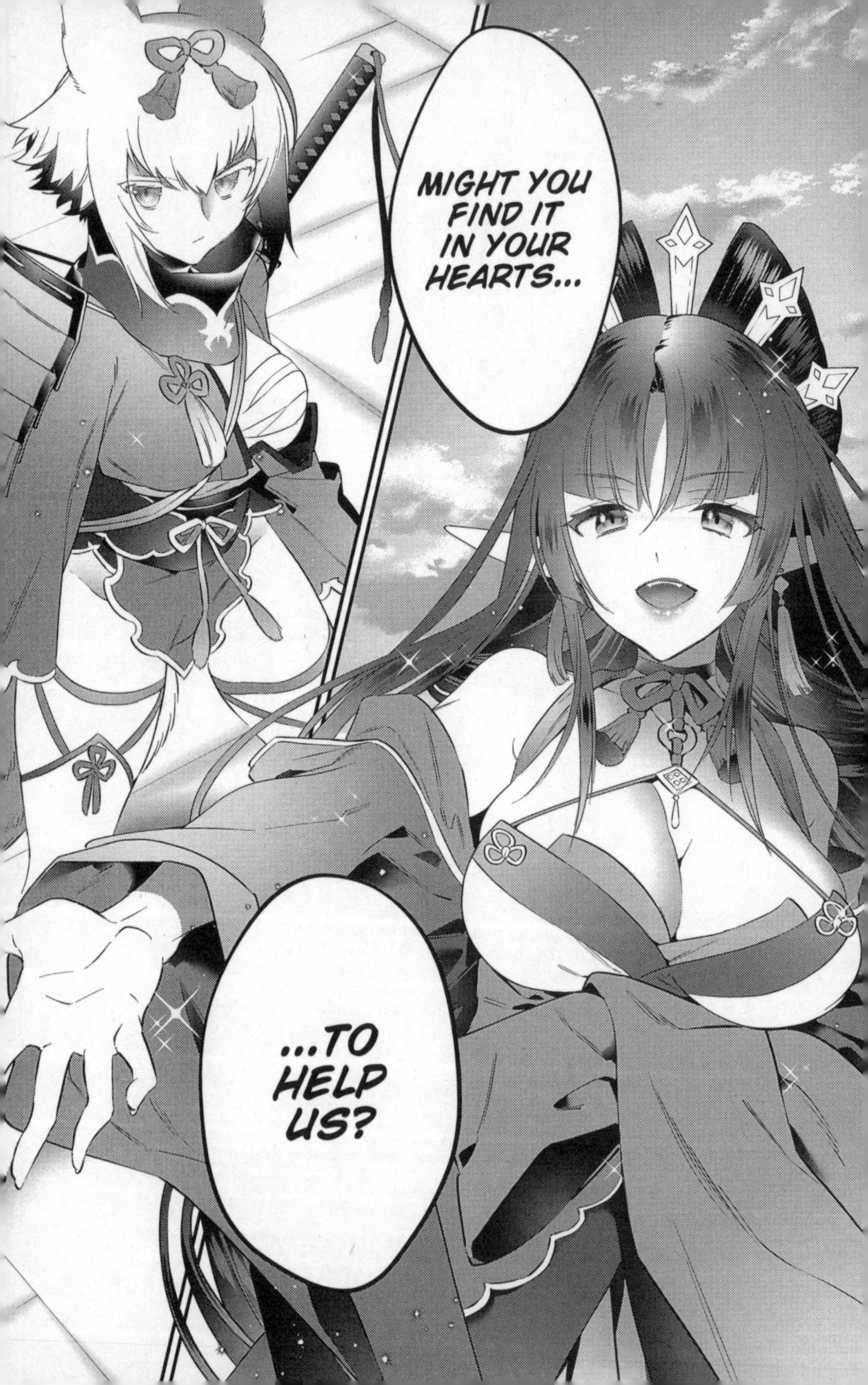
MIGHT YOU FIND IT IN YOUR HEARTS...
...TO HELP US?

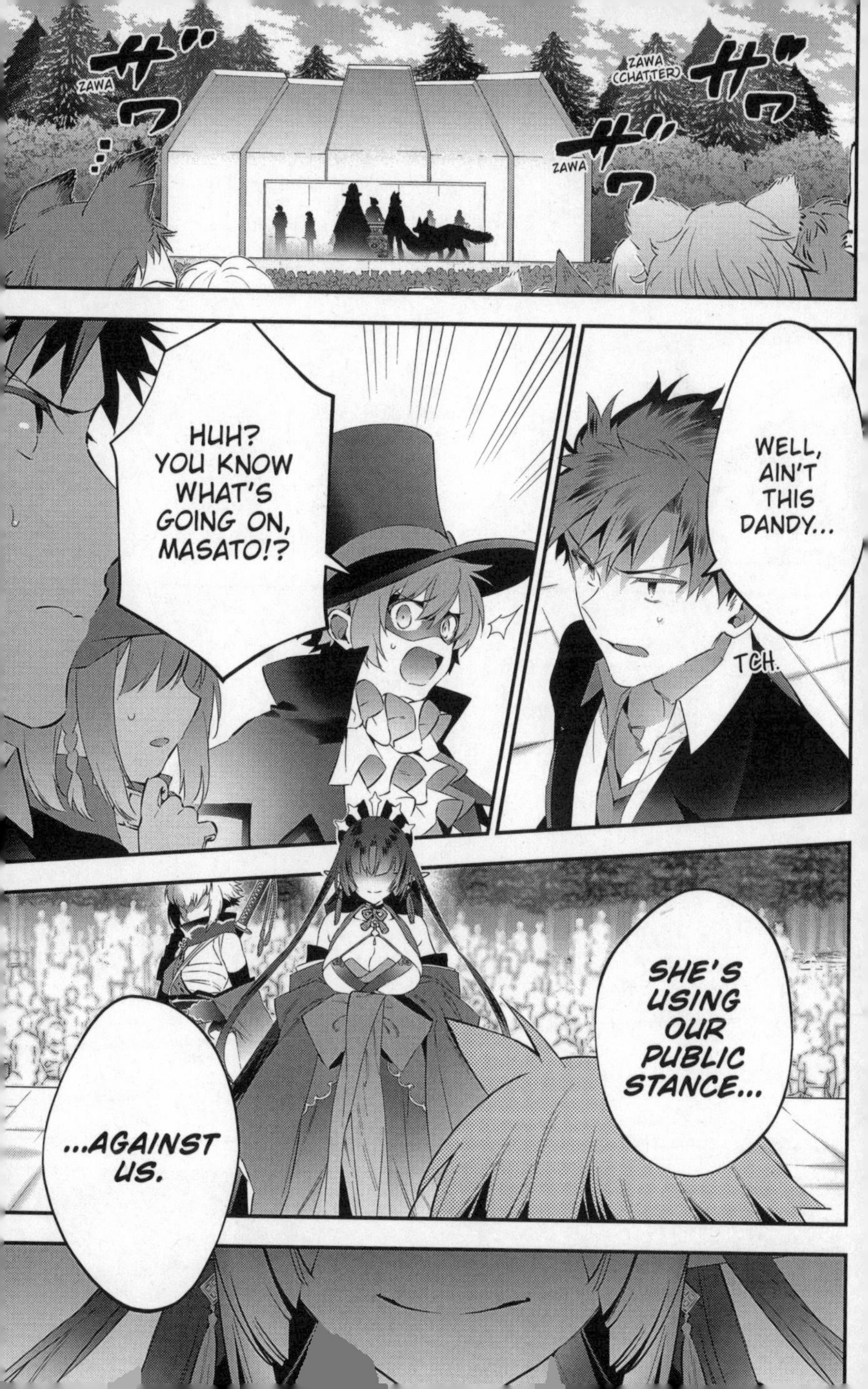
ザワ
ZAWA (CHATTER)
ザワ
ZAWA
ザワ
ZAWA
WELL, AIN'T THIS DANDY...
TCH.
HUH? YOU KNOW WHAT'S GOING ON, MASATO!?
SHE'S USING OUR PUBLIC STANCE...
...AGAINST US.

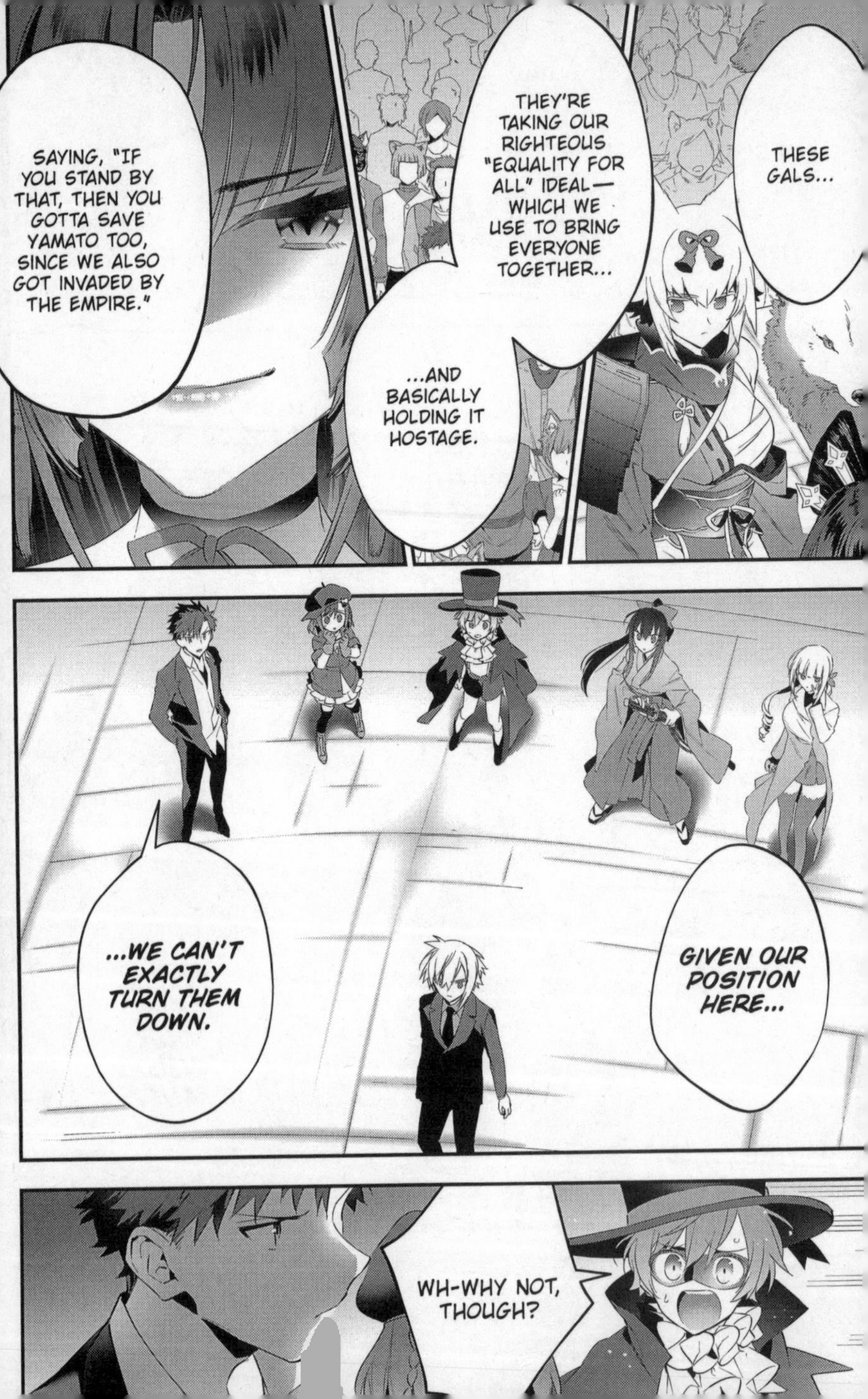
THESE GALS...
THEY'RE TAKING OUR RIGHTEOUS "EQUALITY FOR ALL" IDEAL—WHICH WE USE TO BRING EVERYONE TOGETHER...
...AND BASICALLY HOLDING IT HOSTAGE.
SAYING, "IF YOU STAND BY THAT, THEN YOU GOTTA SAVE YAMATO TOO, SINCE WE ALSO GOT INVADED BY THE EMPIRE."
GIVEN OUR POSITION HERE...
...WE CAN'T EXACTLY TURN THEM DOWN.
WH-WHY NOT, THOUGH?

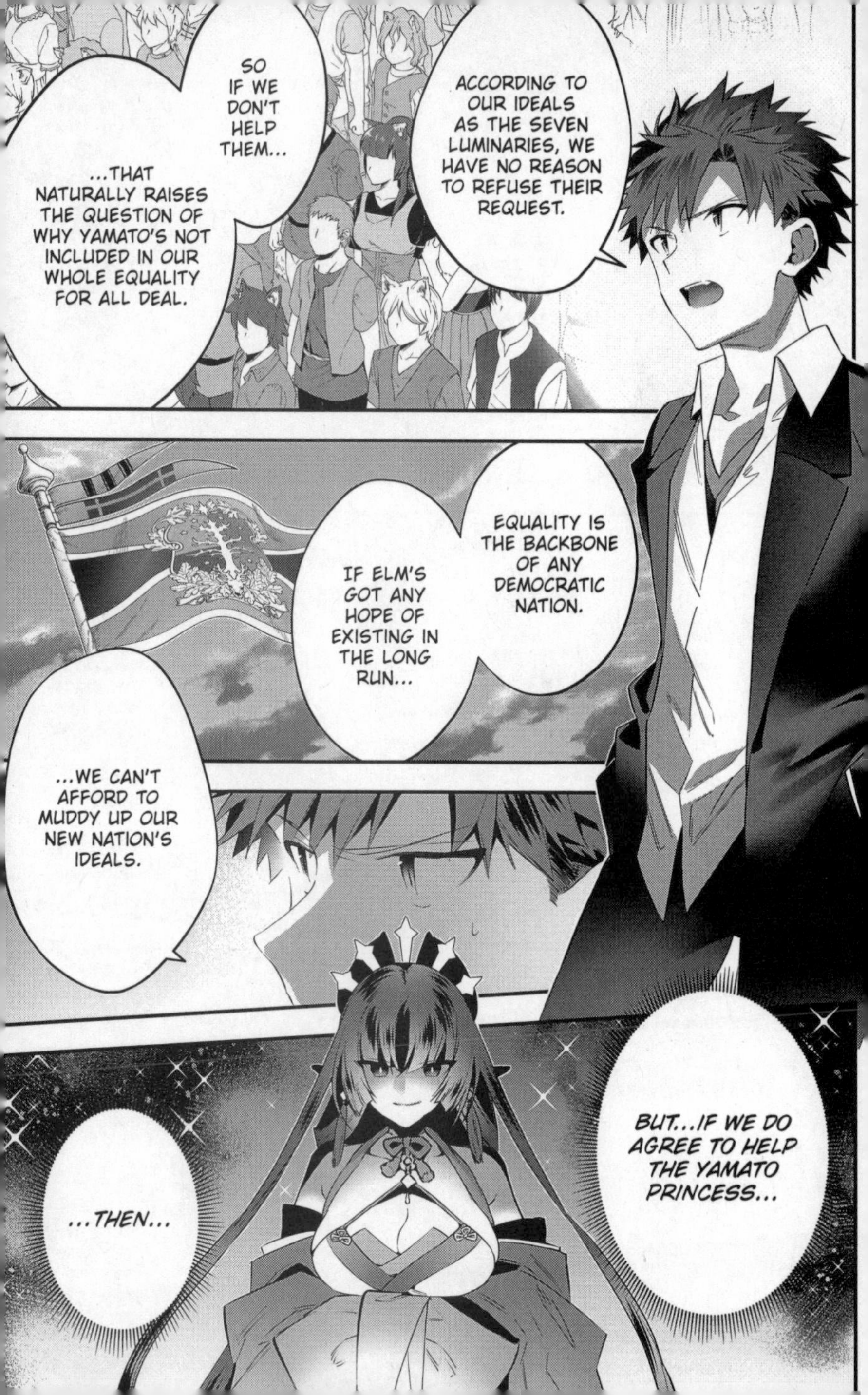
ACCORDING TO OUR IDEALS AS THE SEVEN LUMINARIES, WE HAVE NO REASON TO REFUSE THEIR REQUEST.
SO IF WE DON'T HELP THEM...
...THAT NATURALLY RAISES THE QUESTION OF WHY YAMATO'S NOT INCLUDED IN OUR WHOLE EQUALITY FOR ALL DEAL.
EQUALITY IS THE BACKBONE OF ANY DEMOCRATIC NATION.
IF ELM'S GOT ANY HOPE OF EXISTING IN THE LONG RUN...
...WE CAN'T AFFORD TO MUDDY UP OUR NEW NATION'S IDEALS.
BUT...IF WE DO AGREE TO HELP THE YAMATO PRINCESS...
...THEN...

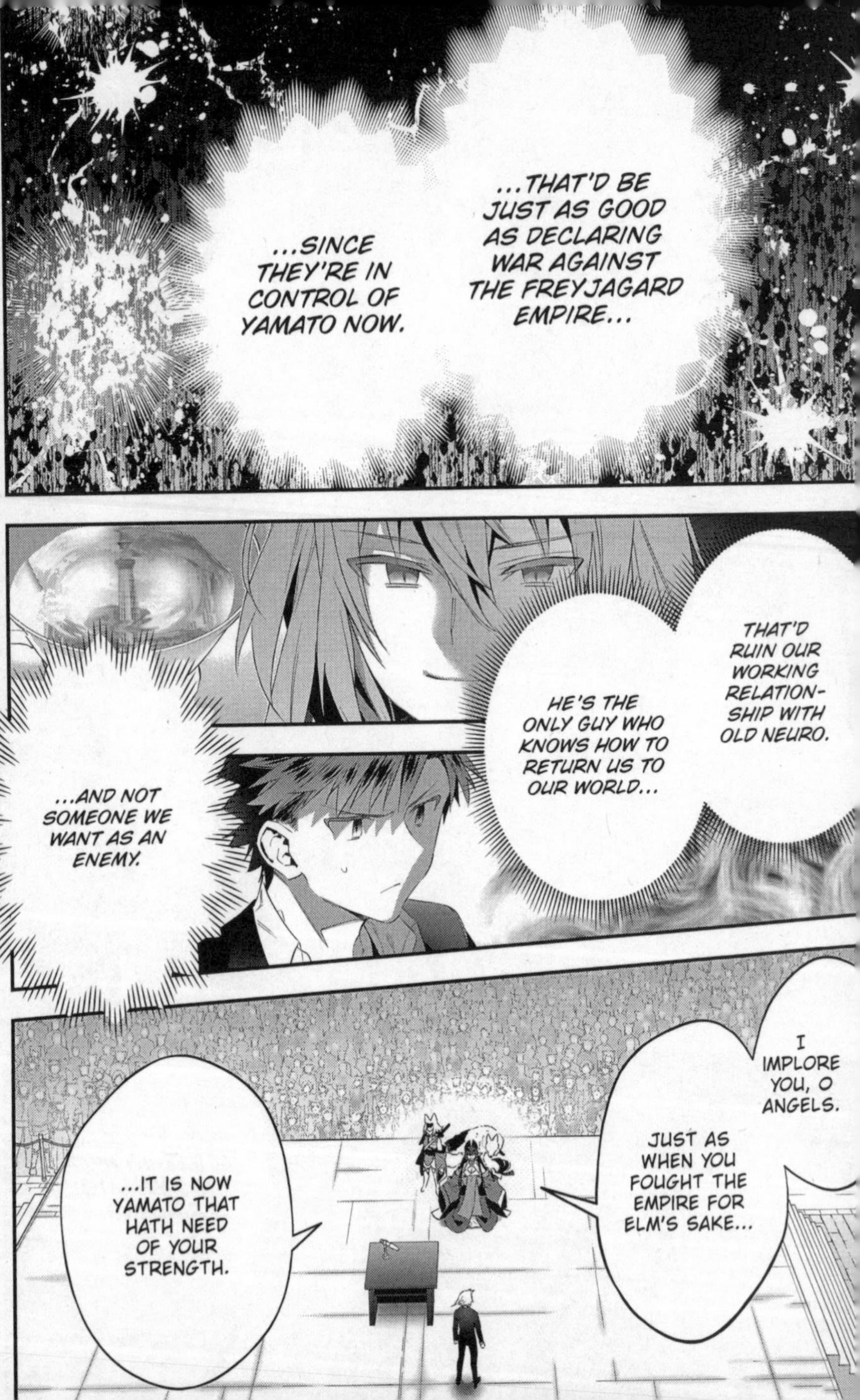
...THAT'D BE JUST AS GOOD AS DECLARING WAR AGAINST THE FREYJAGARD EMPIRE...
...SINCE THEY'RE IN CONTROL OF YAMATO NOW.
THAT'D RUIN OUR WORKING RELATION-SHIP WITH OLD NEURO.
HE'S THE ONLY GUY WHO KNOWS HOW TO RETURN US TO OUR WORLD...
...AND NOT SOMEONE WE WANT AS AN ENEMY.
I IMPLORE YOU, O ANGELS.
JUST AS WHEN YOU FOUGHT THE EMPIRE FOR ELM'S SAKE...
...IT IS NOW YAMATO THAT HATH NEED OF YOUR STRENGTH.

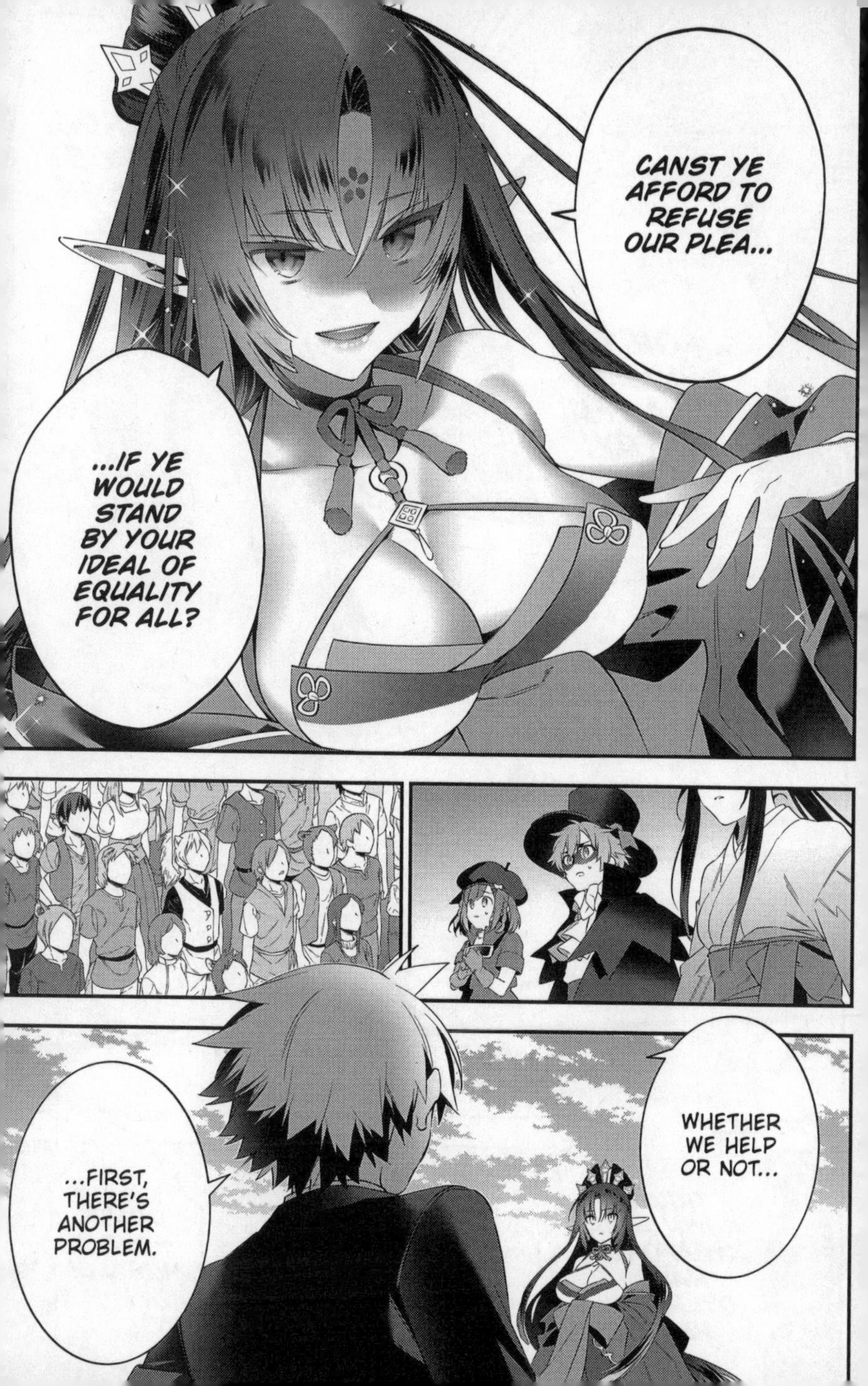
CANST YE AFFORD TO REFUSE OUR PLEA...
...IF YE WOULD STAND BY YOUR IDEAL OF EQUALITY FOR ALL?
WHETHER WE HELP OR NOT...
...FIRST, THERE'S ANOTHER PROBLEM.

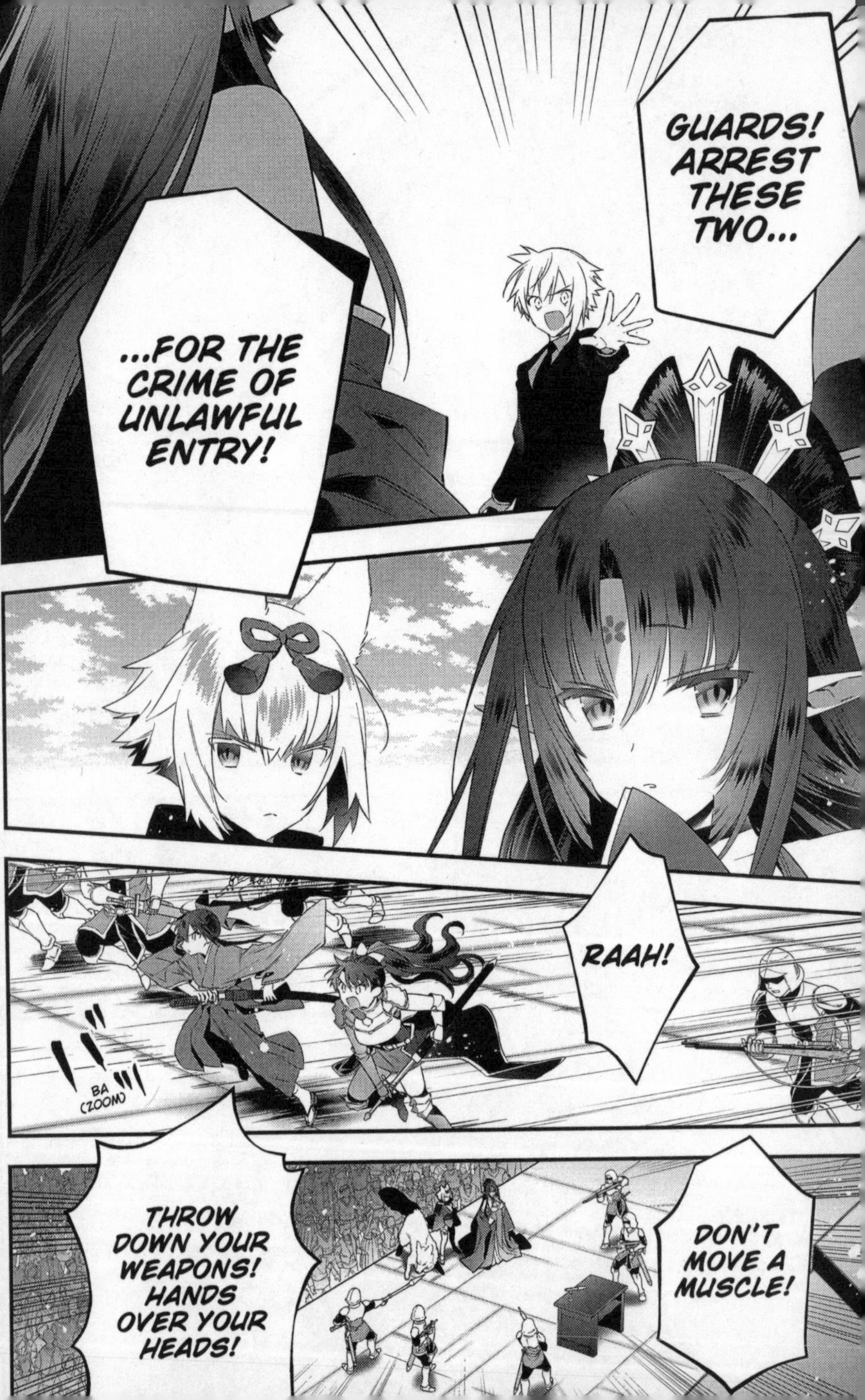
GUARDS! ARREST THESE TWO...
...FOR THE CRIME OF UNLAWFUL ENTRY!
RAAH!
BA (ZOOM)
DON'T MOVE A MUSCLE!
THROW DOWN YOUR WEAPONS! HANDS OVER YOUR HEADS!

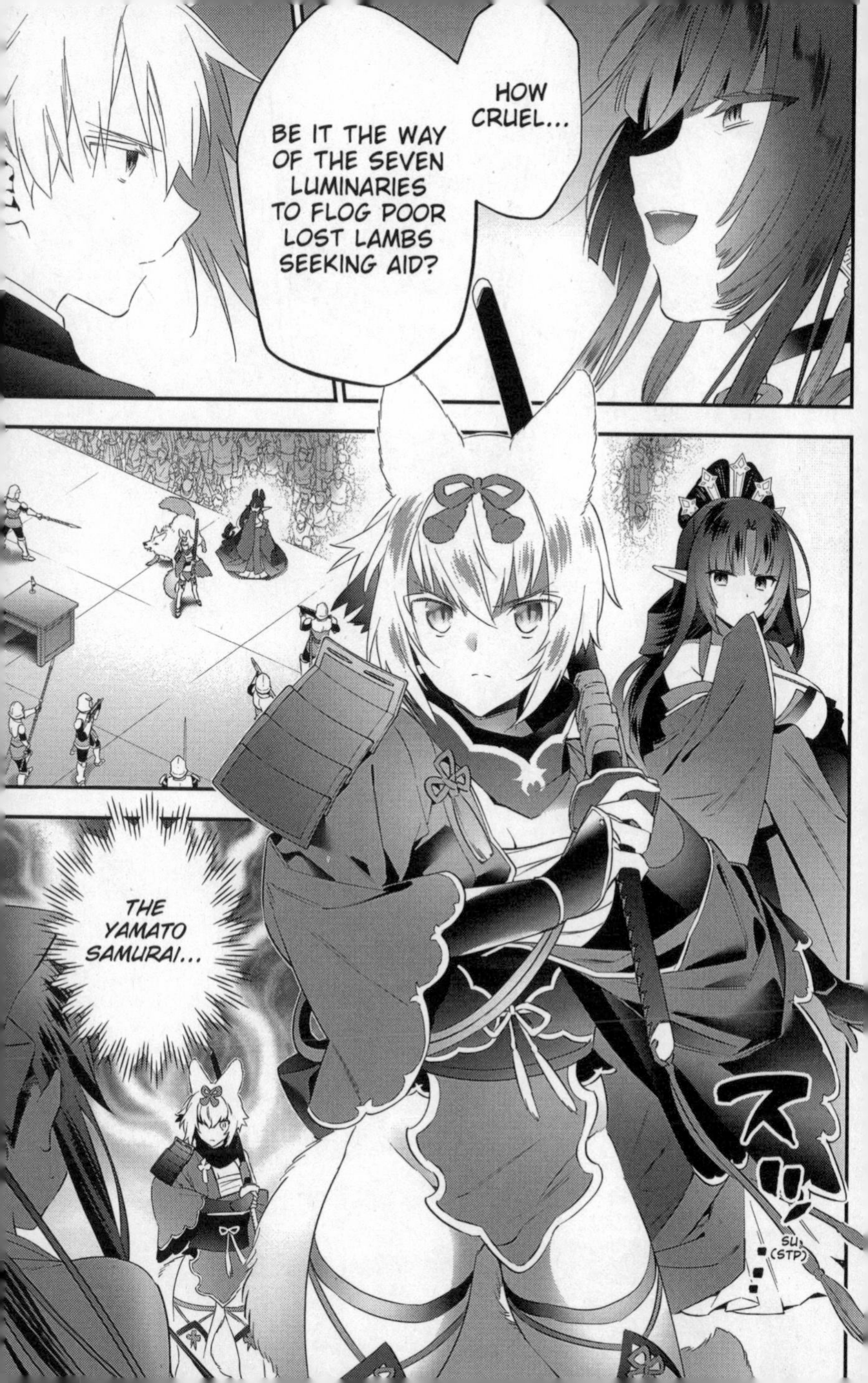

HOW CRUEL...
BE IT THE WAY OF THE SEVEN LUMINARIES TO FLOG POOR LOST LAMBS SEEKING AID?
スッ
SU (STP)
THE YAMATO SAMURAI...

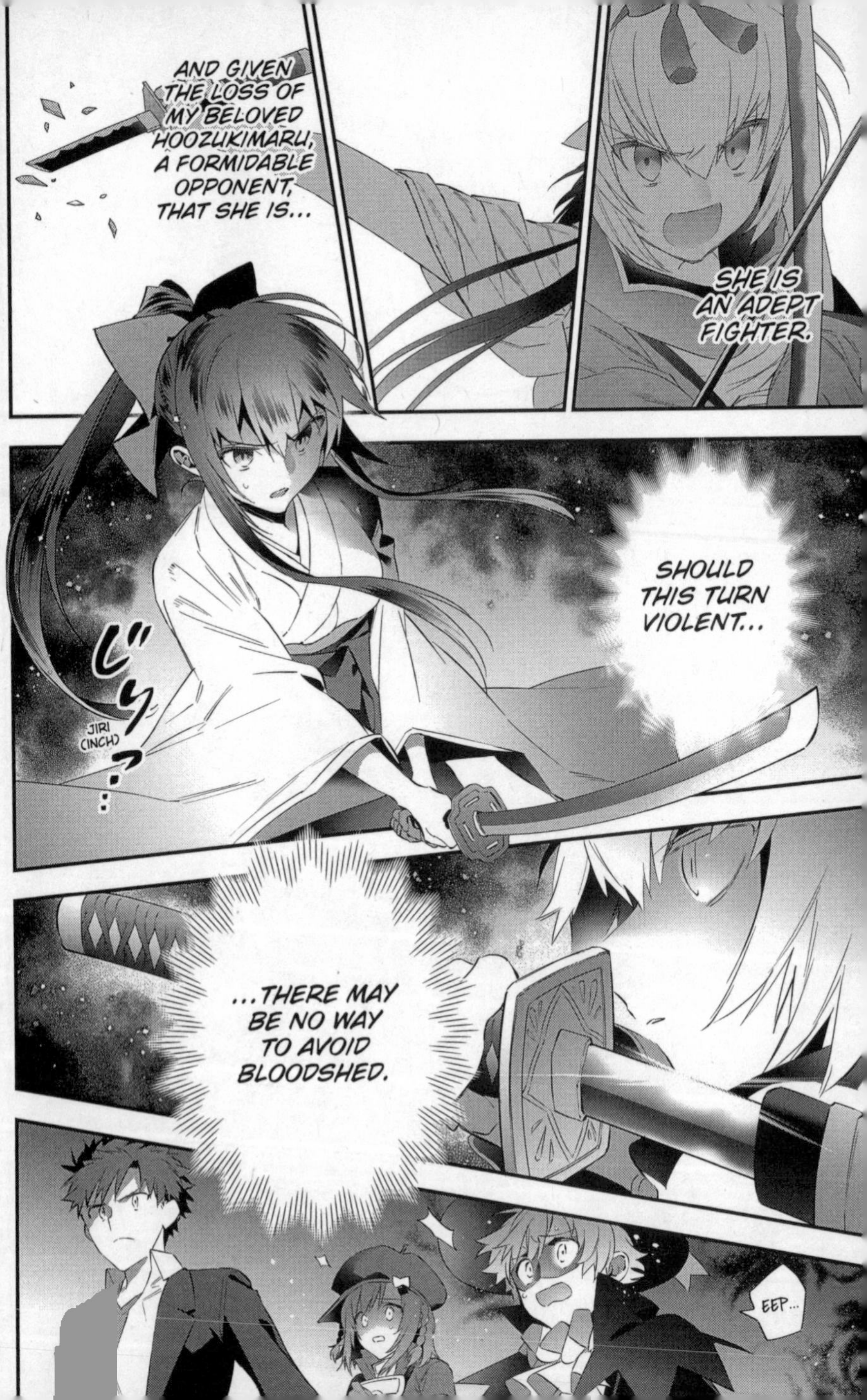
SHE IS AN ADEPT FIGHTER.
AND GIVEN THE LOSS OF MY BELOVED HOOZUKIMARU, A FORMIDABLE OPPONENT, THAT SHE IS...
SHOULD THIS TURN VIOLENT...
JIRI (INCH)
...THERE MAY BE NO WAY TO AVOID BLOODSHED.
EEP...

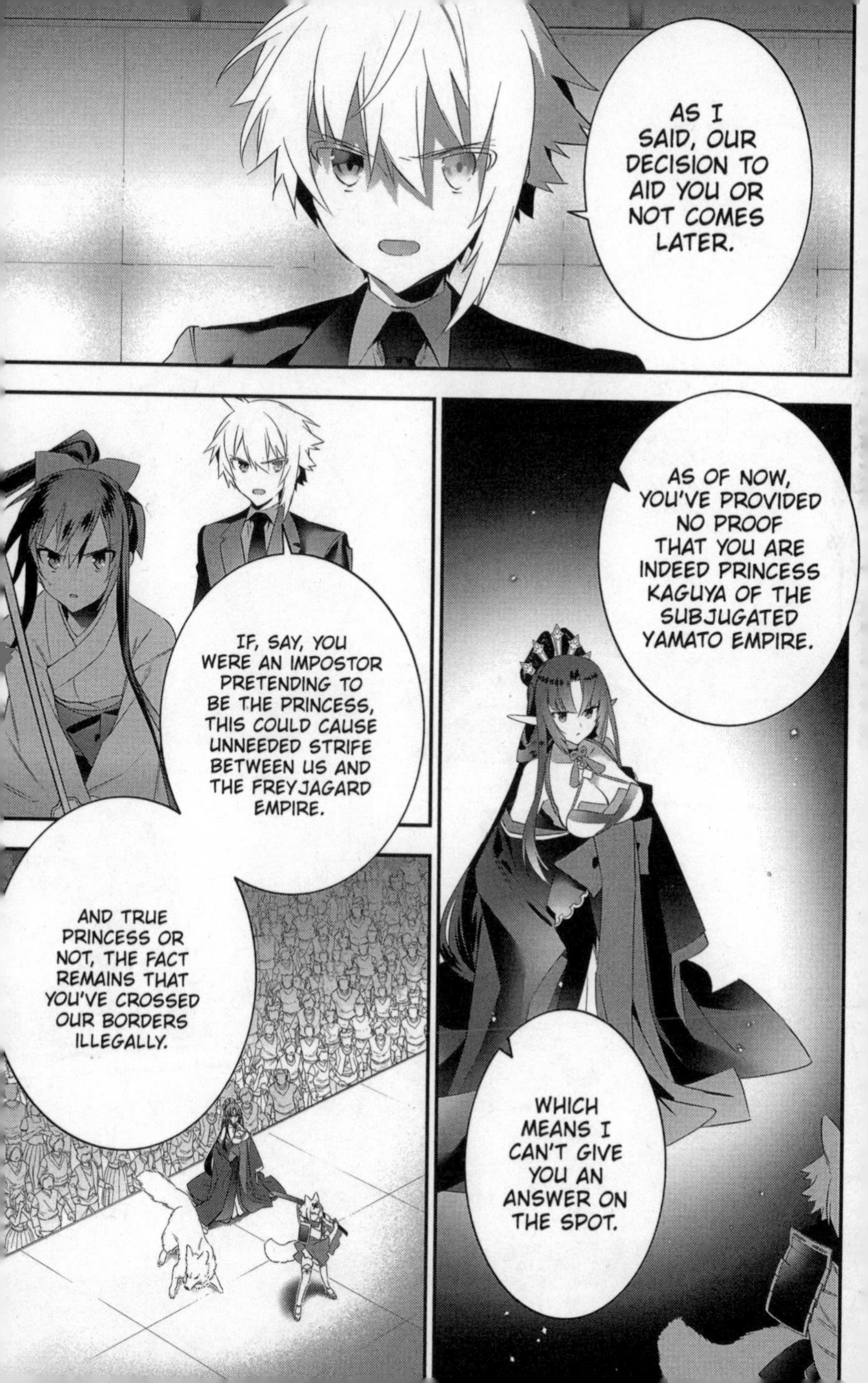
AS I SAID, OUR DECISION TO AID YOU OR NOT COMES LATER.
AS OF NOW, YOU'VE PROVIDED NO PROOF THAT YOU ARE INDEED PRINCESS KAGUYA OF THE SUBJUGATED YAMATO EMPIRE.
WHICH MEANS I CAN'T GIVE YOU AN ANSWER ON THE SPOT.
IF, SAY, YOU WERE AN IMPOSTOR PRETENDING TO BE THE PRINCESS, THIS COULD CAUSE UNNEEDED STRIFE BETWEEN US AND THE FREYJAGARD EMPIRE.
AND TRUE PRINCESS OR NOT, THE FACT REMAINS THAT YOU'VE CROSSED OUR BORDERS ILLEGALLY.

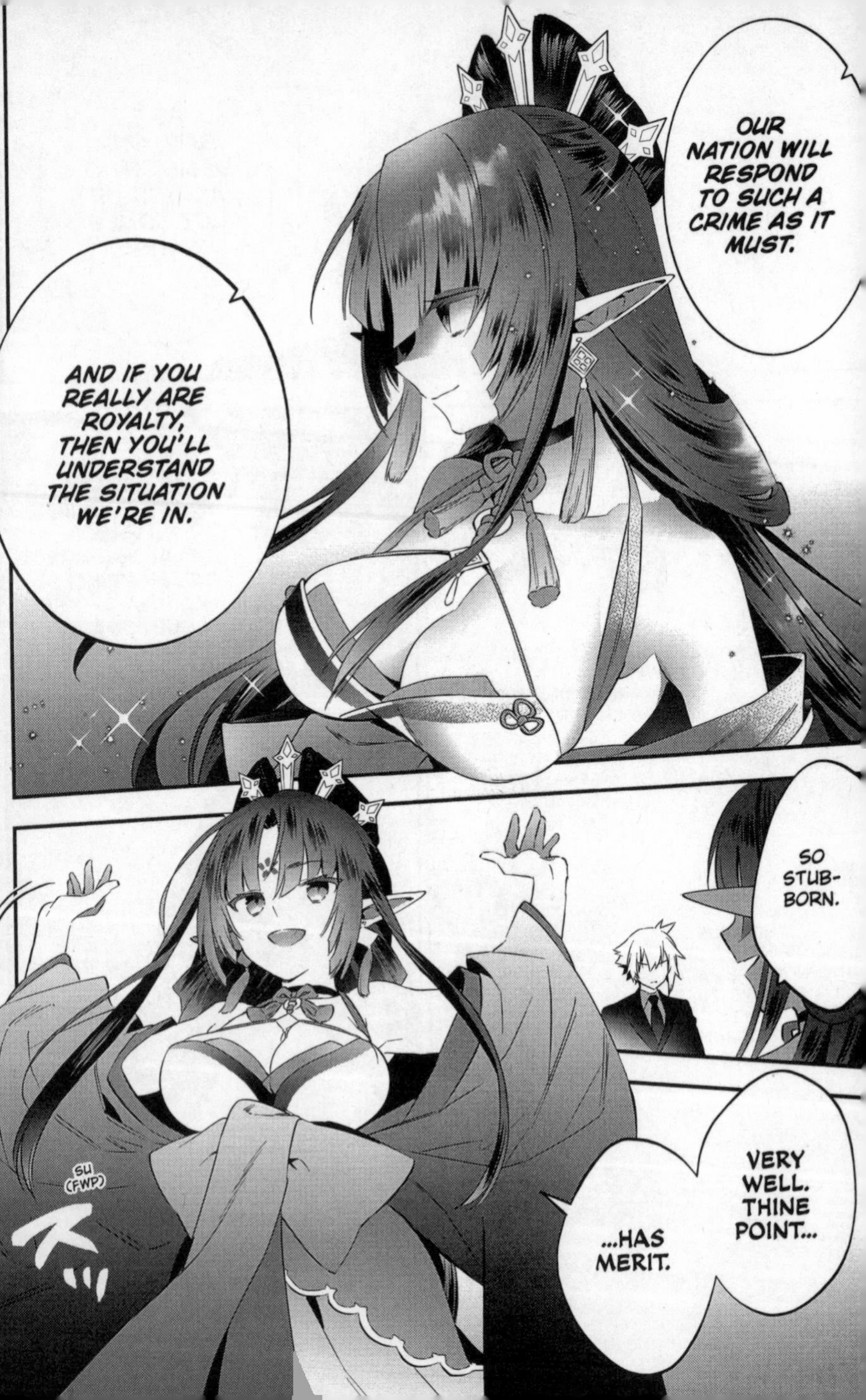
OUR NATION WILL RESPOND TO SUCH A CRIME AS IT MUST.
AND IF YOU REALLY ARE ROYALTY, THEN YOU'LL UNDERSTAND THE SITUATION WE'RE IN.
SO STUB-BORN.
VERY WELL. THINE POINT...
...HAS MERIT.
SU (FWP)
スッ

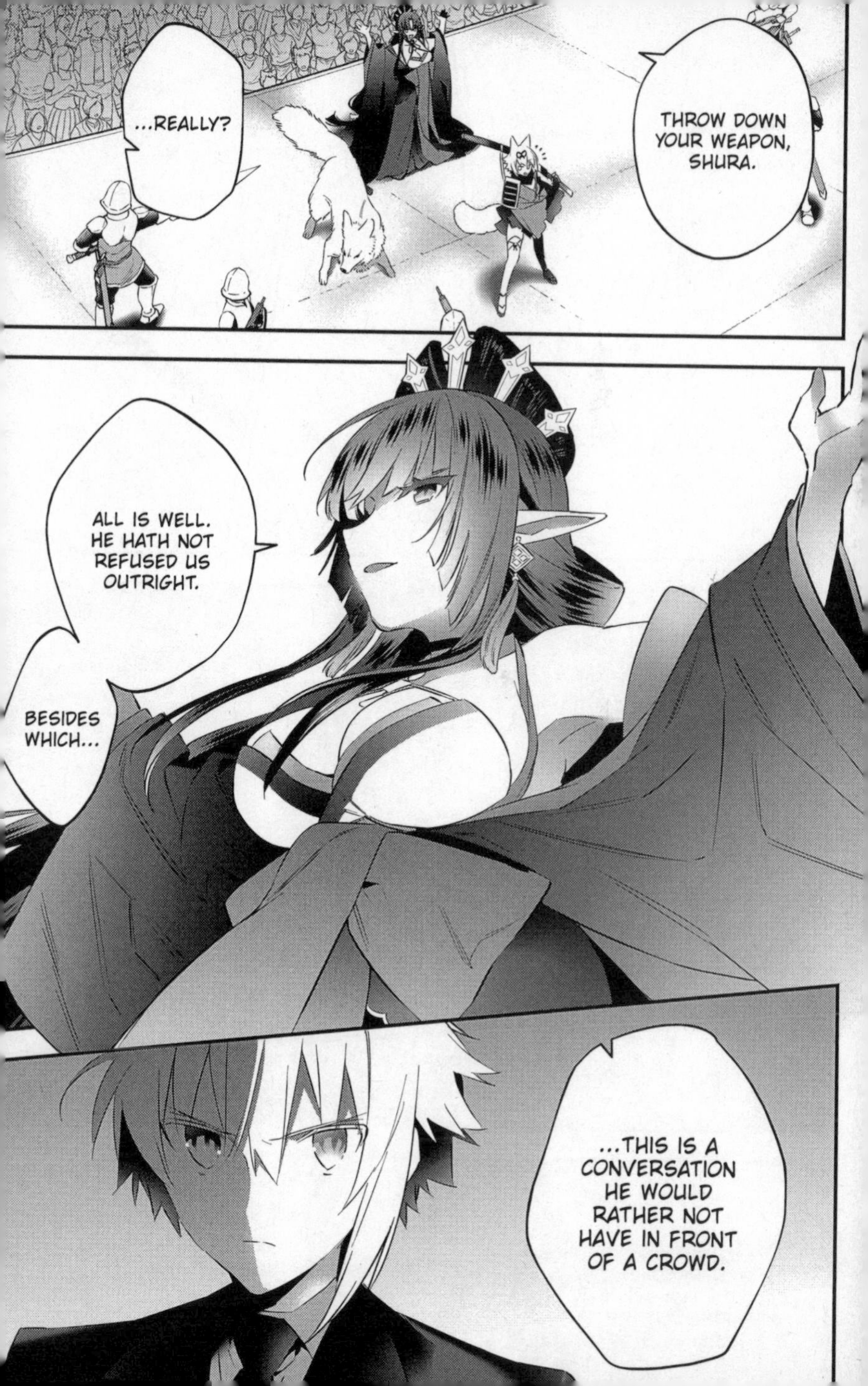
THROW DOWN YOUR WEAPON, SHURA.
...REALLY?
ALL IS WELL. HE HATH NOT REFUSED US OUTRIGHT.
BESIDES WHICH...
...THIS IS A CONVERSATION HE WOULD RATHER NOT HAVE IN FRONT OF A CROWD.

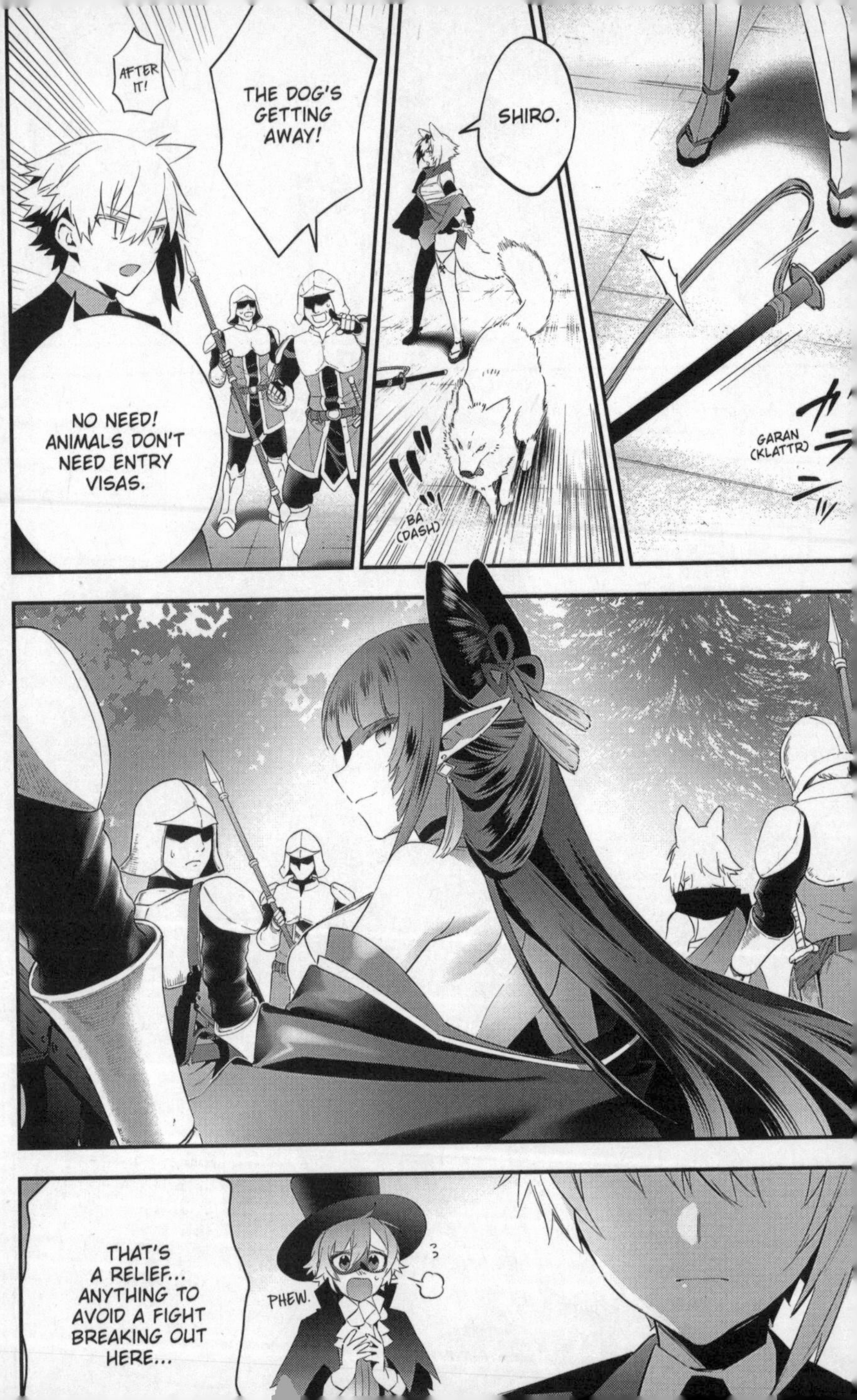
SHIRO.
GARAN (KLATTR)
BA (DASH)
AFTER IT!
THE DOG'S GETTING AWAY!
NO NEED! ANIMALS DON'T NEED ENTRY VISAS.
THAT'S A RELIEF... ANYTHING TO AVOID A FIGHT BREAKING OUT HERE...
PHEW.

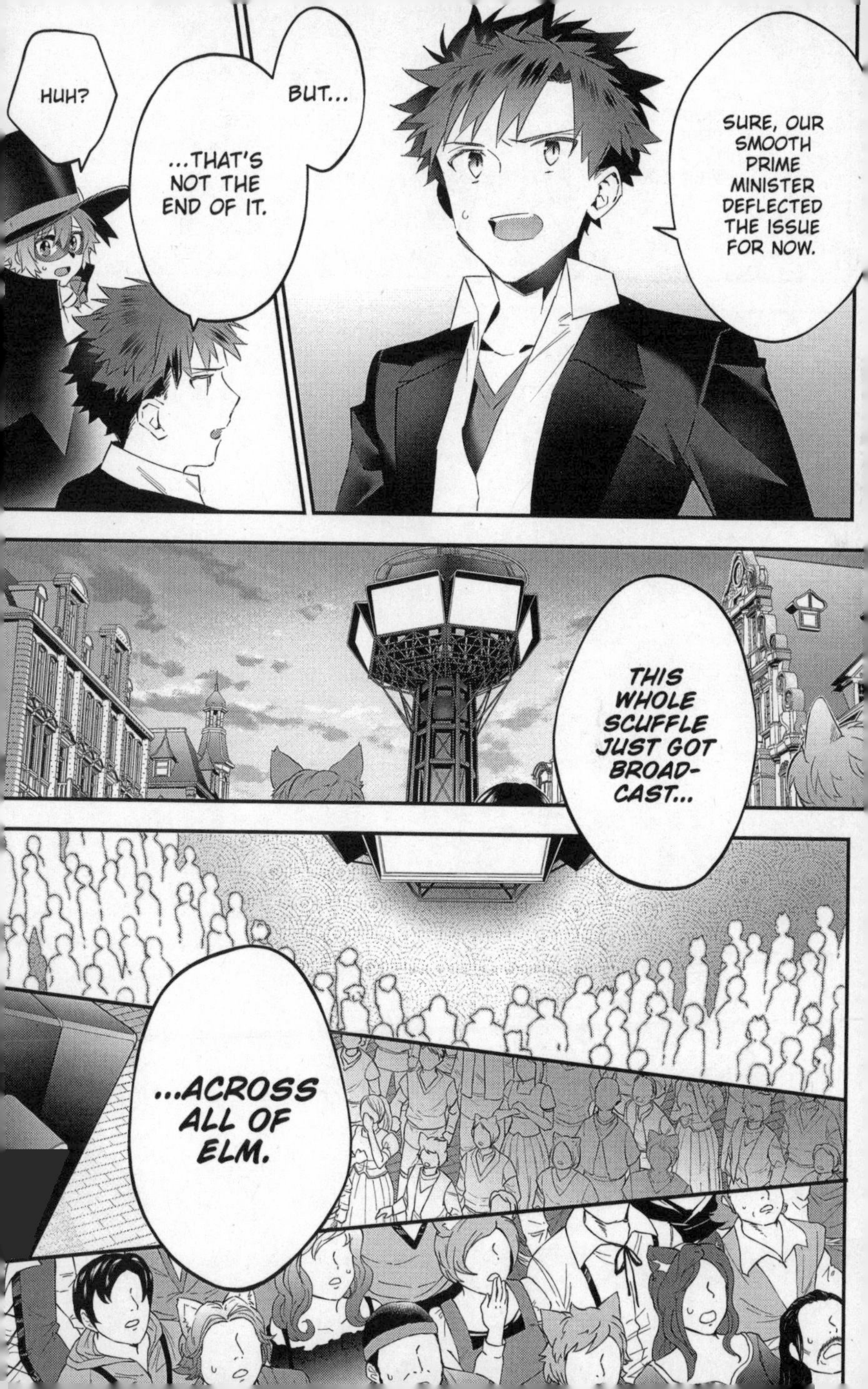
SURE, OUR SMOOTH PRIME MINISTER DEFLECTED THE ISSUE FOR NOW.
BUT...
...THAT'S NOT THE END OF IT.
HUH?
THIS WHOLE SCUFFLE JUST GOT BROAD-CAST...
...ACROSS ALL OF ELM.

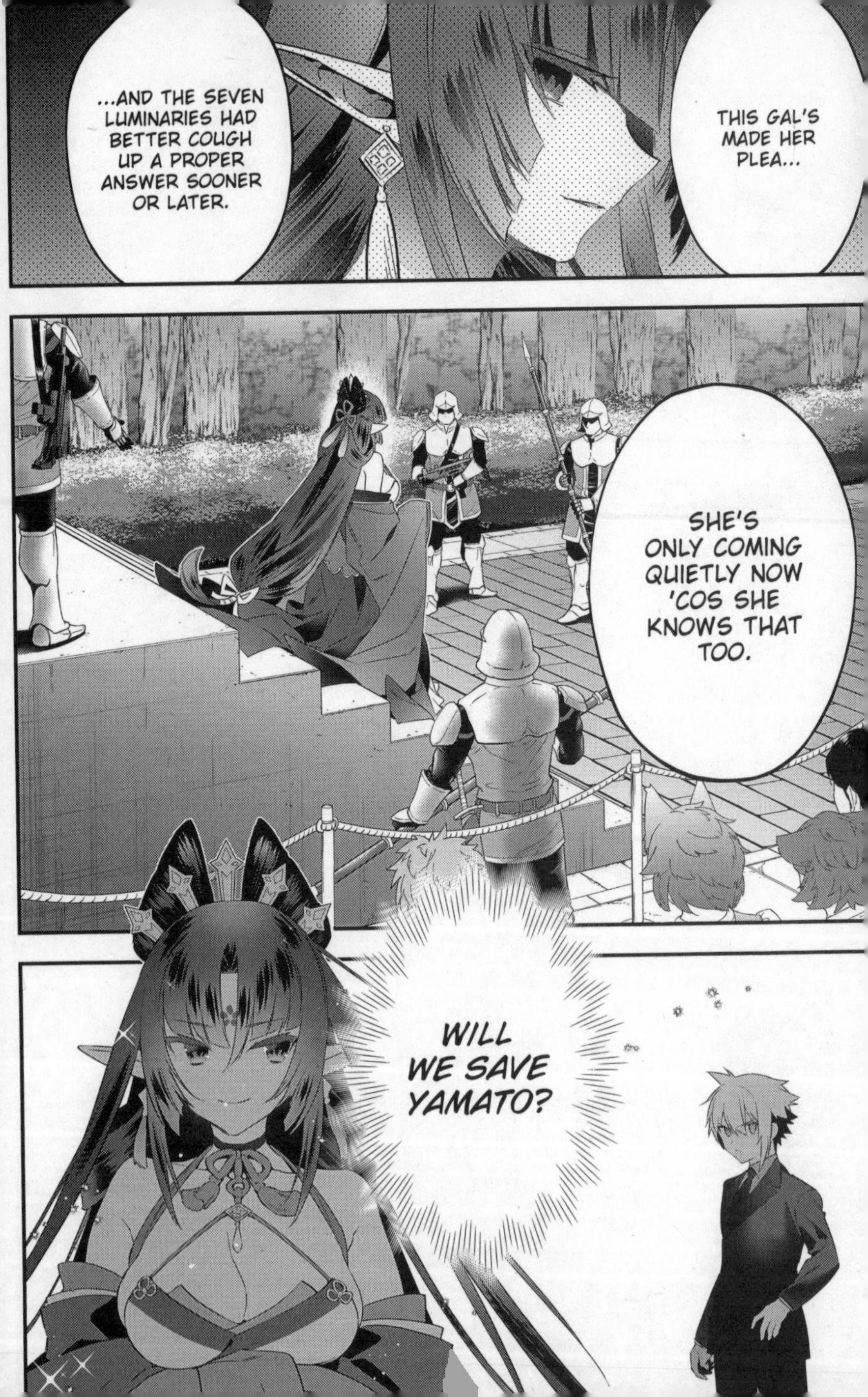
THIS GAL'S MADE HER PLEA...
...AND THE SEVEN LUMINARIES HAD BETTER COUGH UP A PROPER ANSWER SOONER OR LATER.
SHE'S ONLY COMING QUIETLY NOW 'COS SHE KNOWS THAT TOO.
WILL WE SAVE YAMATO?

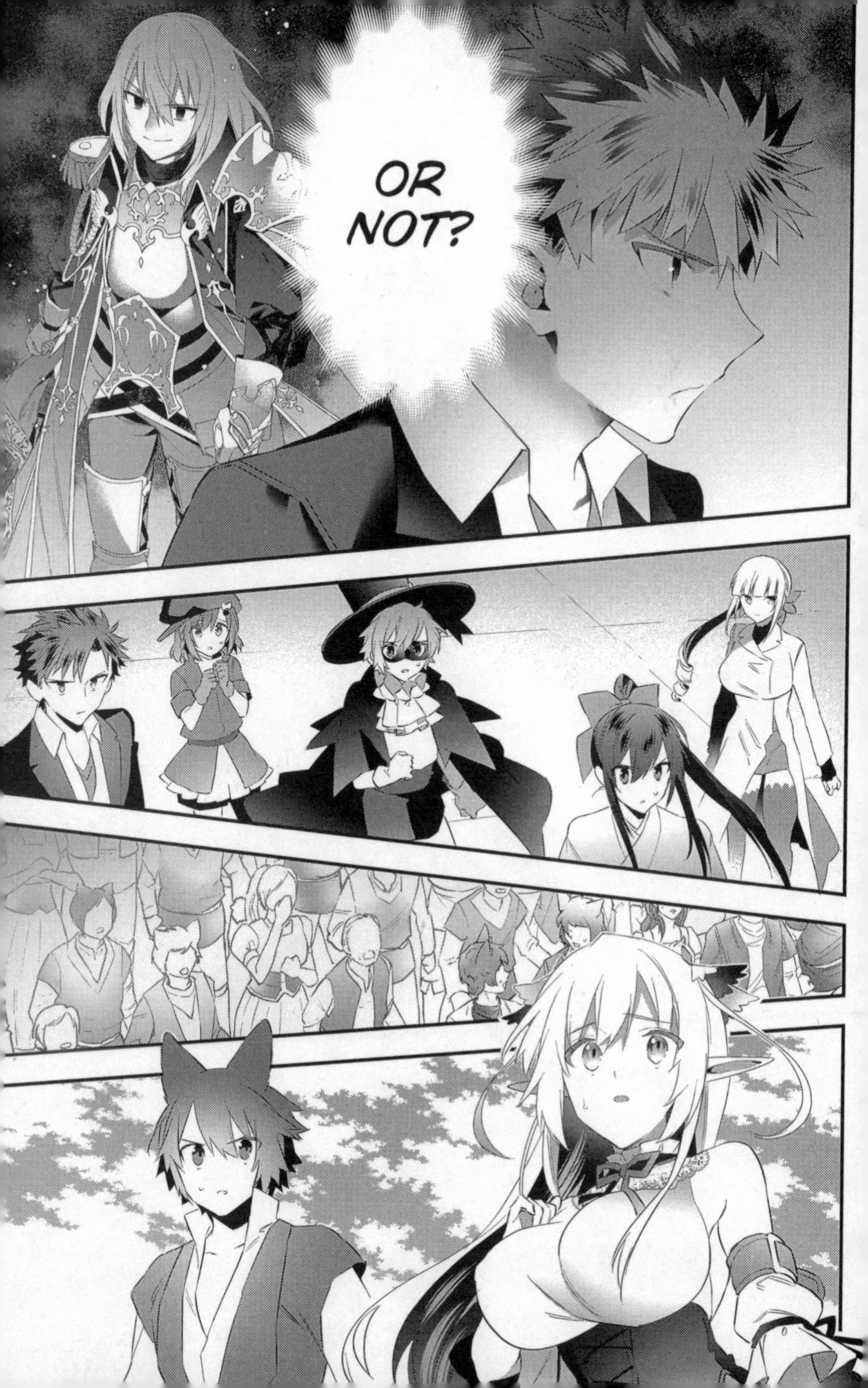
OR NOT?

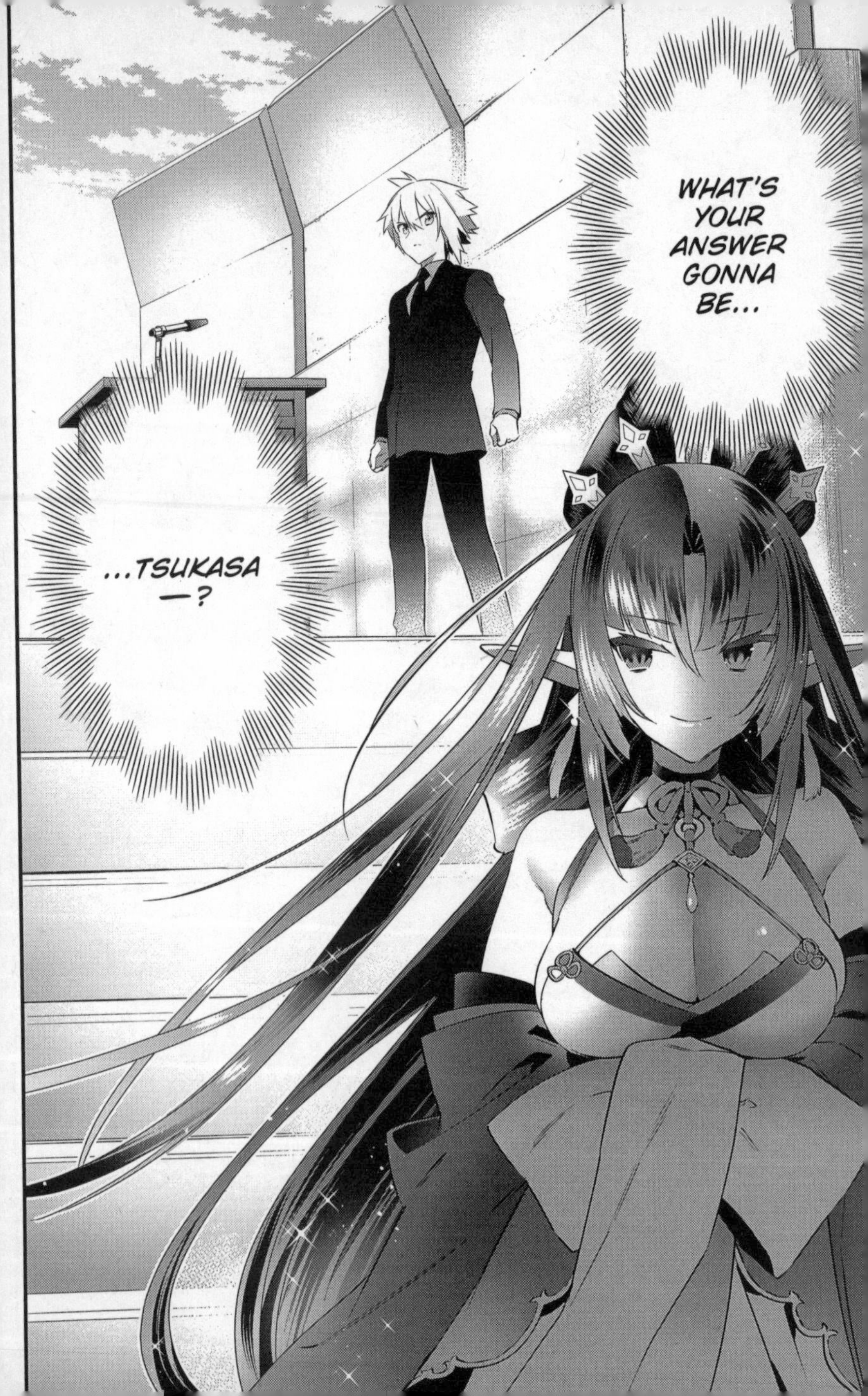
WHAT'S YOUR ANSWER GONNA BE...
...TSUKASA—?

HIGH SCHOOL PRODIGIES HAVE IT EASY EVEN IN ANOTHER WORLD!

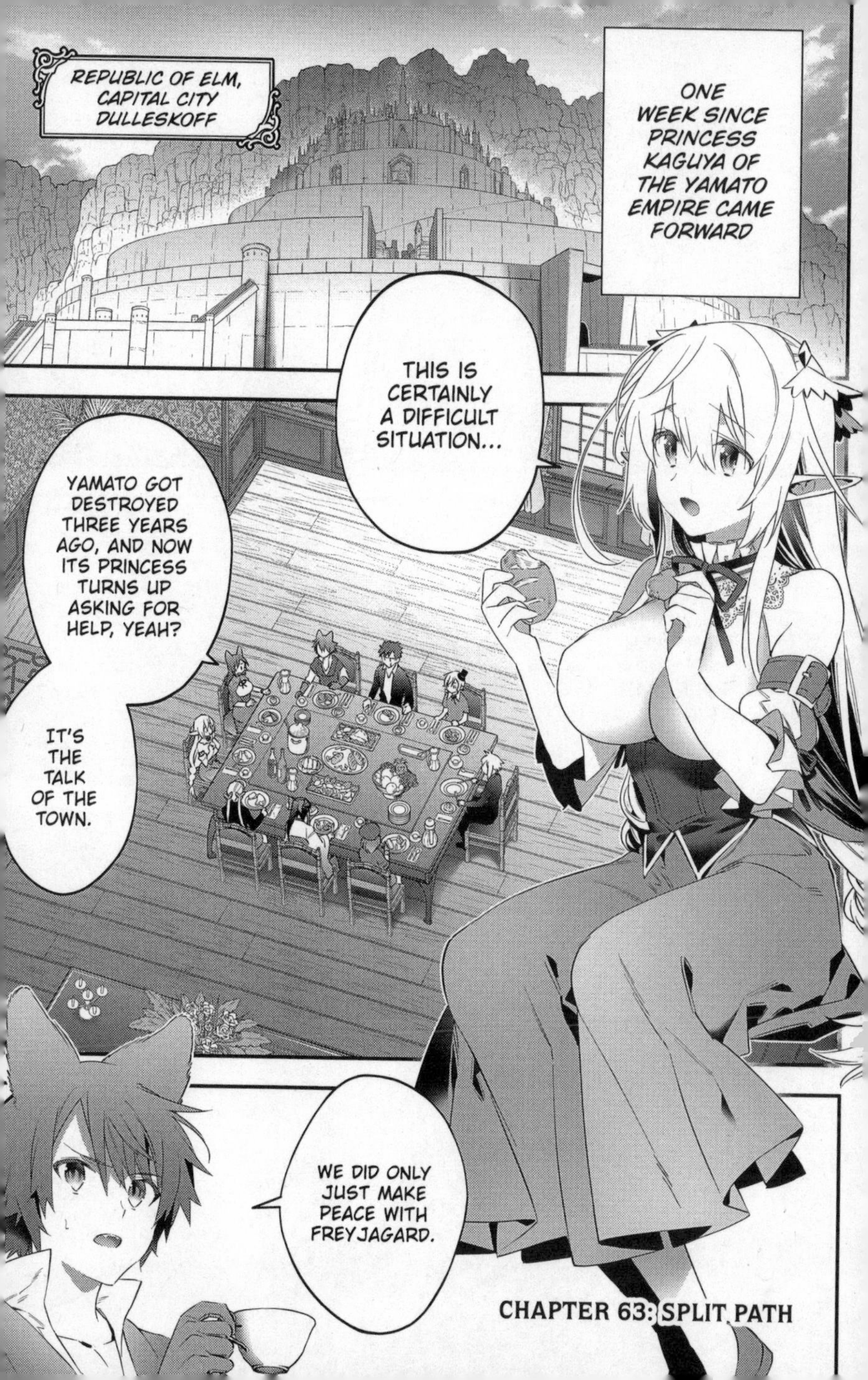
ONE WEEK SINCE PRINCESS KAGUYA OF THE YAMATO EMPIRE CAME FORWARD
REPUBLIC OF ELM, CAPITAL CITY DULLESKOFF
THIS IS CERTAINLY A DIFFICULT SITUATION...
YAMATO GOT DESTROYED THREE YEARS AGO, AND NOW ITS PRINCESS TURNS UP ASKING FOR HELP, YEAH?
IT'S THE TALK OF THE TOWN.
WE DID ONLY JUST MAKE PEACE WITH FREYJAGARD.
CHAPTER 63: SPLIT PATH

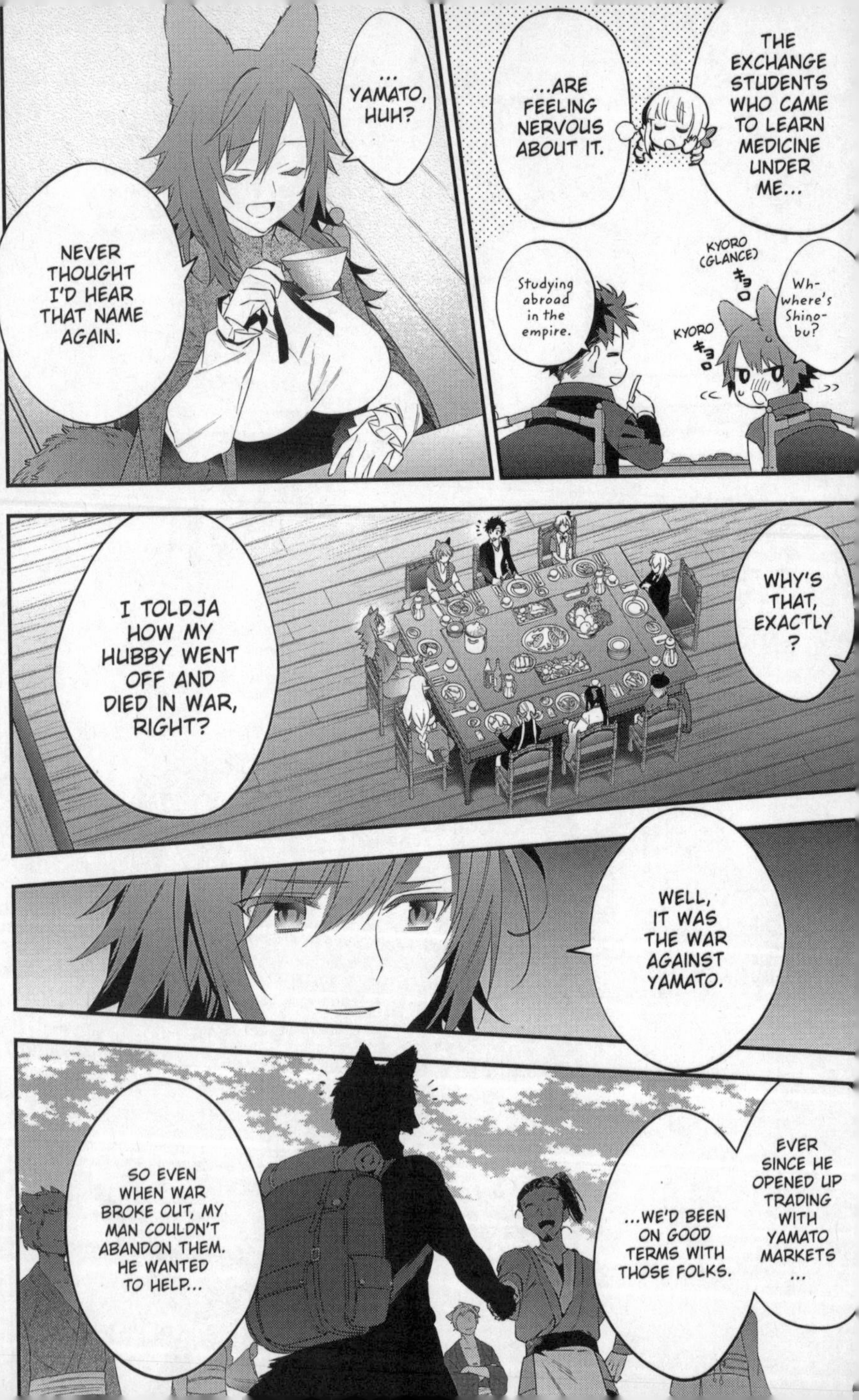
THE EXCHANGE STUDENTS WHO CAME TO LEARN MEDICINE UNDER ME...
...ARE FEELING NERVOUS ABOUT IT.
KYORO (GLANCE)
KYORO
Wh- where's Shino- bu?
Studying abroad in the empire.
... YAMATO, HUH?
NEVER THOUGHT I'D HEAR THAT NAME AGAIN.
WHY'S THAT, EXACTLY?
I TOLDJA HOW MY HUBBY WENT OFF AND DIED IN WAR, RIGHT?
WELL, IT WAS THE WAR AGAINST YAMATO.
EVER SINCE HE OPENED UP TRADING WITH YAMATO MARKETS...
...WE'D BEEN ON GOOD TERMS WITH THOSE FOLKS.
SO EVEN WHEN WAR BROKE OUT, MY MAN COULDN'T ABANDON THEM. HE WANTED TO HELP...

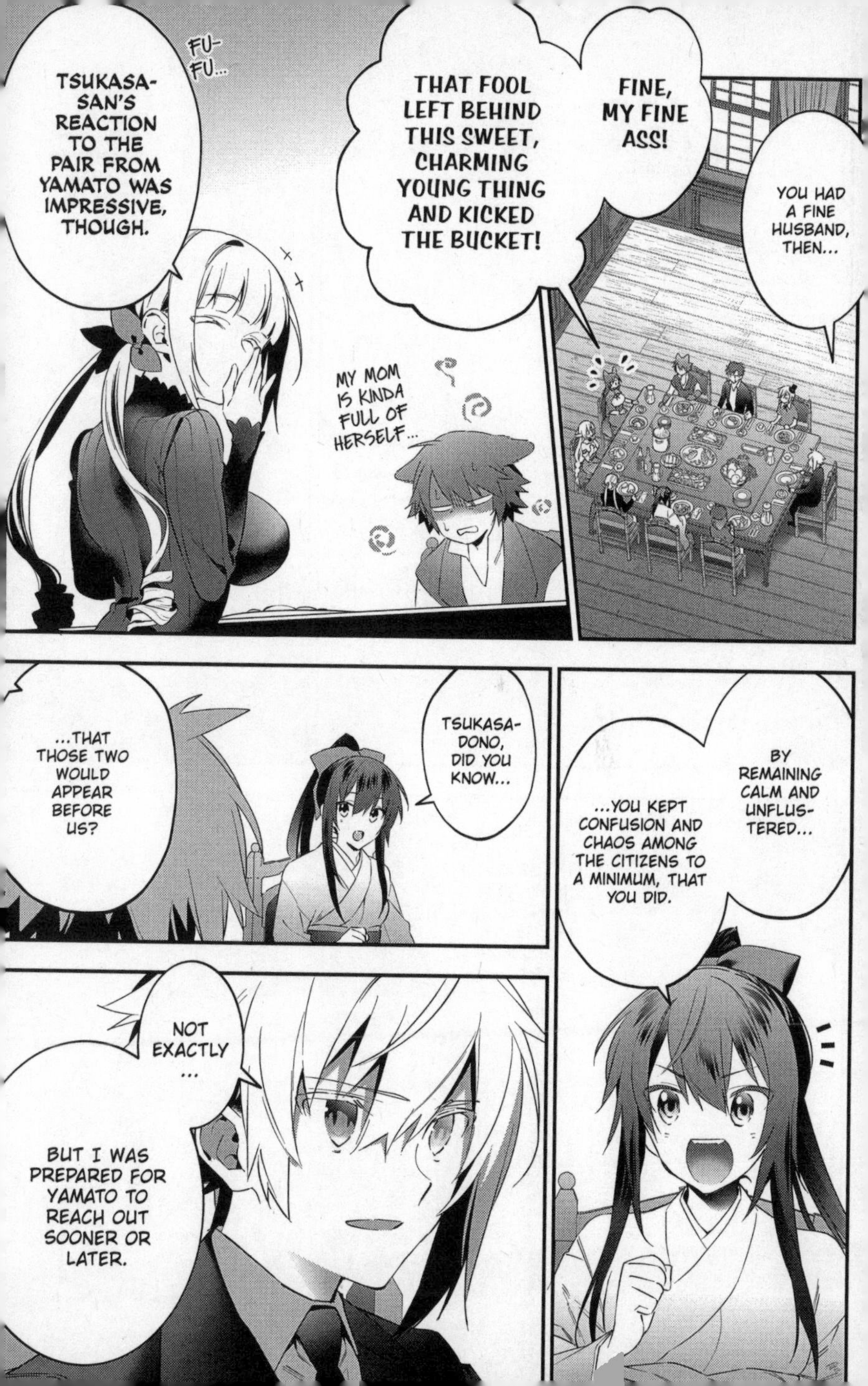
YOU HAD A FINE HUSBAND, THEN...
FINE, MY FINE ASS!
THAT FOOL LEFT BEHIND THIS SWEET, CHARMING YOUNG THING AND KICKED THE BUCKET!
FU-FU...
TSUKASA-SAN'S REACTION TO THE PAIR FROM YAMATO WAS IMPRESSIVE, THOUGH.
MY MOM IS KINDA FULL OF HERSELF...
BY REMAINING CALM AND UNFLUSTERED...
...YOU KEPT CONFUSION AND CHAOS AMONG THE CITIZENS TO A MINIMUM, THAT YOU DID.
TSUKASA-DONO, DID YOU KNOW...
...THAT THOSE TWO WOULD APPEAR BEFORE US?
NOT EXACTLY ...
BUT I WAS PREPARED FOR YAMATO TO REACH OUT SOONER OR LATER.

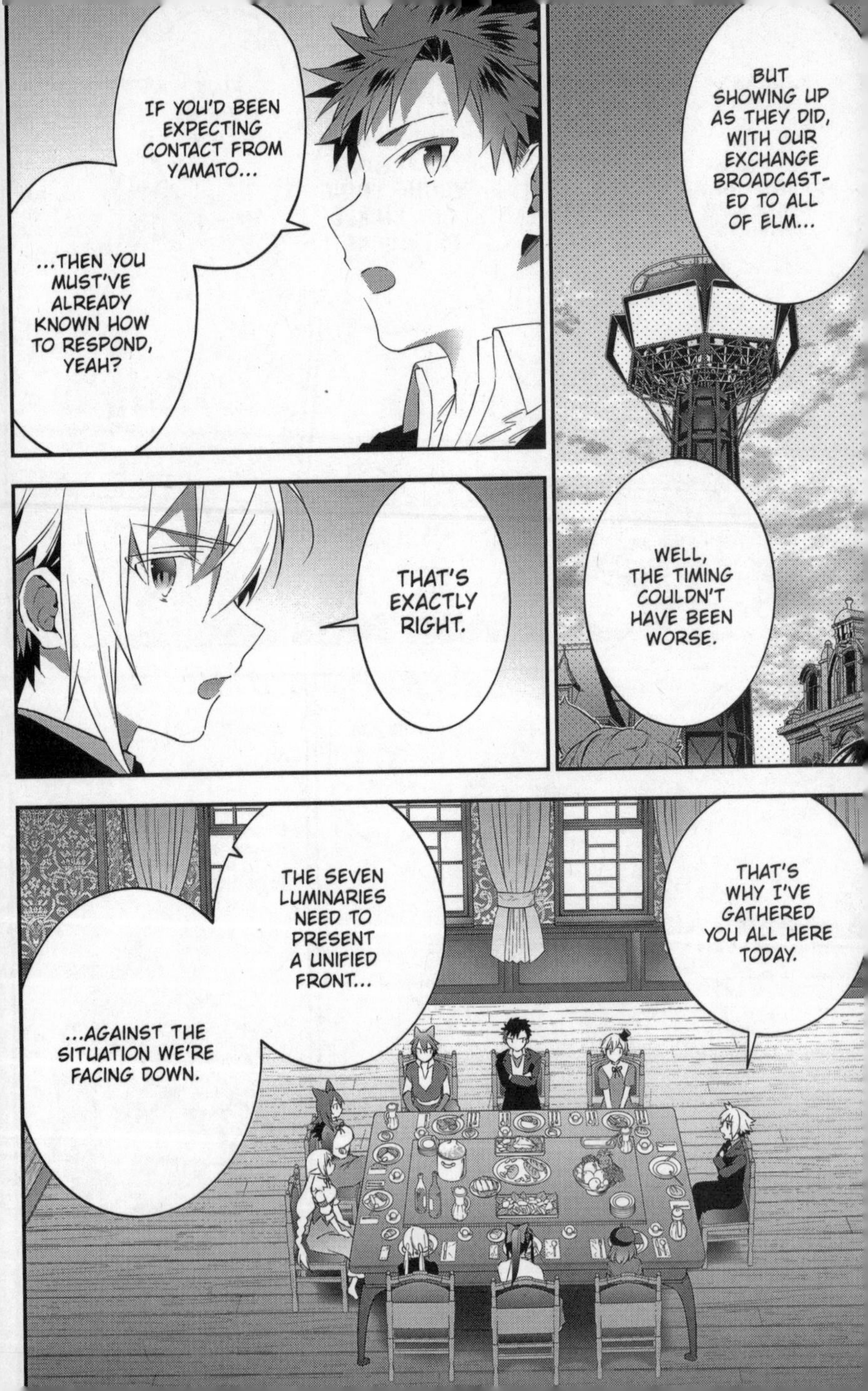
BUT SHOWING UP AS THEY DID, WITH OUR EXCHANGE BROADCAST-ED TO ALL OF ELM...
WELL, THE TIMING COULDN'T HAVE BEEN WORSE.
IF YOU'D BEEN EXPECTING CONTACT FROM YAMATO...
...THEN YOU MUST'VE ALREADY KNOWN HOW TO RESPOND, YEAH?
THAT'S EXACTLY RIGHT.
THAT'S WHY I'VE GATHERED YOU ALL HERE TODAY.
THE SEVEN LUMINARIES NEED TO PRESENT A UNIFIED FRONT...
...AGAINST THE SITUATION WE'RE FACING DOWN.

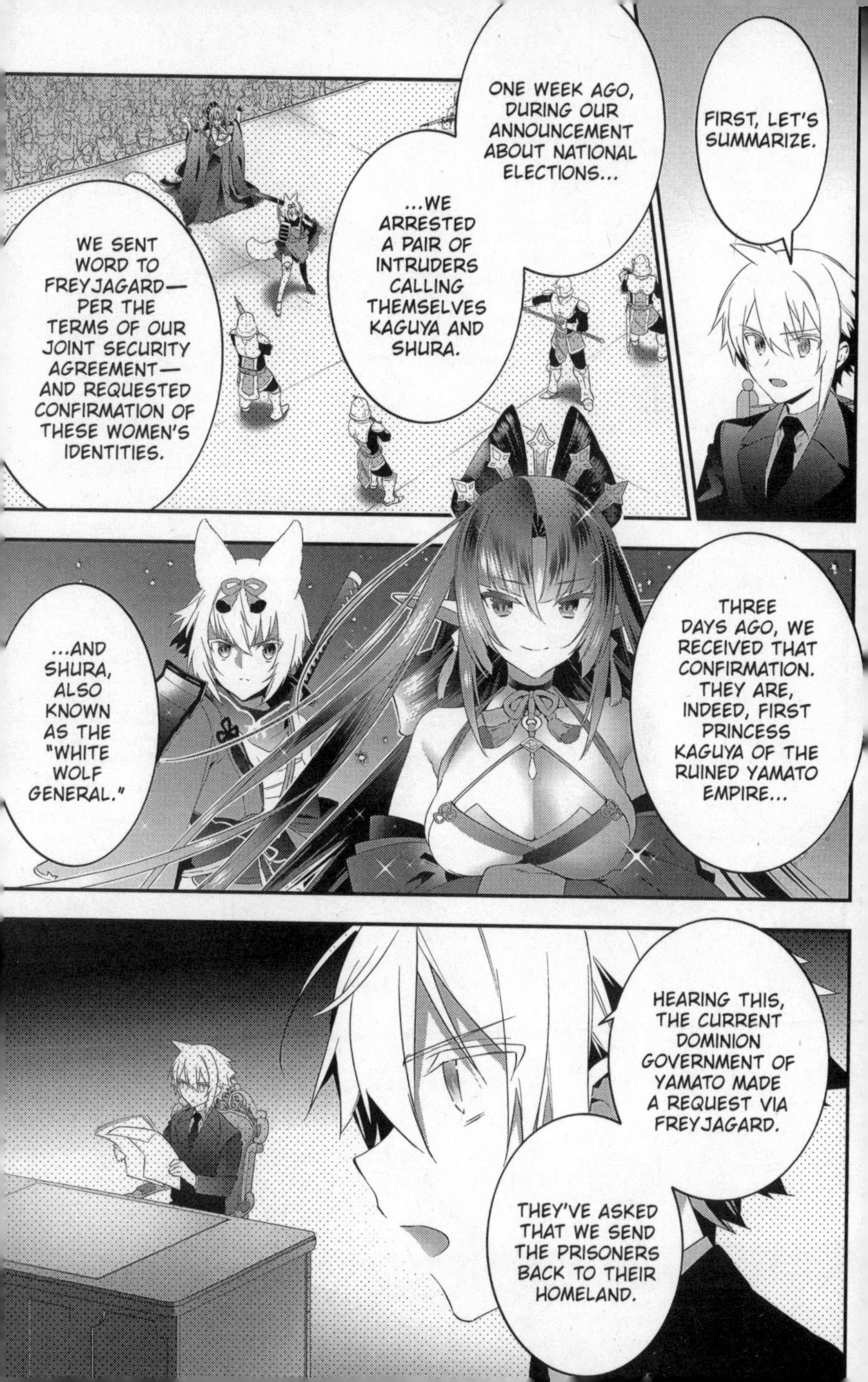
FIRST, LET'S SUMMARIZE.
ONE WEEK AGO, DURING OUR ANNOUNCEMENT ABOUT NATIONAL ELECTIONS...
...WE ARRESTED A PAIR OF INTRUDERS CALLING THEMSELVES KAGUYA AND SHURA.
WE SENT WORD TO FREYJAGARD—PER THE TERMS OF OUR JOINT SECURITY AGREEMENT—AND REQUESTED CONFIRMATION OF THESE WOMEN'S IDENTITIES.
THREE DAYS AGO, WE RECEIVED THAT CONFIRMATION. THEY ARE, INDEED, FIRST PRINCESS KAGUYA OF THE RUINED YAMATO EMPIRE...
...AND SHURA, ALSO KNOWN AS THE "WHITE WOLF GENERAL."
HEARING THIS, THE CURRENT DOMINION GOVERNMENT OF YAMATO MADE A REQUEST VIA FREYJAGARD.
THEY'VE ASKED THAT WE SEND THE PRISONERS BACK TO THEIR HOMELAND.

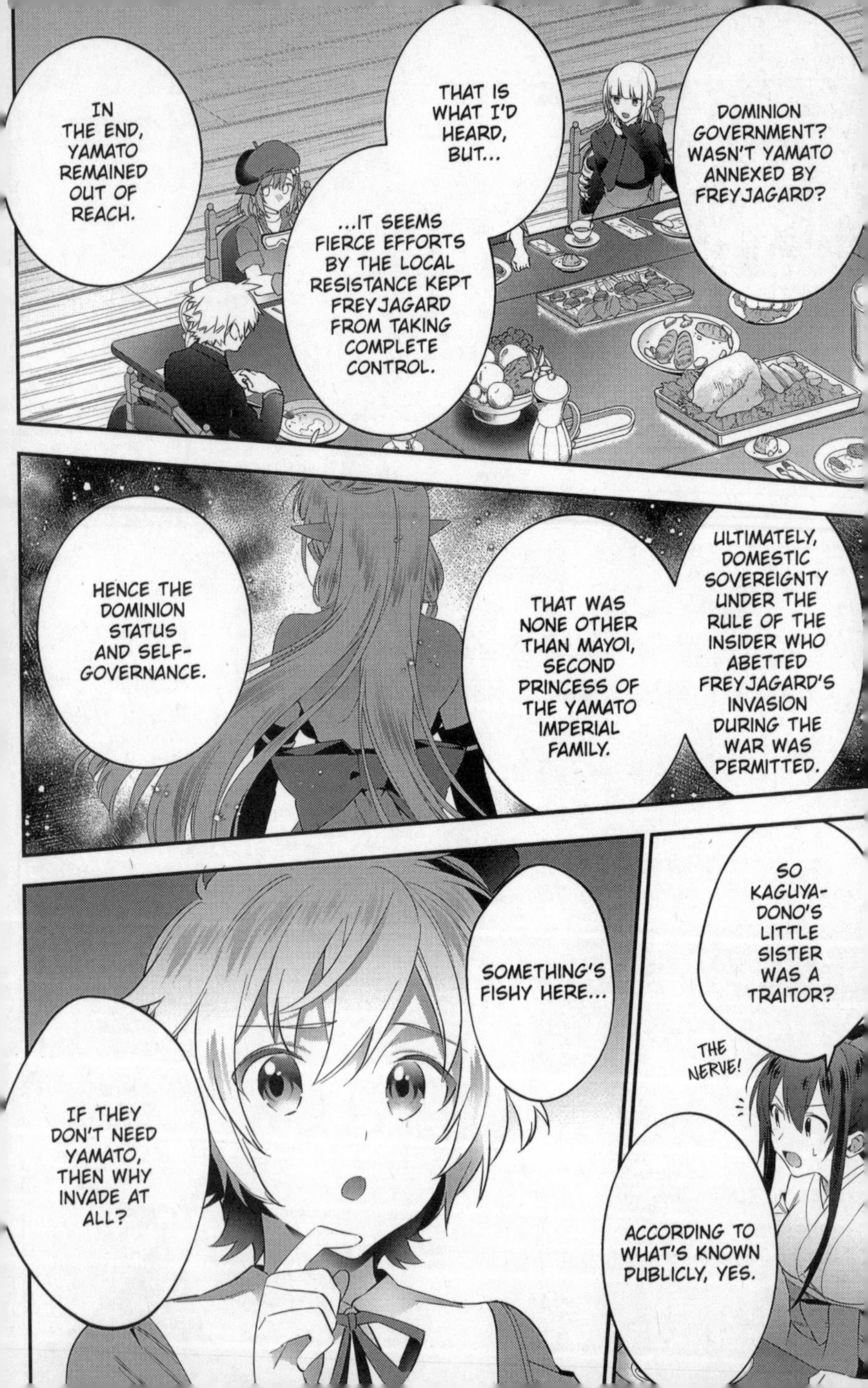
DOMINION GOVERNMENT? WASN'T YAMATO ANNEXED BY FREYJAGARD?
THAT IS WHAT I'D HEARD, BUT...
...IT SEEMS FIERCE EFFORTS BY THE LOCAL RESISTANCE KEPT FREYJAGARD FROM TAKING COMPLETE CONTROL.
IN THE END, YAMATO REMAINED OUT OF REACH.
ULTIMATELY, DOMESTIC SOVEREIGNTY UNDER THE RULE OF THE INSIDER WHO ABETTED FREYJAGARD'S INVASION DURING THE WAR WAS PERMITTED.
THAT WAS NONE OTHER THAN MAYOI, SECOND PRINCESS OF THE YAMATO IMPERIAL FAMILY.
HENCE THE DOMINION STATUS AND SELF-GOVERNANCE.
SO KAGUYA-DONO'S LITTLE SISTER WAS A TRAITOR?
THE NERVE!
ACCORDING TO WHAT'S KNOWN PUBLICLY, YES.
SOMETHING'S FISHY HERE...
IF THEY DON'T NEED YAMATO, THEN WHY INVADE AT ALL?

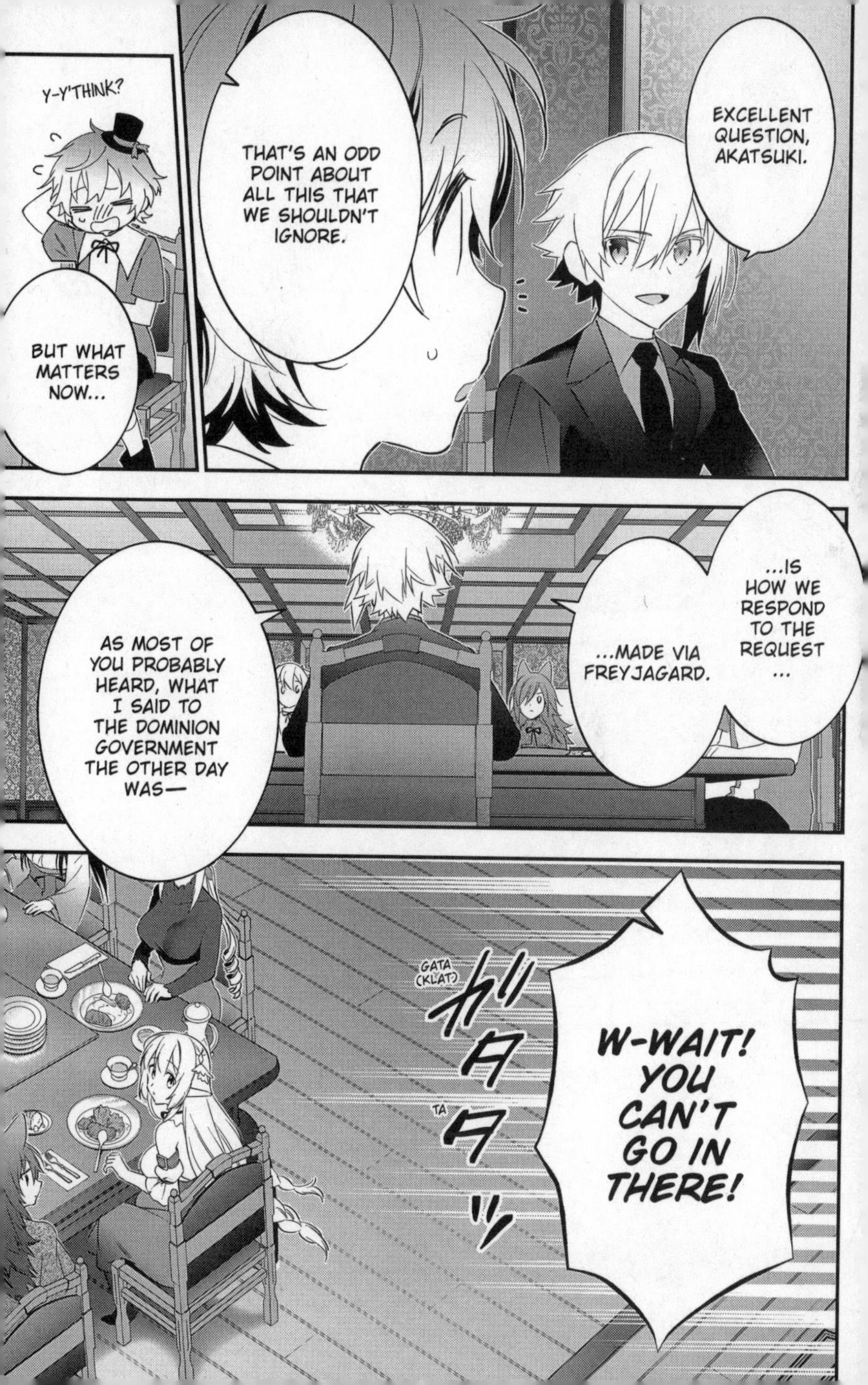
EXCELLENT QUESTION, AKATSUKI.
THAT'S AN ODD POINT ABOUT ALL THIS THAT WE SHOULDN'T IGNORE.
Y-Y'THINK?
BUT WHAT MATTERS NOW...
...IS HOW WE RESPOND TO THE REQUEST ...
...MADE VIA FREYJAGARD.
AS MOST OF YOU PROBABLY HEARD, WHAT I SAID TO THE DOMINION GOVERNMENT THE OTHER DAY WAS—
W-WAIT! YOU CAN'T GO IN THERE!
GATA (KLAT)
TA

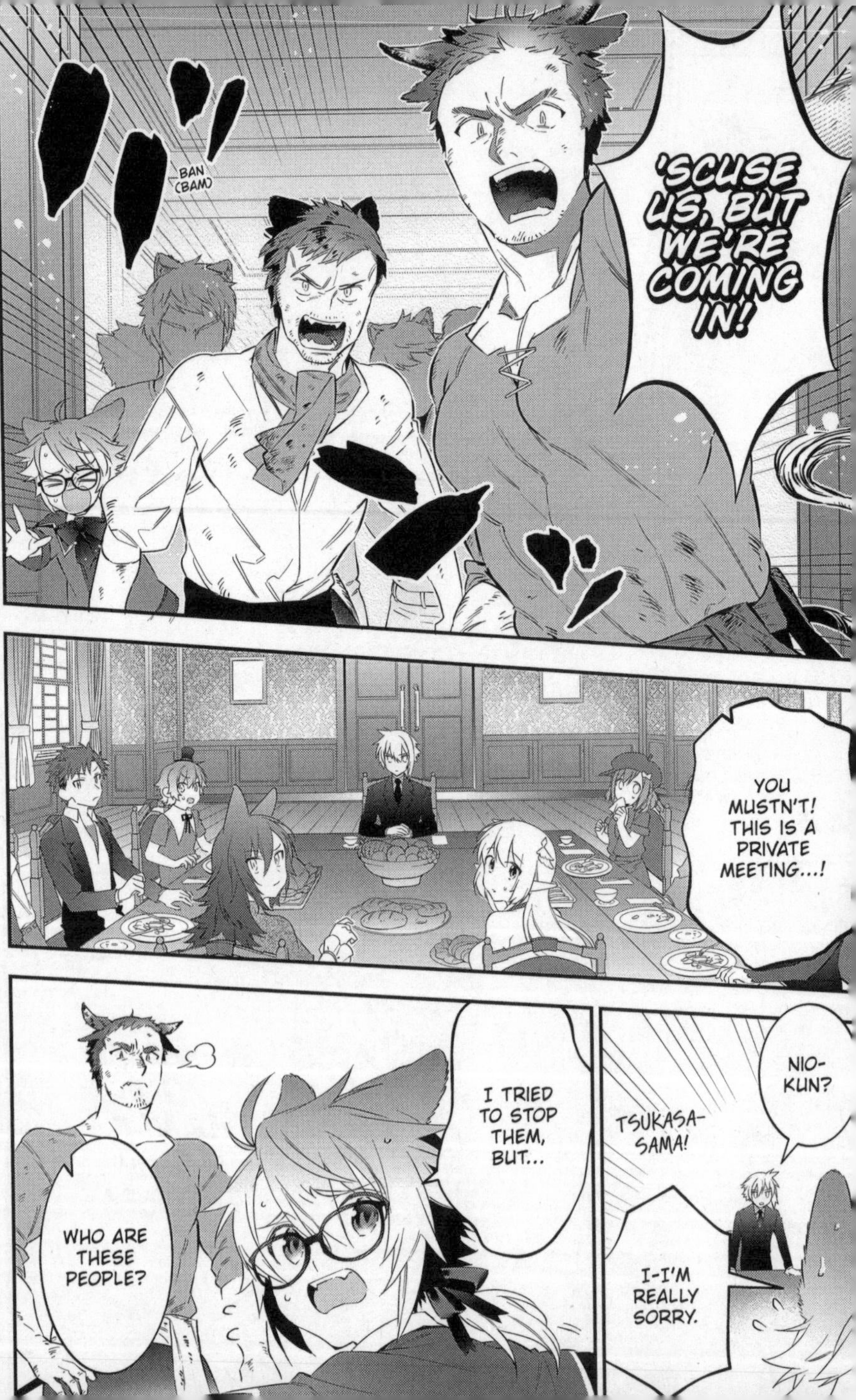
'SCUSE US, BUT WE'RE COMING IN!
BAN (BAM)
YOU MUSTN'T! THIS IS A PRIVATE MEETING...!
NIO-KUN?
TSUKASA-SAMA!
I-I'M REALLY SORRY.
I TRIED TO STOP THEM, BUT...
WHO ARE THESE PEOPLE?

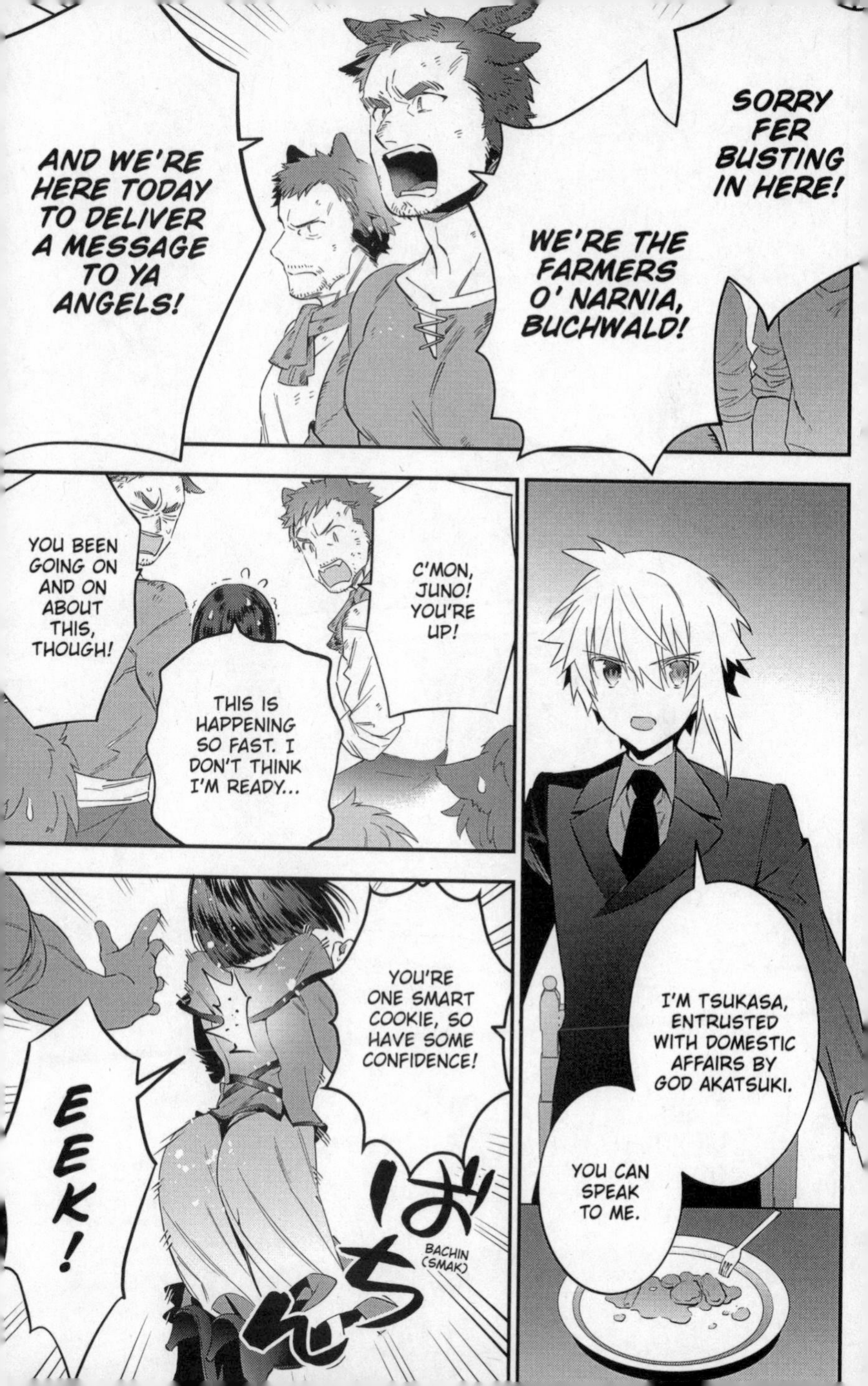
SORRY FER BUSTING IN HERE!
WE'RE THE FARMERS O' NARNIA, BUCHWALD!
AND WE'RE HERE TODAY TO DELIVER A MESSAGE TO YA ANGELS!
I'M TSUKASA, ENTRUSTED WITH DOMESTIC AFFAIRS BY GOD AKATSUKI.
YOU CAN SPEAK TO ME.
C'MON, JUNO! YOU'RE UP!
YOU BEEN GOING ON AND ON ABOUT THIS, THOUGH!
THIS IS HAPPENING SO FAST. I DON'T THINK I'M READY...
YOU'RE ONE SMART COOKIE, SO HAVE SOME CONFIDENCE!
ばちん
BACHIN (SMAK)
EEK!

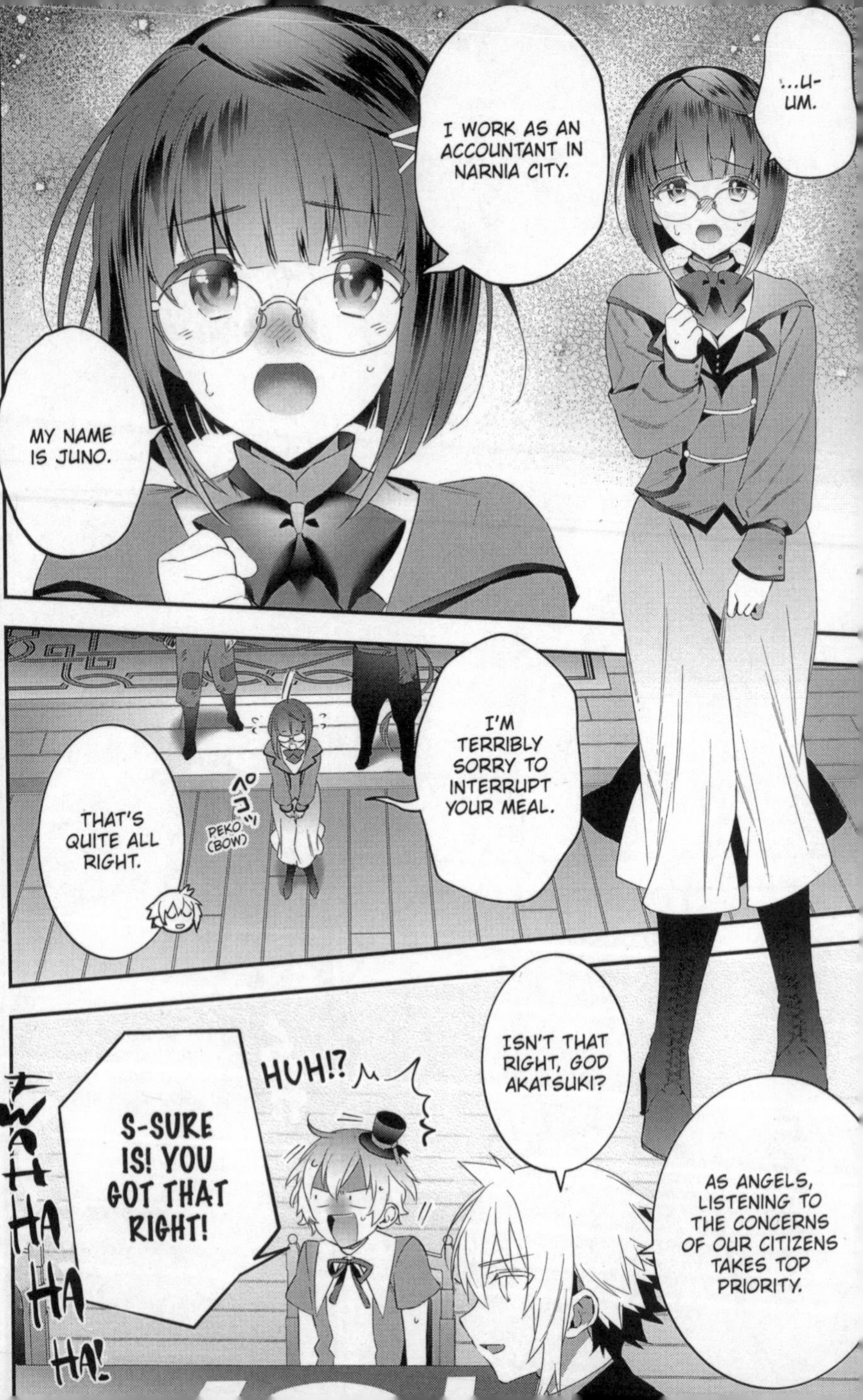
...U-UM.
I WORK AS AN ACCOUNTANT IN NARNIA CITY.
MY NAME IS JUNO.
I'M TERRIBLY SORRY TO INTERRUPT YOUR MEAL.
ペコッ
PEKO (BOW)
THAT'S QUITE ALL RIGHT.
AS ANGELS, LISTENING TO THE CONCERNS OF OUR CITIZENS TAKES TOP PRIORITY.
ISN'T THAT RIGHT, GOD AKATSUKI?
HUH!?
S-SURE IS! YOU GOT THAT RIGHT!
FWAHAHAHA!

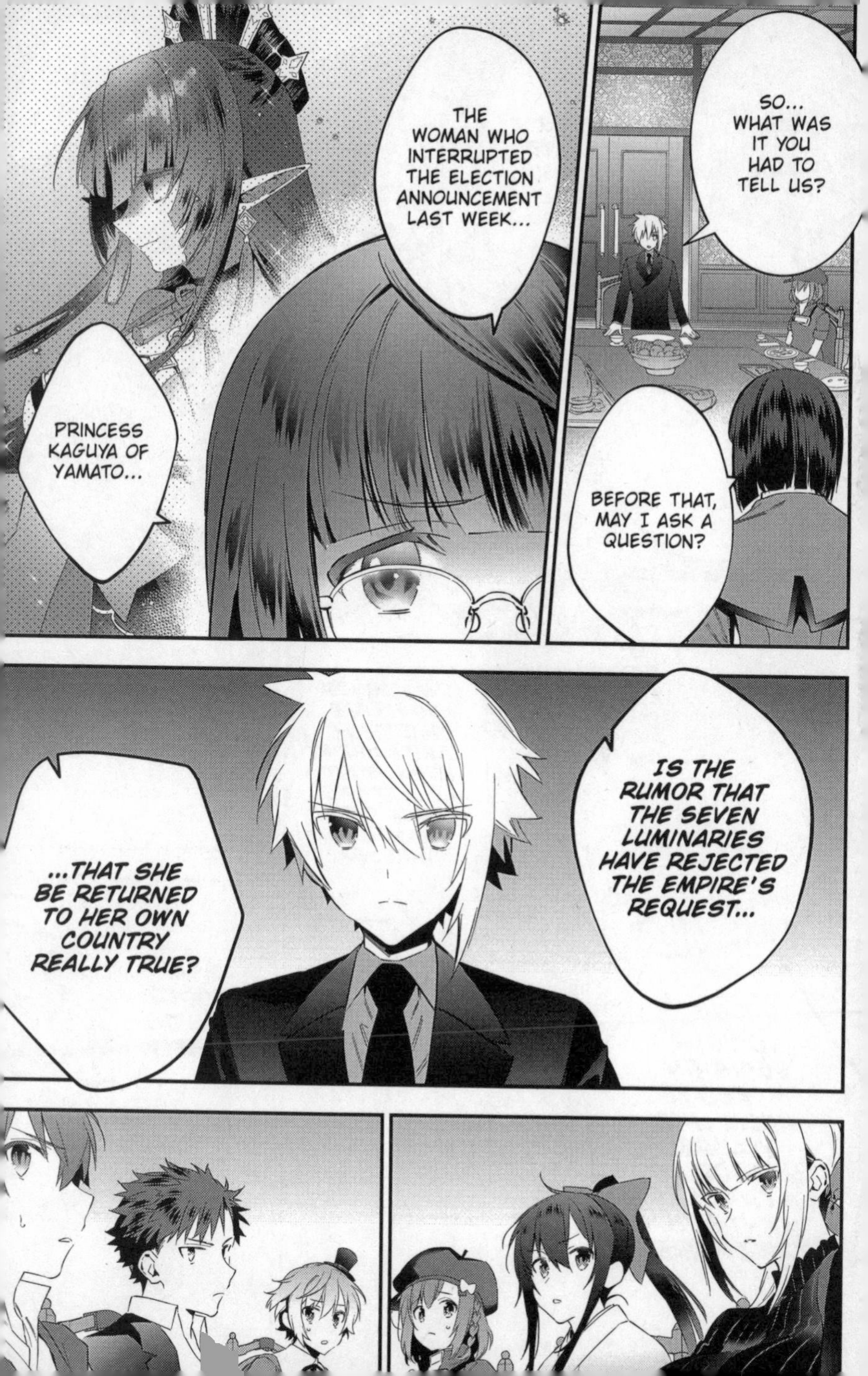
SO... WHAT WAS IT YOU HAD TO TELL US?
BEFORE THAT, MAY I ASK A QUESTION?
THE WOMAN WHO INTERRUPTED THE ELECTION ANNOUNCEMENT LAST WEEK...
PRINCESS KAGUYA OF YAMATO...
IS THE RUMOR THAT THE SEVEN LUMINARIES HAVE REJECTED THE EMPIRE'S REQUEST...
...THAT SHE BE RETURNED TO HER OWN COUNTRY REALLY TRUE?

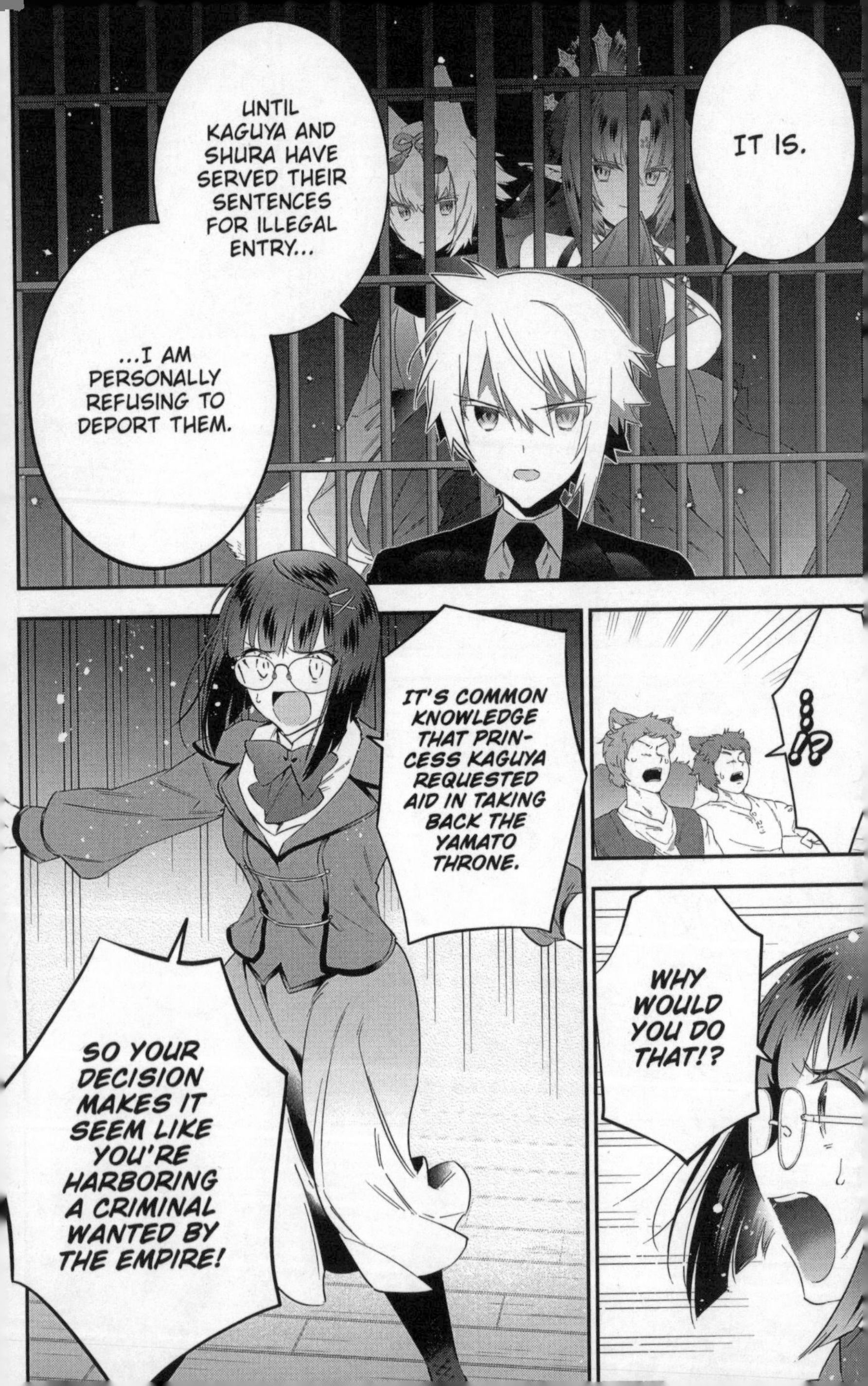
IT IS.
UNTIL KAGUYA AND SHURA HAVE SERVED THEIR SENTENCES FOR ILLEGAL ENTRY...
...I AM PERSONALLY REFUSING TO DEPORT THEM.
...!?
WHY WOULD YOU DO THAT!?
IT'S COMMON KNOWLEDGE THAT PRIN-CESS KAGUYA REQUESTED AID IN TAKING BACK THE YAMATO THRONE.
SO YOUR DECISION MAKES IT SEEM LIKE YOU'RE HARBORING A CRIMINAL WANTED BY THE EMPIRE!

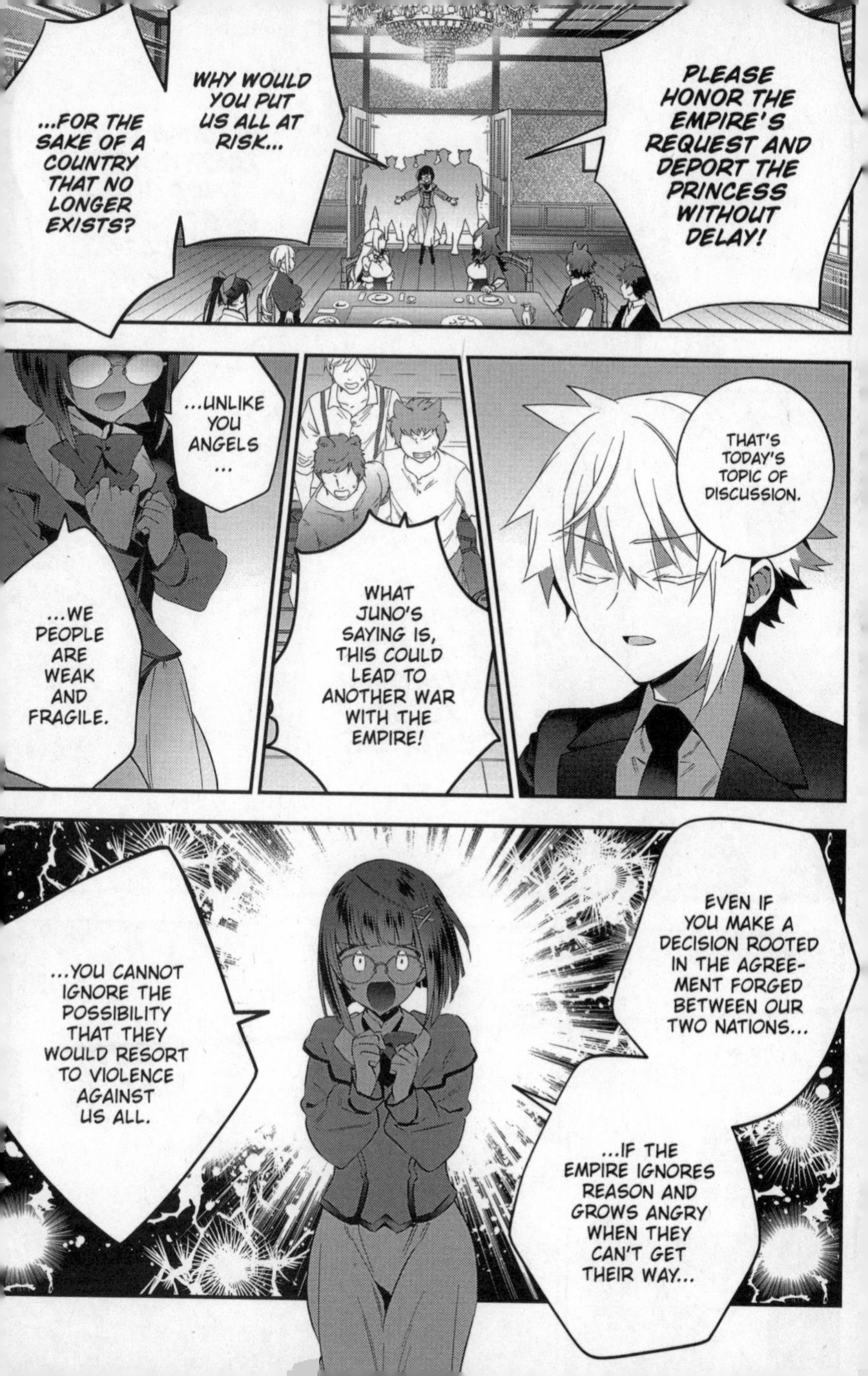
PLEASE HONOR THE EMPIRE'S REQUEST AND DEPORT THE PRINCESS WITHOUT DELAY!
WHY WOULD YOU PUT US ALL AT RISK...
...FOR THE SAKE OF A COUNTRY THAT NO LONGER EXISTS?
THAT'S TODAY'S TOPIC OF DISCUSSION.
WHAT JUNO'S SAYING IS, THIS COULD LEAD TO ANOTHER WAR WITH THE EMPIRE!
...UNLIKE YOU ANGELS ...
...WE PEOPLE ARE WEAK AND FRAGILE.
EVEN IF YOU MAKE A DECISION ROOTED IN THE AGREE-MENT FORGED BETWEEN OUR TWO NATIONS...
...IF THE EMPIRE IGNORES REASON AND GROWS ANGRY WHEN THEY CAN'T GET THEIR WAY...
...YOU CANNOT IGNORE THE POSSIBILITY THAT THEY WOULD RESORT TO VIOLENCE AGAINST US ALL.

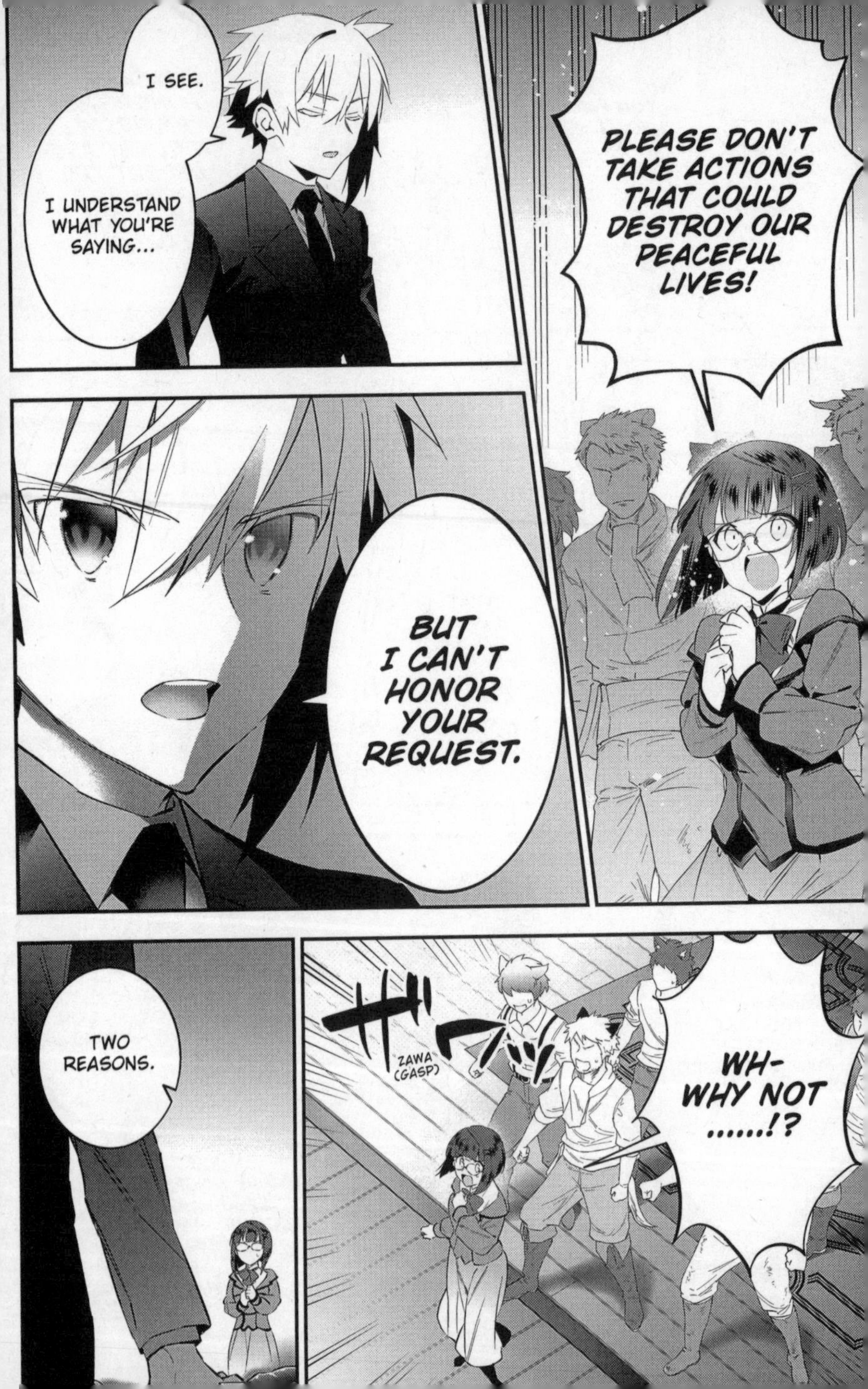
PLEASE DON'T TAKE ACTIONS THAT COULD DESTROY OUR PEACEFUL LIVES!
I SEE.
I UNDERSTAND WHAT YOU'RE SAYING...
BUT I CAN'T HONOR YOUR REQUEST.
WH-WHY NOT ......!?
ZAWA (GASP)
TWO REASONS.

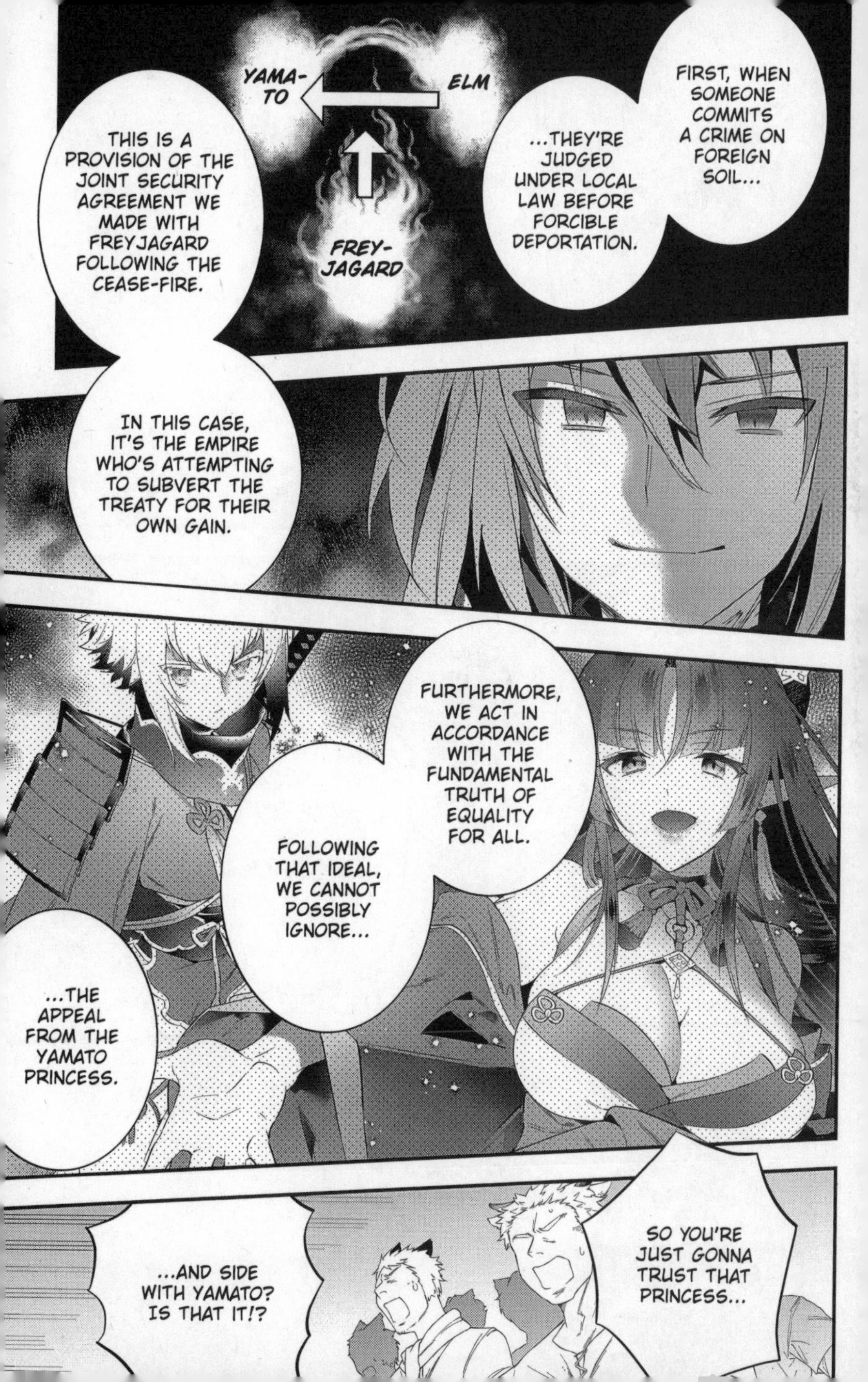
FIRST, WHEN SOMEONE COMMITS A CRIME ON FOREIGN SOIL...
...THEY'RE JUDGED UNDER LOCAL LAW BEFORE FORCIBLE DEPORTATION.
ELM
YAMA-TO
FREY-JAGARD
THIS IS A PROVISION OF THE JOINT SECURITY AGREEMENT WE MADE WITH FREYJAGARD FOLLOWING THE CEASE-FIRE.
IN THIS CASE, IT'S THE EMPIRE WHO'S ATTEMPTING TO SUBVERT THE TREATY FOR THEIR OWN GAIN.
FURTHERMORE, WE ACT IN ACCORDANCE WITH THE FUNDAMENTAL TRUTH OF EQUALITY FOR ALL.
FOLLOWING THAT IDEAL, WE CANNOT POSSIBLY IGNORE...
...THE APPEAL FROM THE YAMATO PRINCESS.
SO YOU'RE JUST GONNA TRUST THAT PRINCESS...
...AND SIDE WITH YAMATO? IS THAT IT!?

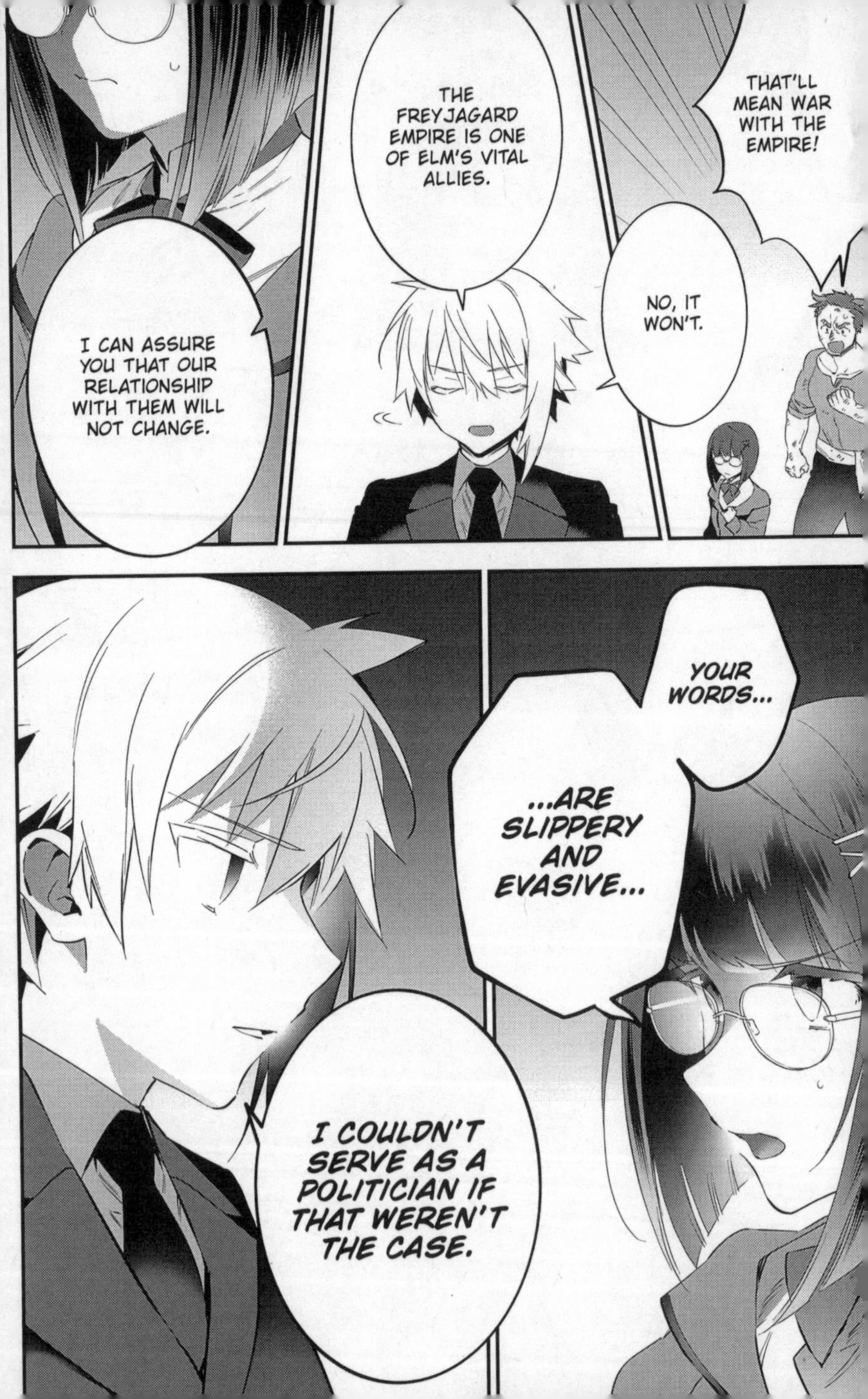
THAT'LL MEAN WAR WITH THE EMPIRE!
NO, IT WON'T.
THE FREYJAGARD EMPIRE IS ONE OF ELM'S VITAL ALLIES.
I CAN ASSURE YOU THAT OUR RELATIONSHIP WITH THEM WILL NOT CHANGE.
YOUR WORDS...
...ARE SLIPPERY AND EVASIVE...
I COULDN'T SERVE AS A POLITICIAN IF THAT WEREN'T THE CASE.

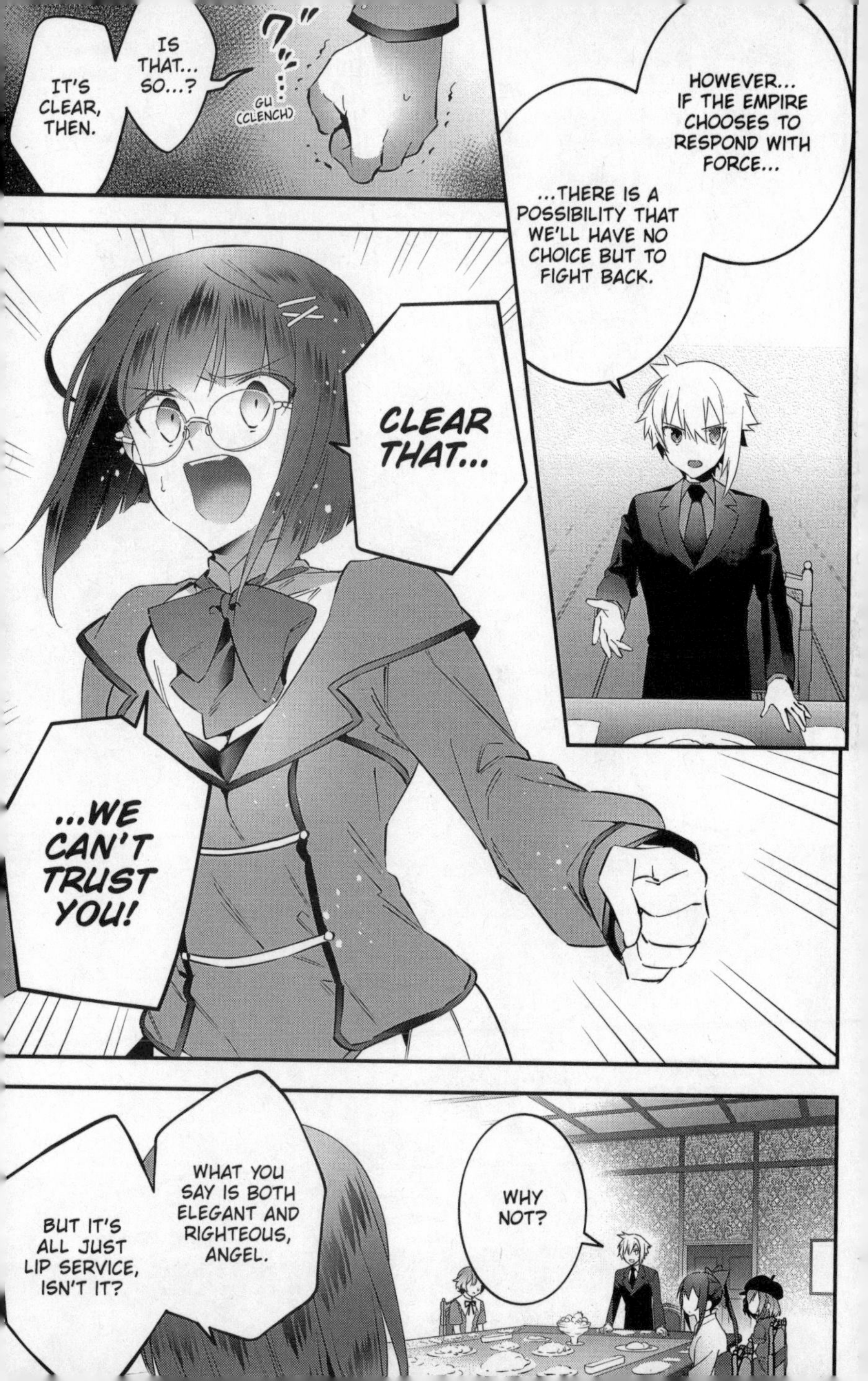
HOWEVER... IF THE EMPIRE CHOOSES TO RESPOND WITH FORCE...
...THERE IS A POSSIBILITY THAT WE'LL HAVE NO CHOICE BUT TO FIGHT BACK.
GU (CLENCH)
IS THAT... SO...?
IT'S CLEAR, THEN.
CLEAR THAT...
...WE CAN'T TRUST YOU!
WHY NOT?
WHAT YOU SAY IS BOTH ELEGANT AND RIGHTEOUS, ANGEL.
BUT IT'S ALL JUST LIP SERVICE, ISN'T IT?

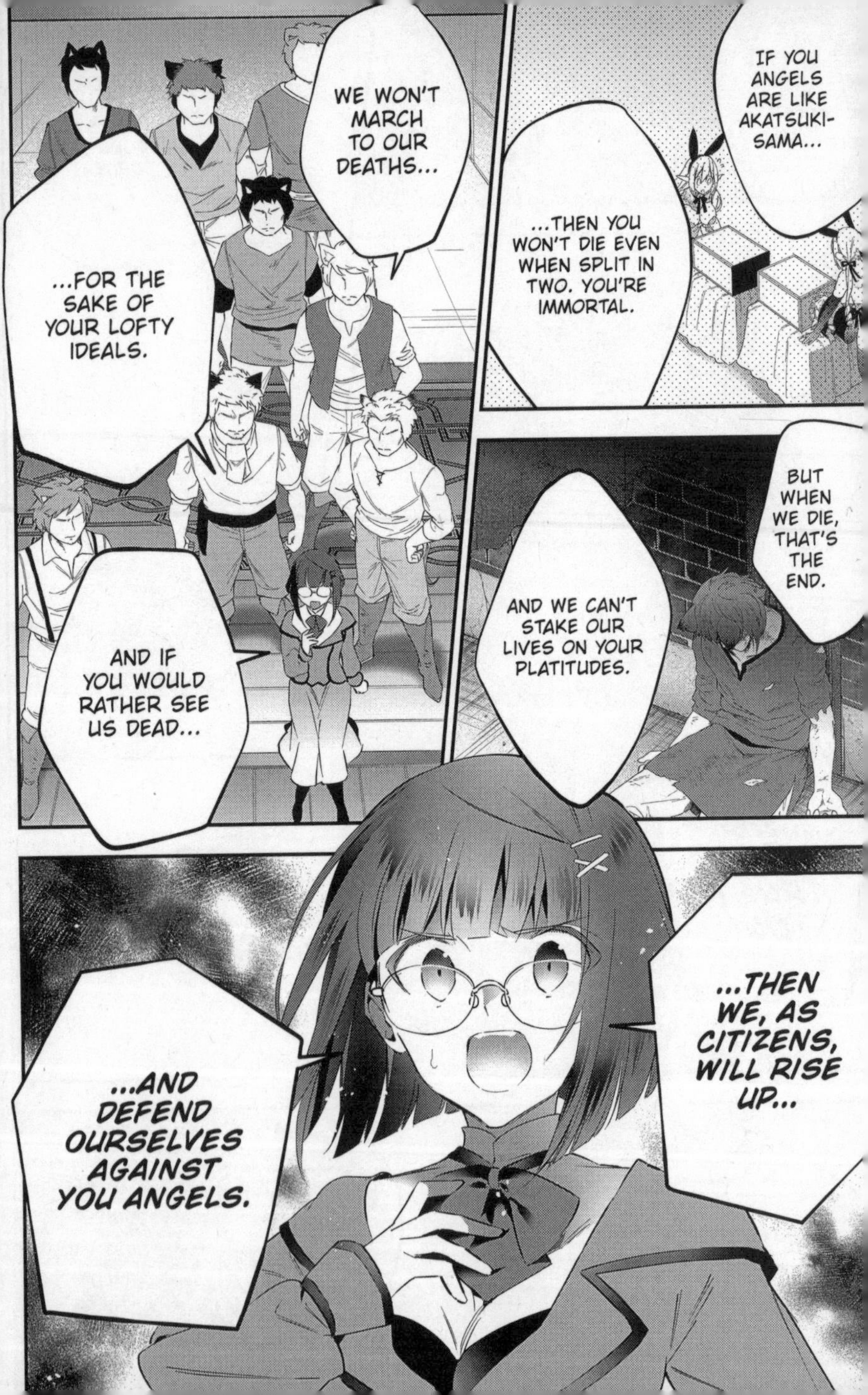
IF YOU ANGELS ARE LIKE AKATSUKI-SAMA...
...THEN YOU WON'T DIE EVEN WHEN SPLIT IN TWO. YOU'RE IMMORTAL.
BUT WHEN WE DIE, THAT'S THE END.
AND WE CAN'T STAKE OUR LIVES ON YOUR PLATITUDES.
WE WON'T MARCH TO OUR DEATHS...
...FOR THE SAKE OF YOUR LOFTY IDEALS.
AND IF YOU WOULD RATHER SEE US DEAD...
...THEN WE, AS CITIZENS, WILL RISE UP...
...AND DEFEND OURSELVES AGAINST YOU ANGELS.

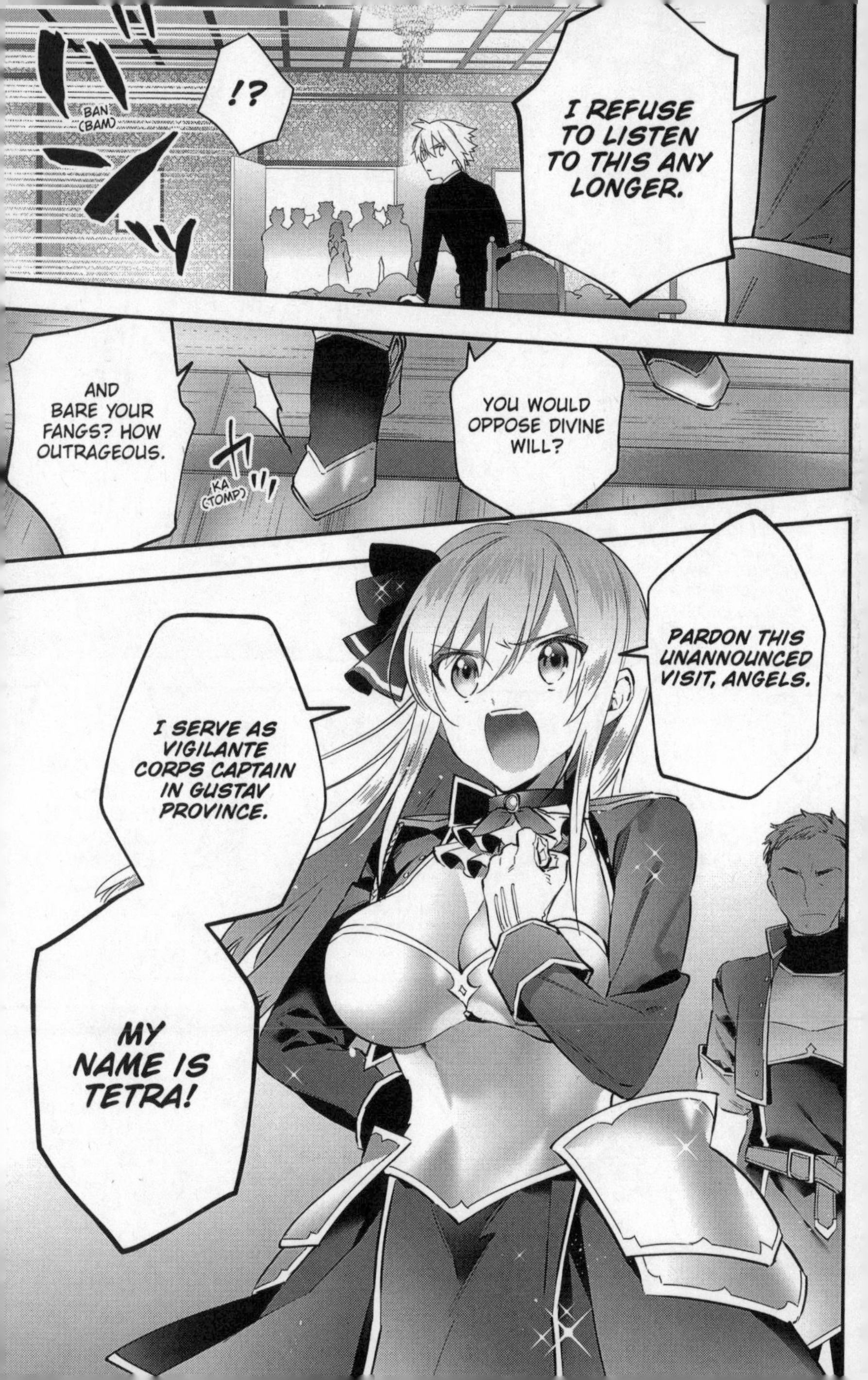
I REFUSE TO LISTEN TO THIS ANY LONGER.
!?
BAN (BAM)
YOU WOULD OPPOSE DIVINE WILL?
KA (TOMP)
AND BARE YOUR FANGS? HOW OUTRAGEOUS.
PARDON THIS UNANNOUNCED VISIT, ANGELS.
I SERVE AS VIGILANTE CORPS CAPTAIN IN GUSTAV PROVINCE.
MY NAME IS TETRA!

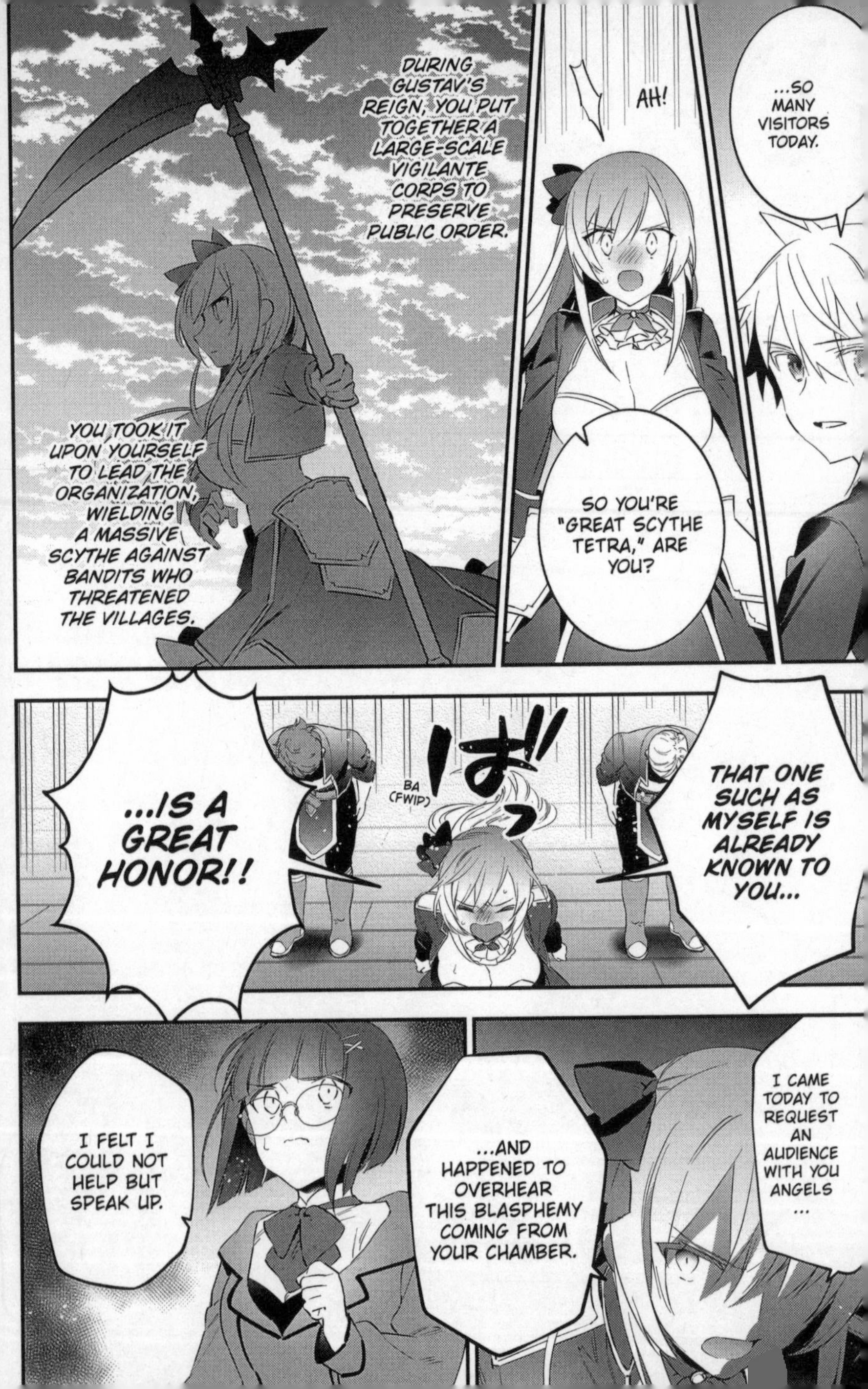
...SO MANY VISITORS TODAY.
AH!
SO YOU'RE "GREAT SCYTHE TETRA," ARE YOU?
DURING GUSTAV'S REIGN, YOU PUT TOGETHER A LARGE-SCALE VIGILANTE CORPS TO PRESERVE PUBLIC ORDER.
YOU TOOK IT UPON YOURSELF TO LEAD THE ORGANIZATION, WIELDING A MASSIVE SCYTHE AGAINST BANDITS WHO THREATENED THE VILLAGES.
THAT ONE SUCH AS MYSELF IS ALREADY KNOWN TO YOU...
ばっ
BA (FWIP)
...IS A GREAT HONOR!!
I CAME TODAY TO REQUEST AN AUDIENCE WITH YOU ANGELS ...
...AND HAPPENED TO OVERHEAR THIS BLASPHEMY COMING FROM YOUR CHAMBER.
I FELT I COULD NOT HELP BUT SPEAK UP.

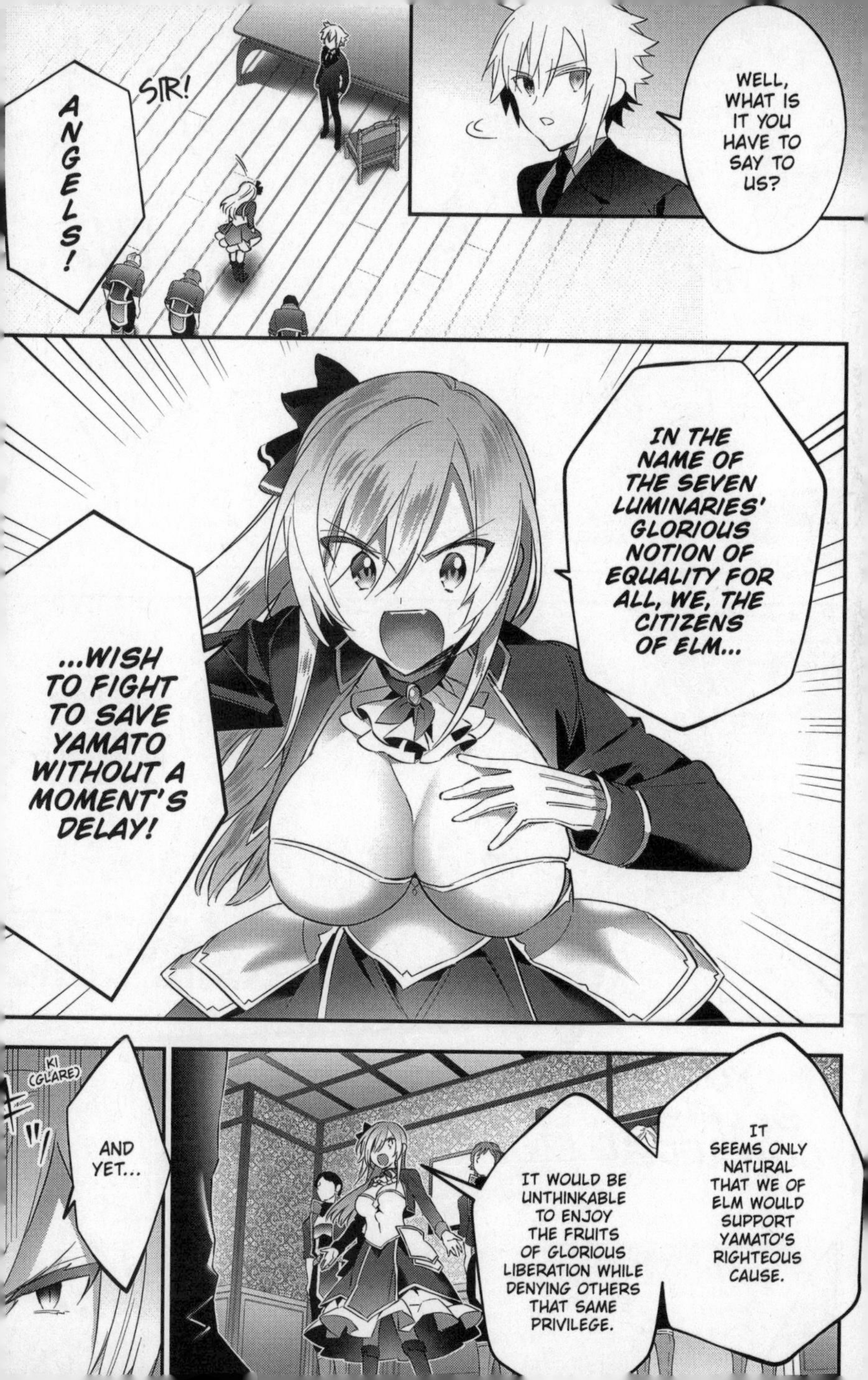
WELL, WHAT IS IT YOU HAVE TO SAY TO US?
SIR!
ANGELS!
IN THE NAME OF THE SEVEN LUMINARIES' GLORIOUS NOTION OF EQUALITY FOR ALL, WE, THE CITIZENS OF ELM...
...WISH TO FIGHT TO SAVE YAMATO WITHOUT A MOMENT'S DELAY!
IT SEEMS ONLY NATURAL THAT WE OF ELM WOULD SUPPORT YAMATO'S RIGHTEOUS CAUSE.
IT WOULD BE UNTHINKABLE TO ENJOY THE FRUITS OF GLORIOUS LIBERATION WHILE DENYING OTHERS THAT SAME PRIVILEGE.
KI (GLARE)
AND YET...

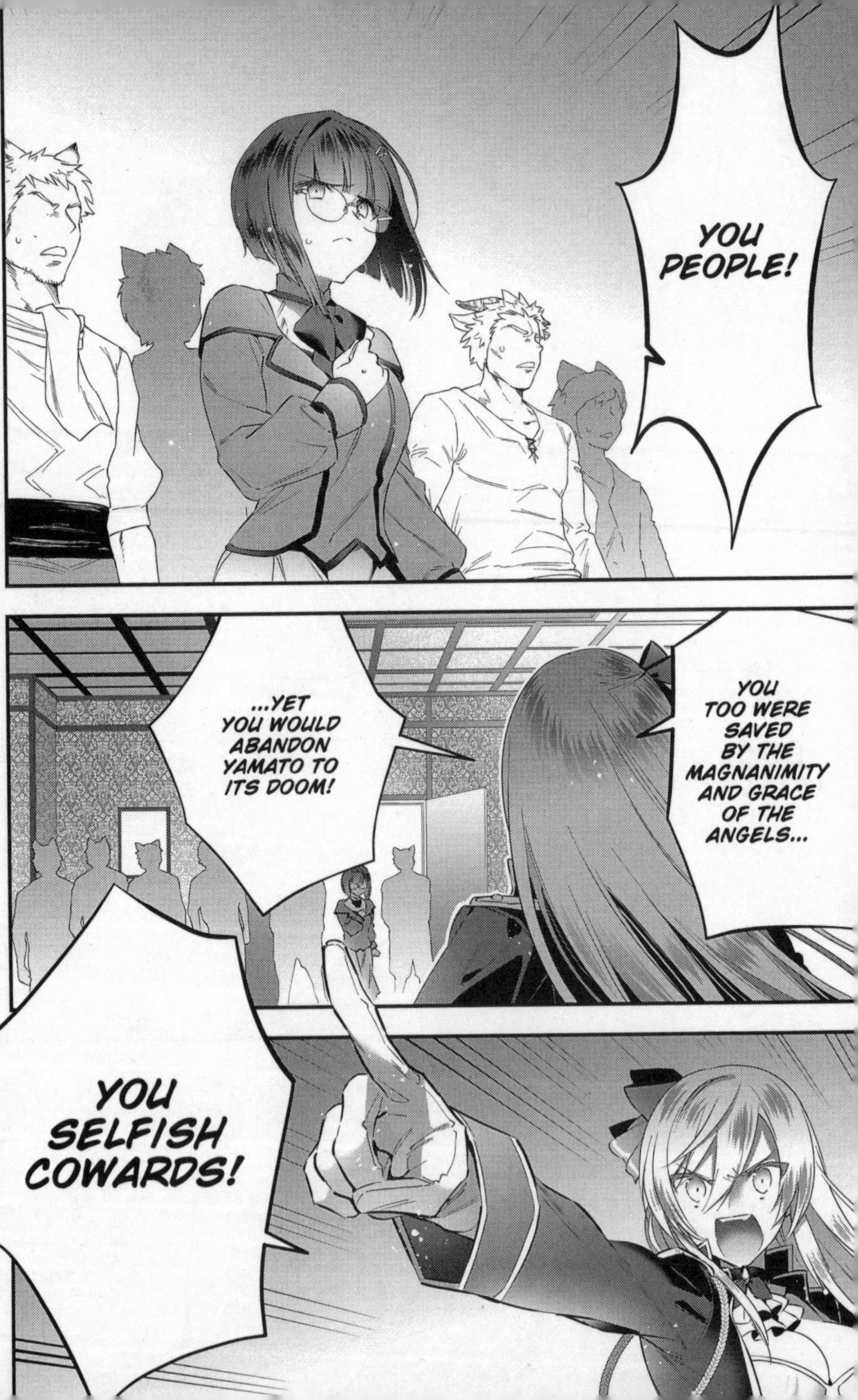
YOU PEOPLE!
YOU TOO WERE SAVED BY THE MAGNANIMITY AND GRACE OF THE ANGELS...
...YET YOU WOULD ABANDON YAMATO TO ITS DOOM!
YOU SELFISH COWARDS!

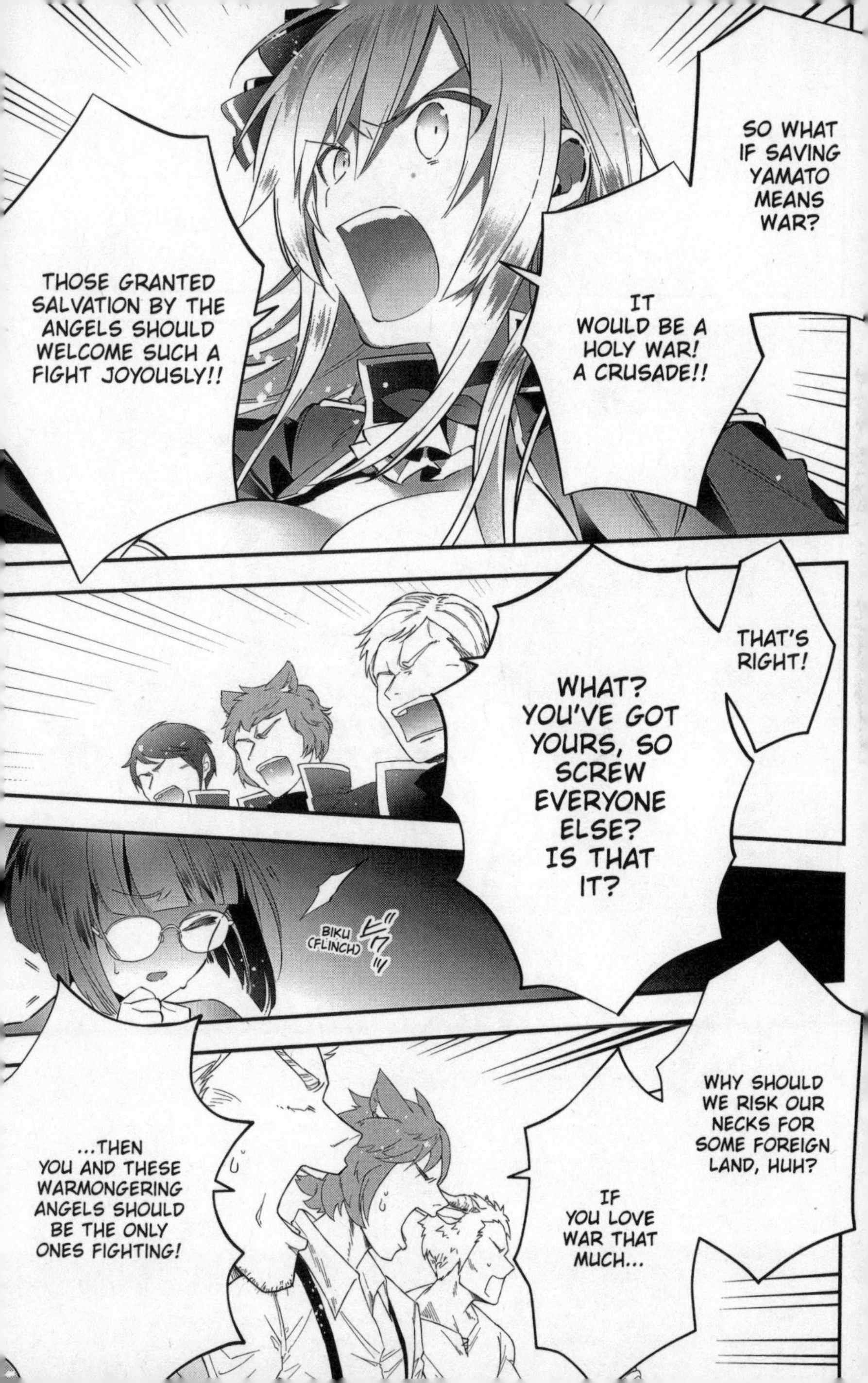
SO WHAT IF SAVING YAMATO MEANS WAR?
IT WOULD BE A HOLY WAR! A CRUSADE!!
THOSE GRANTED SALVATION BY THE ANGELS SHOULD WELCOME SUCH A FIGHT JOYOUSLY!!
THAT'S RIGHT!
WHAT? YOU'VE GOT YOURS, SO SCREW EVERYONE ELSE? IS THAT IT?
BIKU (FLINCH)
WHY SHOULD WE RISK OUR NECKS FOR SOME FOREIGN LAND, HUH?
IF YOU LOVE WAR THAT MUCH...
...THEN YOU AND THESE WARMONGERING ANGELS SHOULD BE THE ONLY ONES FIGHTING!

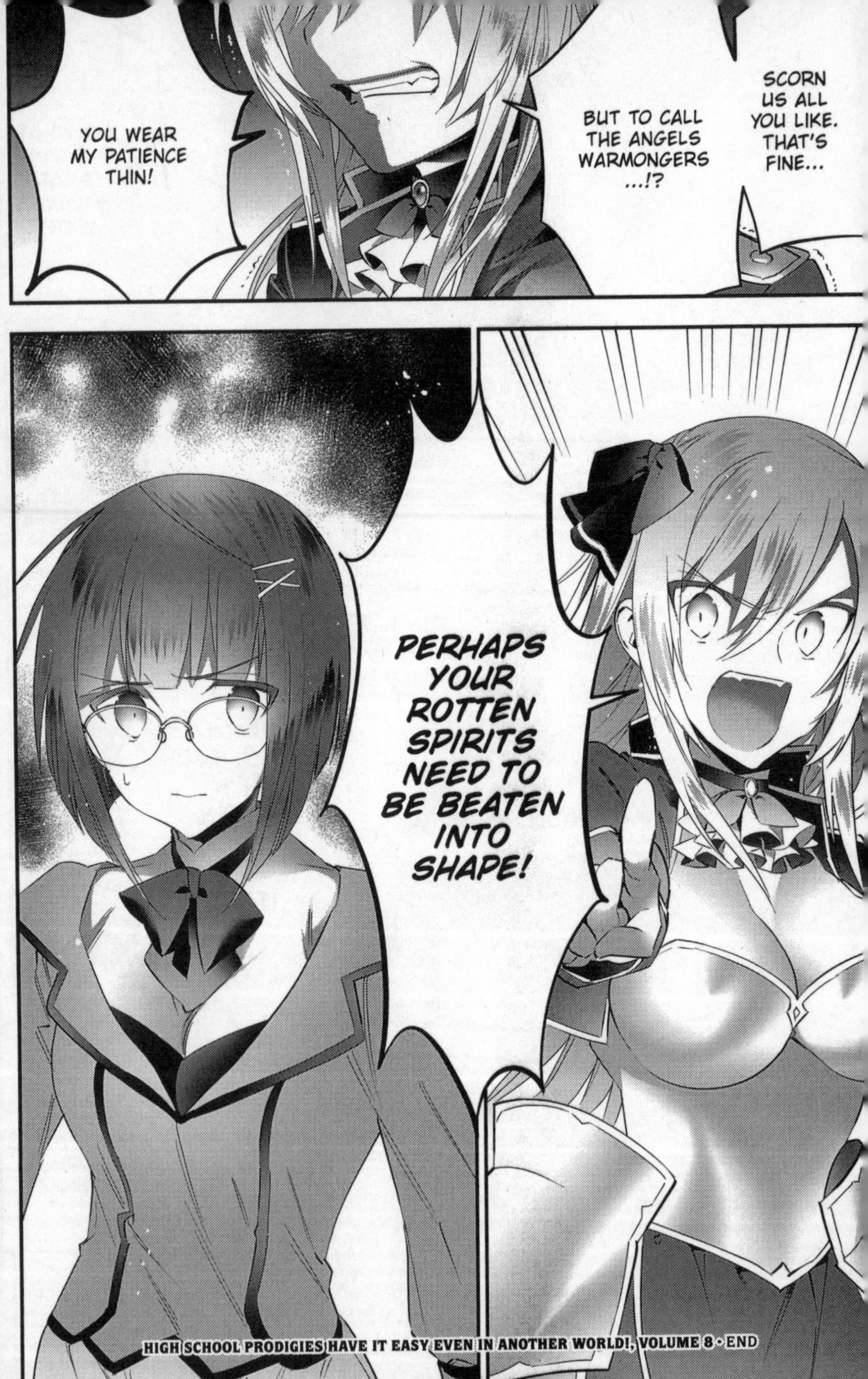
SCORN US ALL YOU LIKE. THAT'S FINE...
BUT TO CALL THE ANGELS WARMONGERS ...!?
YOU WEAR MY PATIENCE THIN!
PERHAPS YOUR ROTTEN SPIRITS NEED TO BE BEATEN INTO SHAPE!
HIGH SCHOOL PRODIGIES HAVE IT EASY EVEN IN ANOTHER WORLD!, VOLUME 8 • END

TRANSLATION NOTES

COMMON HONORIFICS

no honorific: Indicates familiarity or closeness; if used without permission or reason, addressing someone in this manner would constitute an insult.

-san: The Japanese equivalent of Mr./Mrs./Miss. If a situation calls for politeness, this is the fail-safe honorific.

-sama: Conveys great respect; may also indicate that the social status of the speaker is lower than that of the addressee.

-kun: Used most often when referring to boys, this indicates affection or familiarity. Occasionally used by older men among their peers, but it may also be used by anyone referring to a person of lower standing.

-sensei: A respectful term for teachers, artists, or high-level professionals.

-dono: A respectful term typically equated with "lord" or "master," this honorific has an archaic spin to it when used in colloquial parlance.

Page 117
The town of **Narnia** is a nod to C. S. Lewis's *The Chronicles of Narnia*, which also features a group of teenagers inexplicably transported to another world full of magic and sentient non-humans.

Page 139
Kirin, the name the sound director accidentally calls instead of Ringo, is the Japanese word for "giraffe."

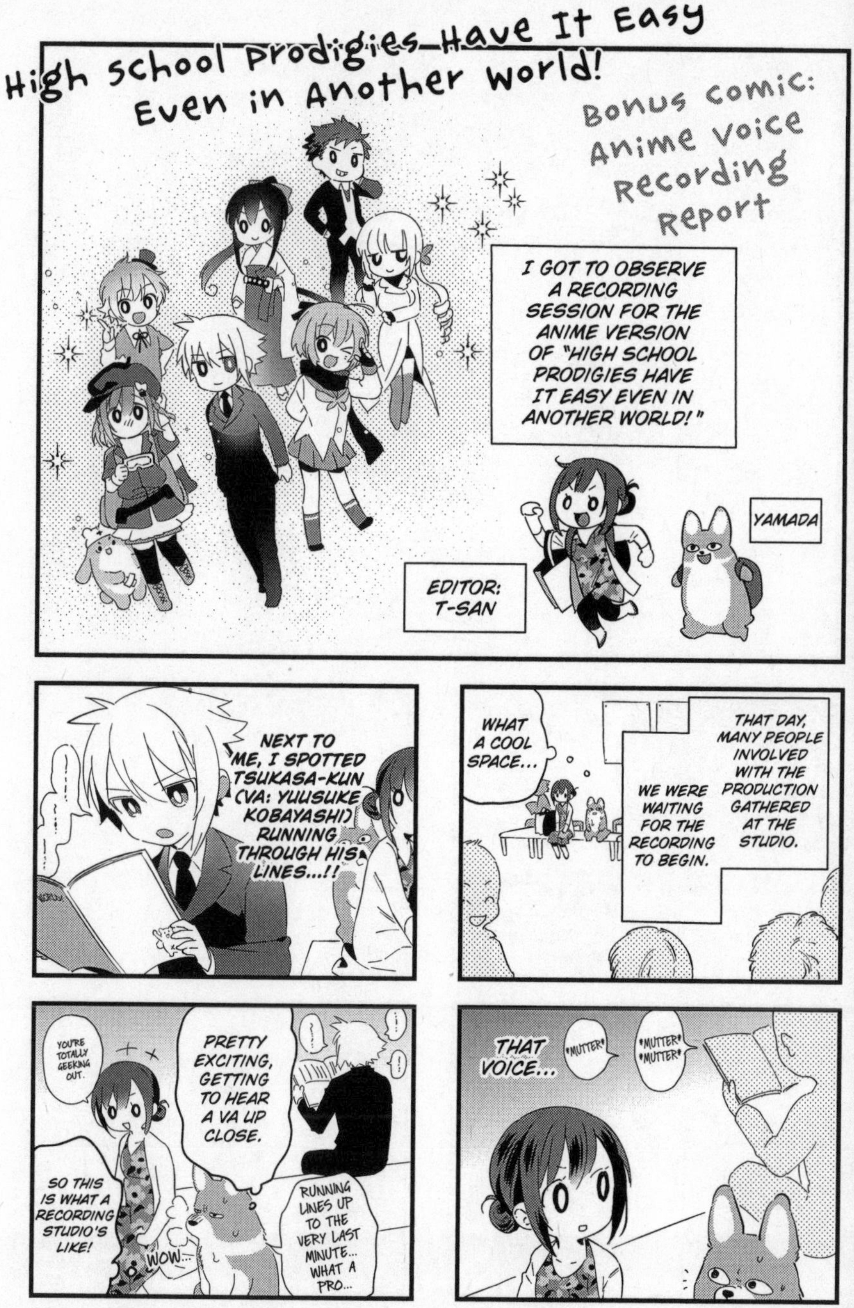
High School Prodigies Have It Easy Even in Another World!
Bonus comic: Anime Voice Recording Report
I GOT TO OBSERVE A RECORDING SESSION FOR THE ANIME VERSION OF "HIGH SCHOOL PRODIGIES HAVE IT EASY EVEN IN ANOTHER WORLD!"
YAMADA
EDITOR: T-SAN
THAT DAY, MANY PEOPLE INVOLVED WITH THE PRODUCTION GATHERED AT THE STUDIO.
WE WERE WAITING FOR THE RECORDING TO BEGIN.
WHAT A COOL SPACE...
NEXT TO ME, I SPOTTED TSUKASA-KUN (VA: YUUSUKE KOBAYASHI) RUNNING THROUGH HIS LINES...!!
MUTTER *MUTTER*
MUTTER
THAT VOICE...
PRETTY EXCITING, GETTING TO HEAR A VA UP CLOSE.
YOU'RE TOTALLY GEEKING OUT.
RUNNING LINES UP TO THE VERY LAST MINUTE... WHAT A PRO...
SO THIS IS WHAT A RECORDING STUDIO'S LIKE!
WOW...

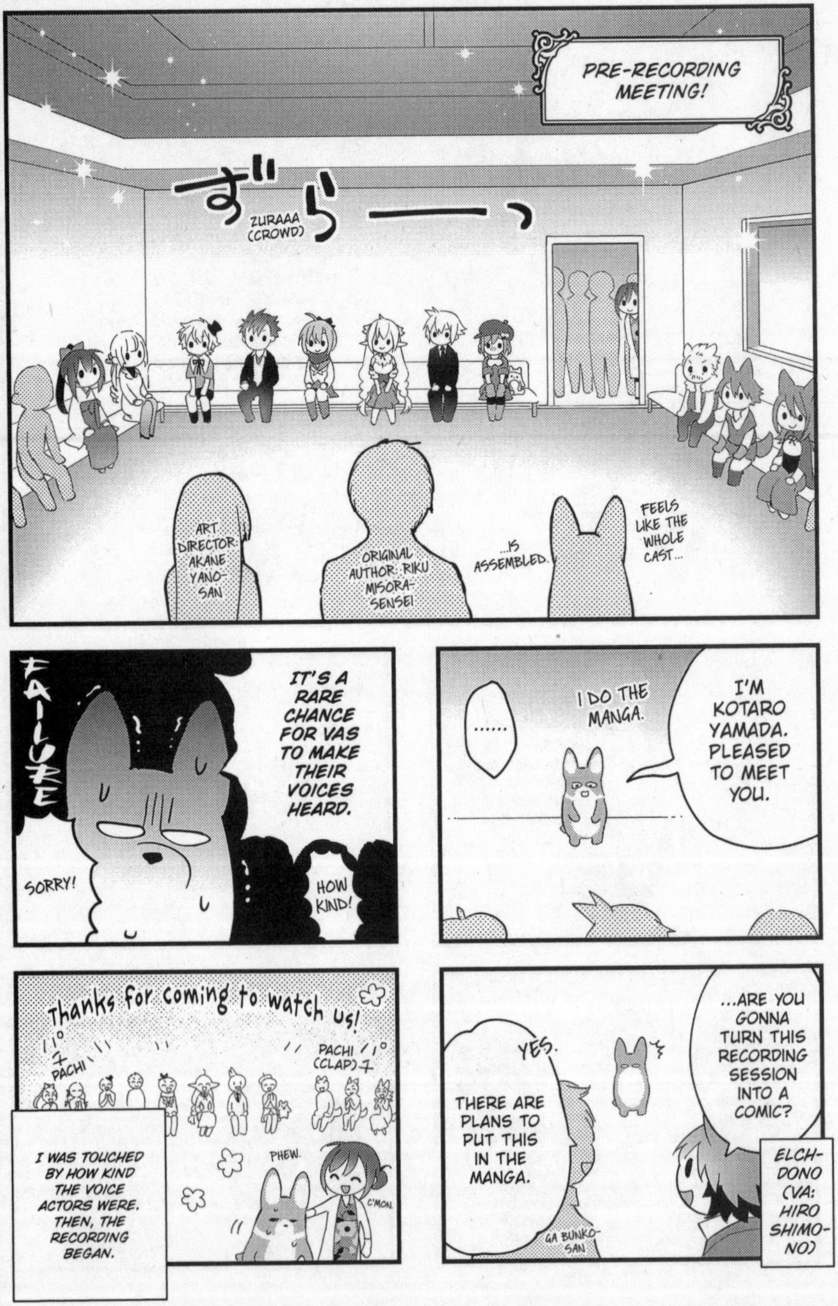
PRE-RECORDING MEETING!
ずらーーっ
ZURAAA (CROWD)
FEELS LIKE THE WHOLE CAST...
...IS ASSEMBLED.
ORIGINAL AUTHOR: RIKU MISORA-SENSEI
ART DIRECTOR: AKANE YANO-SAN
I'M KOTARO YAMADA. PLEASED TO MEET YOU.
I DO THE MANGA.
......
IT'S A RARE CHANCE FOR VAS TO MAKE THEIR VOICES HEARD.
HOW KIND!
FAILURE
SORRY!
...ARE YOU GONNA TURN THIS RECORDING SESSION INTO A COMIC?
ELCH-DONO (VA: HIRO SHIMONO)
YES.
THERE ARE PLANS TO PUT THIS IN THE MANGA.
GA BUNKO-SAN
Thanks for coming to watch us!
パチ
PACHI (CLAP)
パチ
PACHI
PHEW.
C'MON.
I WAS TOUCHED BY HOW KIND THE VOICE ACTORS WERE. THEN, THE RECORDING BEGAN.

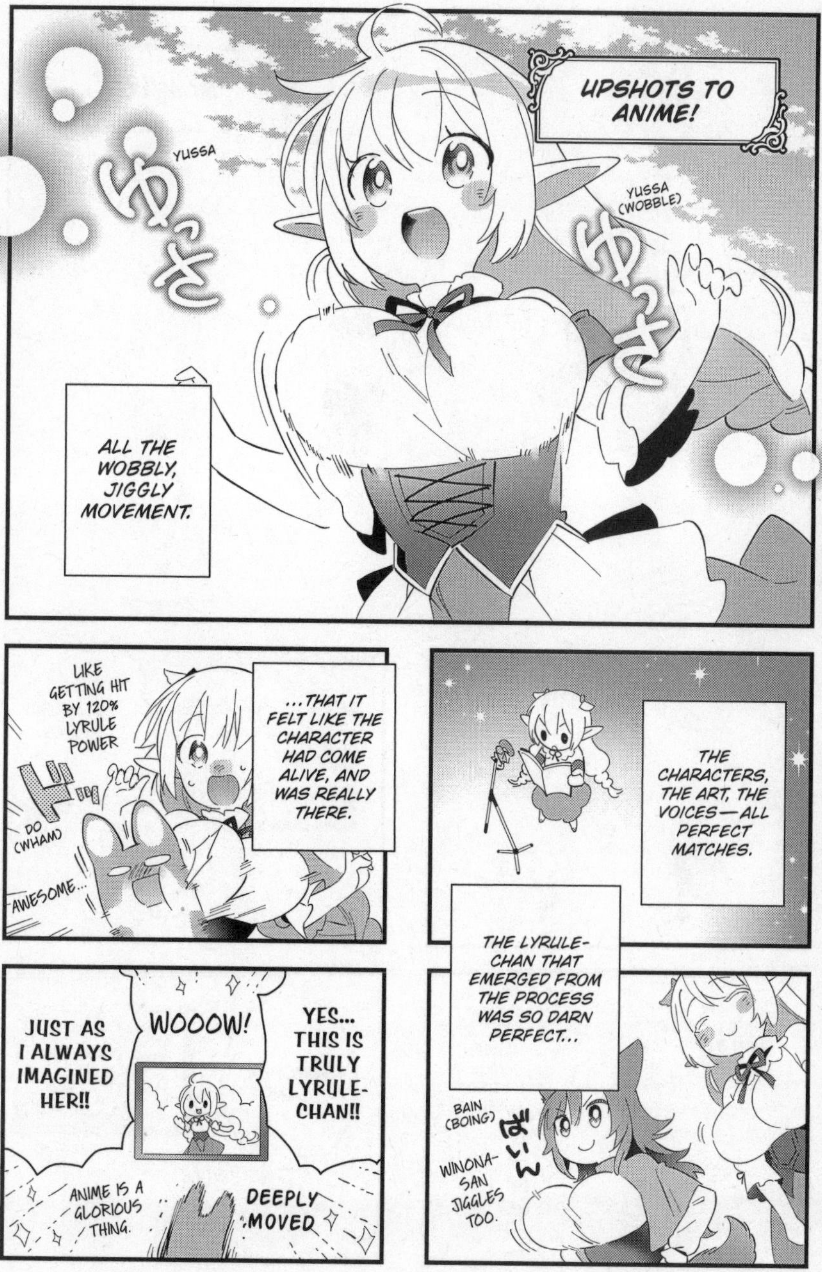
UPSHOTS TO ANIME!
YUSSA (WOBBLE)
ゆっさ
YUSSA
ゆっさ
ALL THE WOBBLY, JIGGLY MOVEMENT.
THE CHARACTERS, THE ART, THE VOICES—ALL PERFECT MATCHES.
...THAT IT FELT LIKE THE CHARACTER HAD COME ALIVE, AND WAS REALLY THERE.
LIKE GETTING HIT BY 120% LYRULE POWER
ド
DO (WHAM)
AWESOME...
THE LYRULE-CHAN THAT EMERGED FROM THE PROCESS WAS SO DARN PERFECT...
BAIN (BOING)
ばいん
WINONA-SAN JIGGLES TOO.
YES... THIS IS TRULY LYRULE-CHAN!!
WOOOW!
JUST AS I ALWAYS IMAGINED HER!!
DEEPLY MOVED
ANIME IS A GLORIOUS THING.

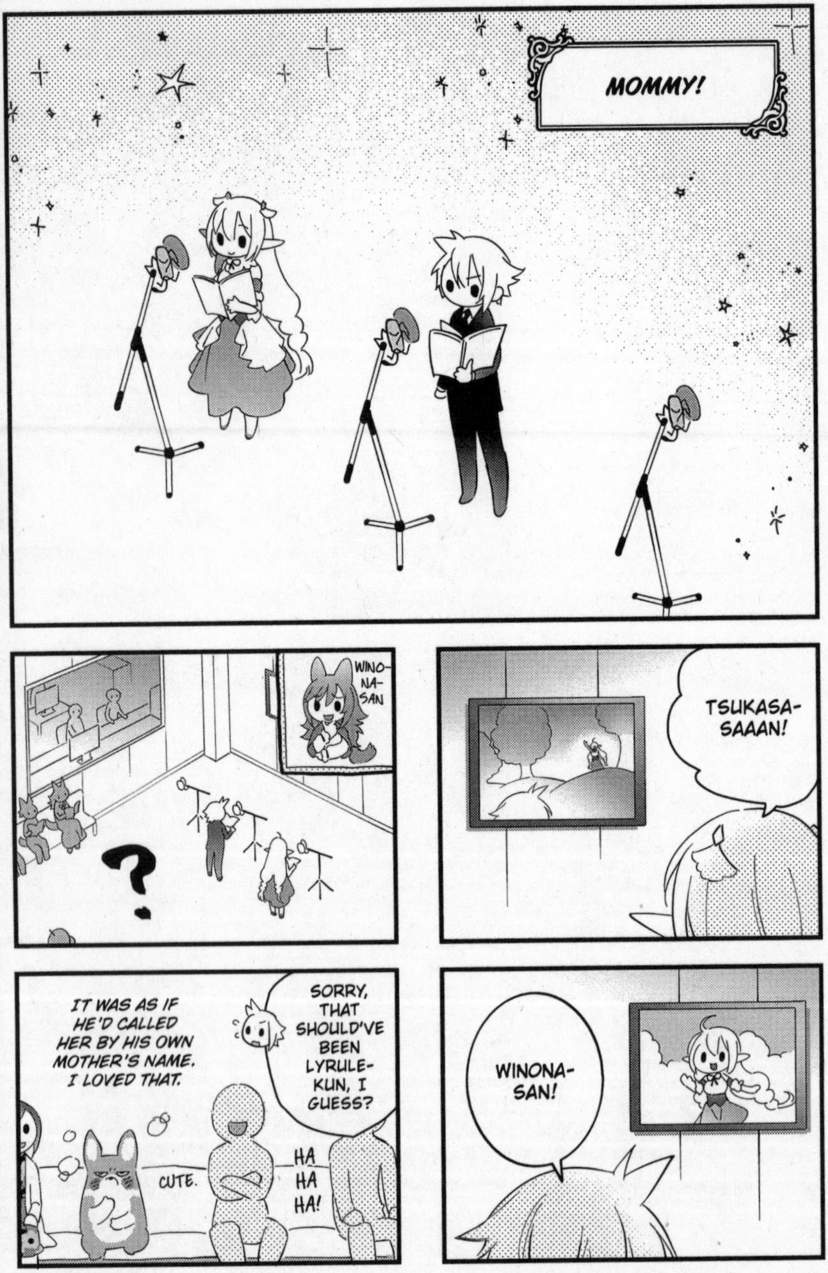
MOMMY!
TSUKASA-SAAAN!
WINO-NA-SAN
WINONA-SAN!
SORRY, THAT SHOULD'VE BEEN LYRULE-KUN, I GUESS?
IT WAS AS IF HE'D CALLED HER BY HIS OWN MOTHER'S NAME. I LOVED THAT.
HA HA HA!
CUTE.

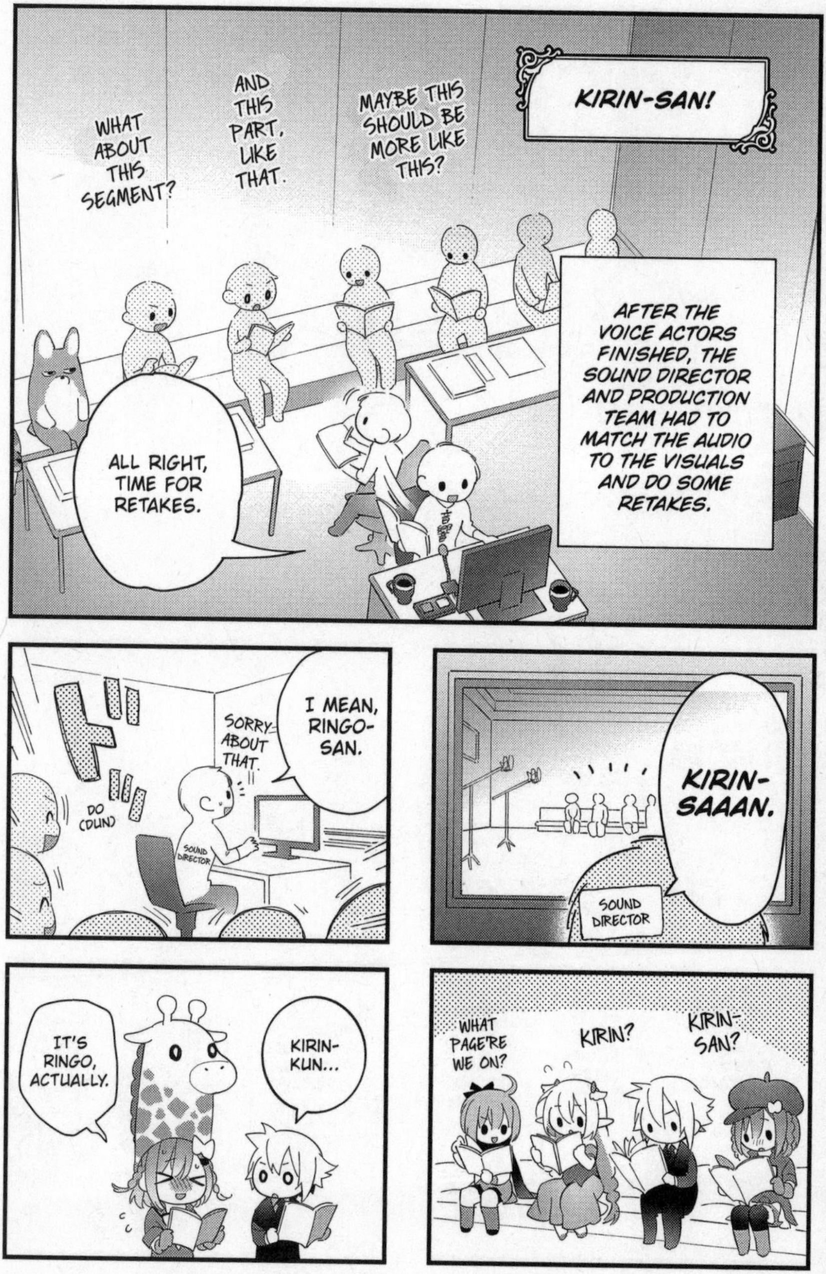
KIRIN-SAN!
MAYBE THIS SHOULD BE MORE LIKE THIS?
AND THIS PART, LIKE THAT.
WHAT ABOUT THIS SEGMENT?
AFTER THE VOICE ACTORS FINISHED, THE SOUND DIRECTOR AND PRODUCTION TEAM HAD TO MATCH THE AUDIO TO THE VISUALS AND DO SOME RETAKES.
ALL RIGHT, TIME FOR RETAKES.
KIRIN-SAAAN.
SOUND DIRECTOR
I MEAN, RINGO-SAN.
SORRY ABOUT THAT.
DO (DUN)
SOUND DIRECTOR
KIRIN-SAN?
KIRIN?
WHAT PAGE'RE WE ON?
KIRIN-KUN...
IT'S RINGO, ACTUALLY.

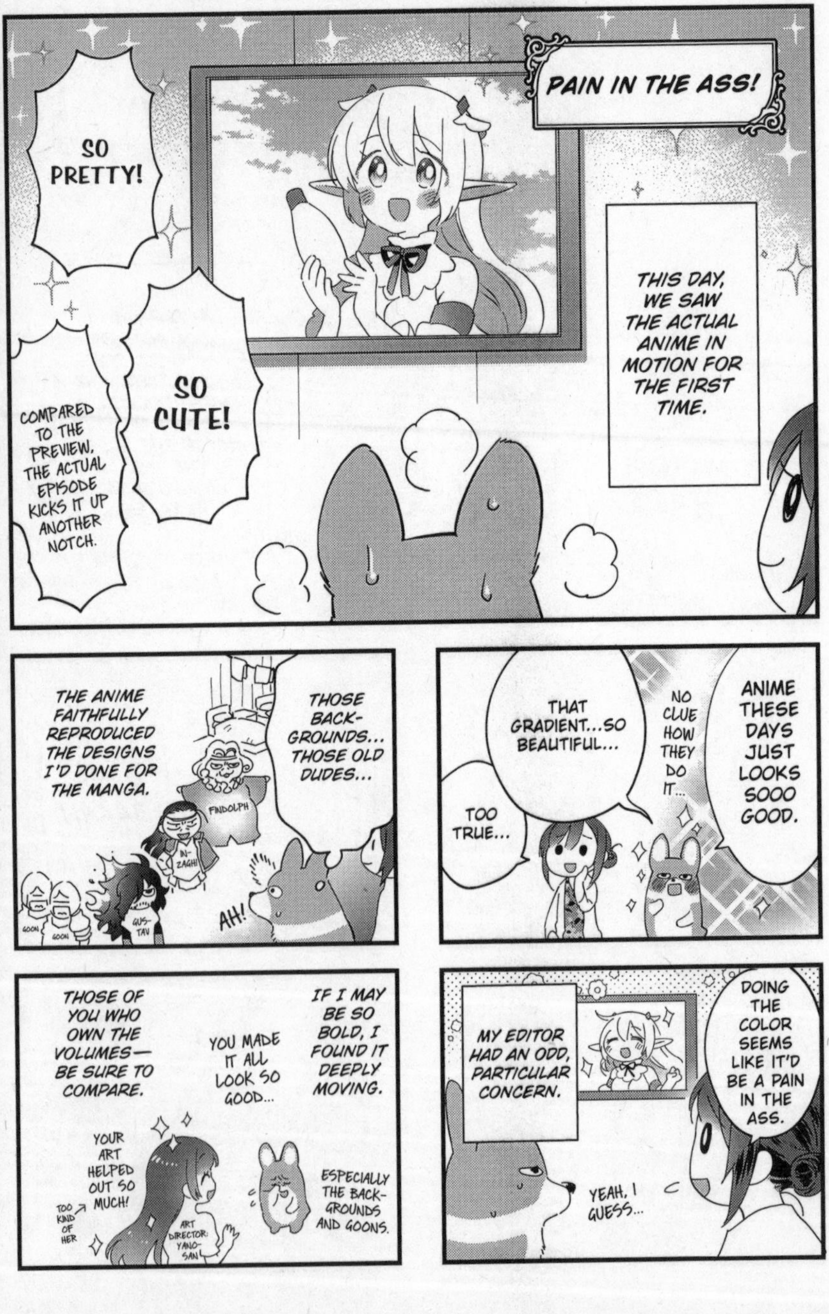
PAIN IN THE ASS!
THIS DAY, WE SAW THE ACTUAL ANIME IN MOTION FOR THE FIRST TIME.
SO PRETTY!
SO CUTE!
COMPARED TO THE PREVIEW, THE ACTUAL EPISODE KICKS IT UP ANOTHER NOTCH.
ANIME THESE DAYS JUST LOOKS SOOO GOOD.
NO CLUE HOW THEY DO IT...
THAT GRADIENT...SO BEAUTIFUL...
TOO TRUE...
THOSE BACK-GROUNDS... THOSE OLD DUDES...
THE ANIME FAITHFULLY REPRODUCED THE DESIGNS I'D DONE FOR THE MANGA.
FINDOLPH
IN-ZAGHI
AH!
GUS-TAV
GOON
GOON
DOING THE COLOR SEEMS LIKE IT'D BE A PAIN IN THE ASS.
MY EDITOR HAD AN ODD, PARTICULAR CONCERN.
YEAH, I GUESS...
IF I MAY BE SO BOLD, I FOUND IT DEEPLY MOVING.
YOU MADE IT ALL LOOK SO GOOD...
THOSE OF YOU WHO OWN THE VOLUMES—BE SURE TO COMPARE.
ESPECIALLY THE BACK-GROUNDS AND GOONS.
YOUR ART HELPED OUT SO MUCH!
TOO KIND OF HER
ART DIRECTOR: YANO-SAN

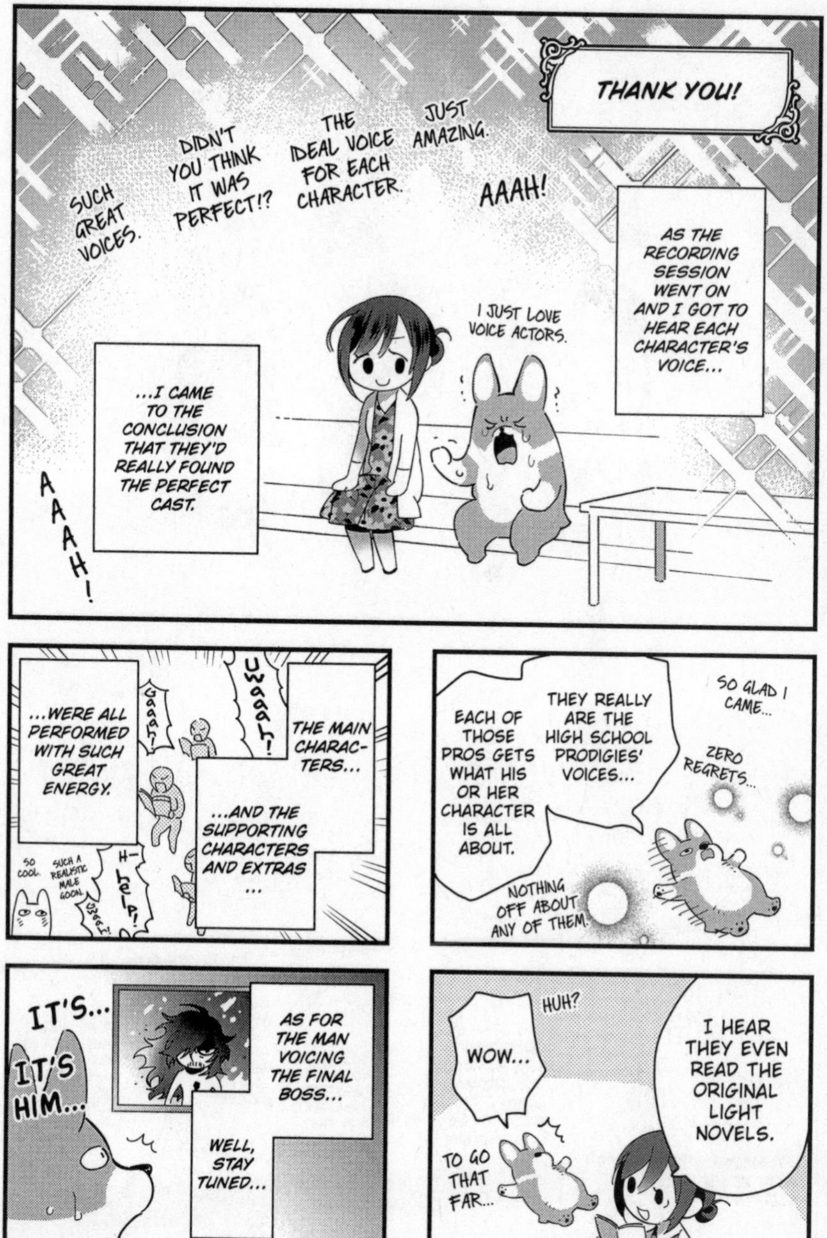
THANK YOU!
AS THE RECORDING SESSION WENT ON AND I GOT TO HEAR EACH CHARACTER'S VOICE...
JUST AMAZING.
AAAH!
THE IDEAL VOICE FOR EACH CHARACTER.
DIDN'T YOU THINK IT WAS PERFECT!?
SUCH GREAT VOICES.
I JUST LOVE VOICE ACTORS.
...I CAME TO THE CONCLUSION THAT THEY'D REALLY FOUND THE PERFECT CAST.
AAAH!
SO GLAD I CAME...
ZERO REGRETS...
THEY REALLY ARE THE HIGH SCHOOL PRODIGIES' VOICES...
EACH OF THOSE PROS GETS WHAT HIS OR HER CHARACTER IS ALL ABOUT.
NOTHING OFF ABOUT ANY OF THEM.
THE MAIN CHARACTERS...
Uwaaah!
Gaaah!
...AND THE SUPPORTING CHARACTERS AND EXTRAS...
...WERE ALL PERFORMED WITH SUCH GREAT ENERGY.
H-help!
Gwaah!
SUCH A REALISTIC MALE GOON.
SO COOL.
I HEAR THEY EVEN READ THE ORIGINAL LIGHT NOVELS.
HUH?
WOW...
TO GO THAT FAR...
AS FOR THE MAN VOICING THE FINAL BOSS...
WELL, STAY TUNED...
IT'S...
IT'S HIM...

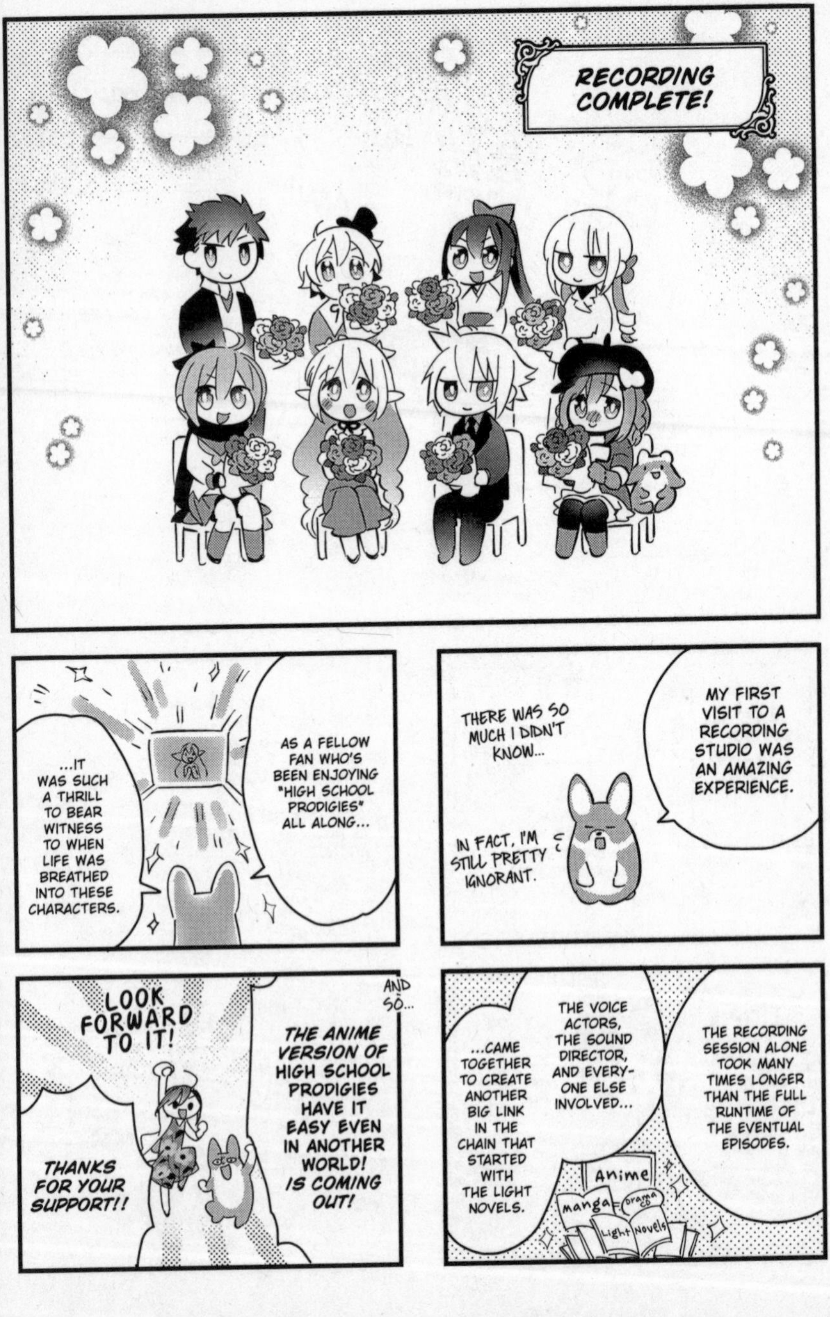
RECORDING COMPLETE!
MY FIRST VISIT TO A RECORDING STUDIO WAS AN AMAZING EXPERIENCE.
THERE WAS SO MUCH I DIDN'T KNOW...
IN FACT, I'M STILL PRETTY IGNORANT.
AS A FELLOW FAN WHO'S BEEN ENJOYING "HIGH SCHOOL PRODIGIES" ALL ALONG...
...IT WAS SUCH A THRILL TO BEAR WITNESS TO WHEN LIFE WAS BREATHED INTO THESE CHARACTERS.
THE RECORDING SESSION ALONE TOOK MANY TIMES LONGER THAN THE FULL RUNTIME OF THE EVENTUAL EPISODES.
THE VOICE ACTORS, THE SOUND DIRECTOR, AND EVERYONE ELSE INVOLVED...
...CAME TOGETHER TO CREATE ANOTHER BIG LINK IN THE CHAIN THAT STARTED WITH THE LIGHT NOVELS.
Anime
manga
Drama CD
Light Novels
AND SO...
THE ANIME VERSION OF HIGH SCHOOL PRODIGIES HAVE IT EASY EVEN IN ANOTHER WORLD! IS COMING OUT!
LOOK FORWARD TO IT!
THANKS FOR YOUR SUPPORT!!

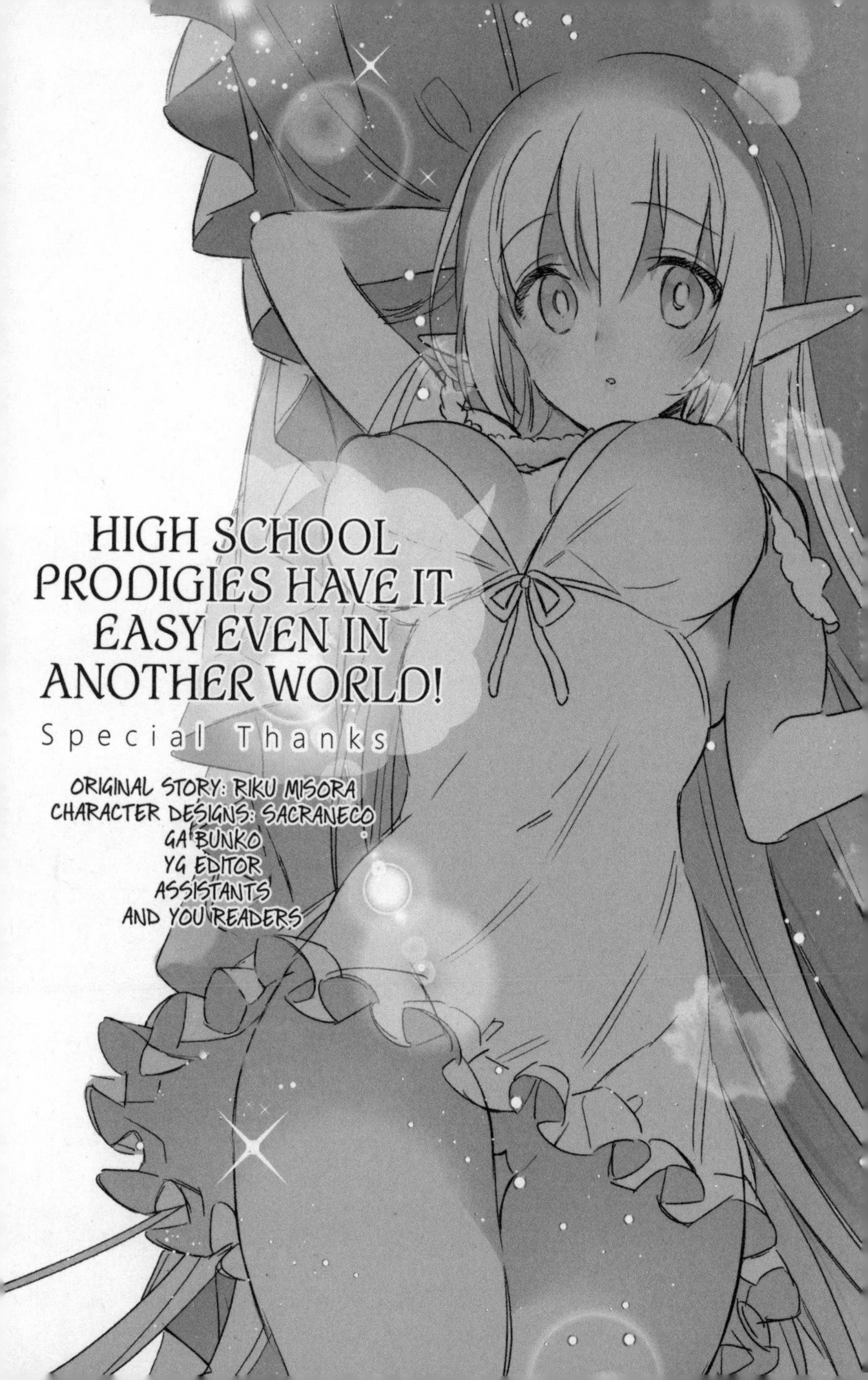
HIGH SCHOOL PRODIGIES HAVE IT EASY EVEN IN ANOTHER WORLD!
Special Thanks
ORIGINAL STORY: RIKU MISORA
CHARACTER DESIGNS: SACRANECO
GA BUNKO
YG EDITOR
ASSISTANTS
AND YOU READERS

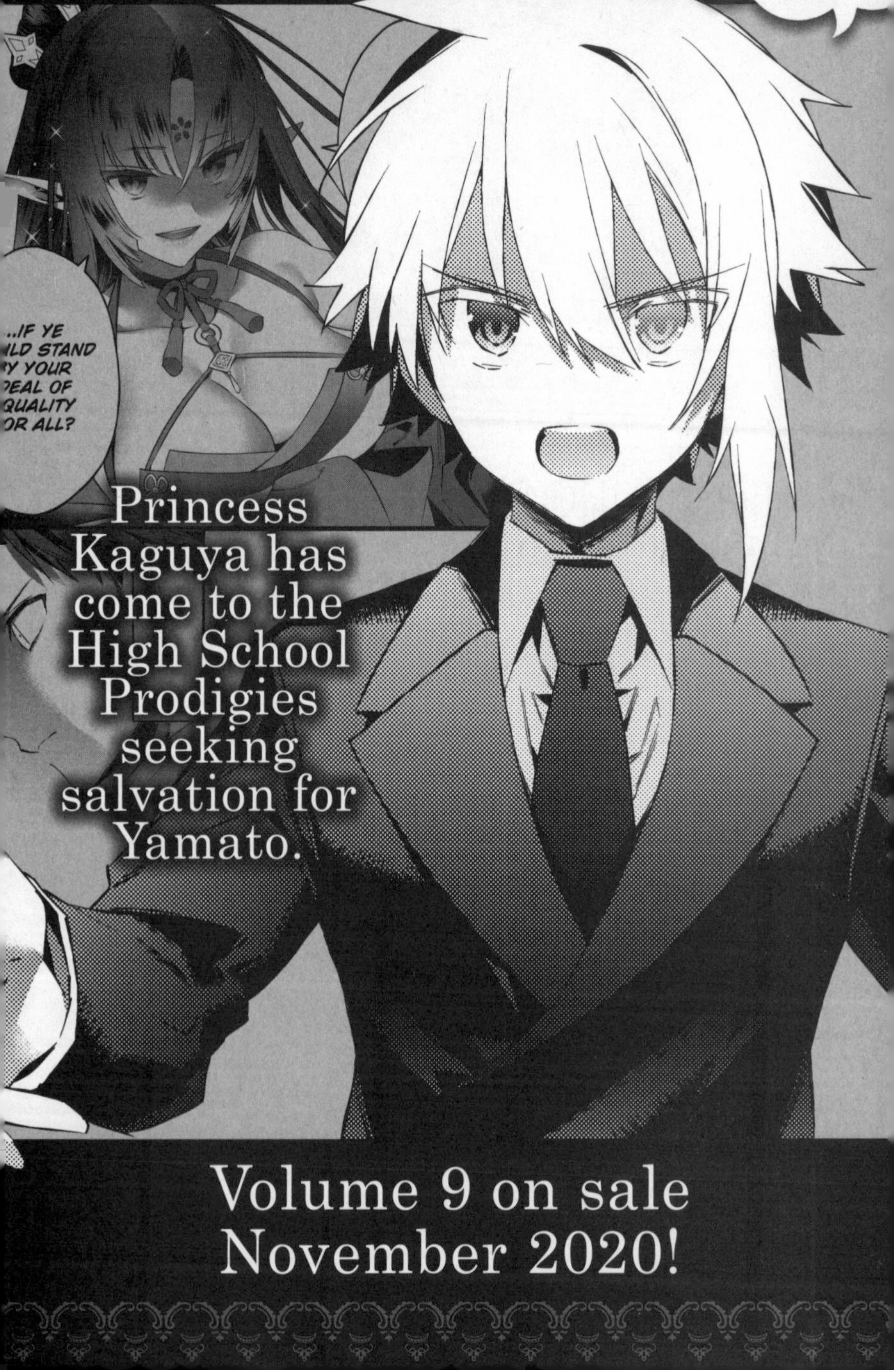
NEXT VOLUME PREVIEW!
..IF YE ILD STAND Y YOUR EAL OF QUALITY OR ALL?
Princess Kaguya has come to the High School Prodigies seeking salvation for Yamato.

Volume 9 on sale November 2020!

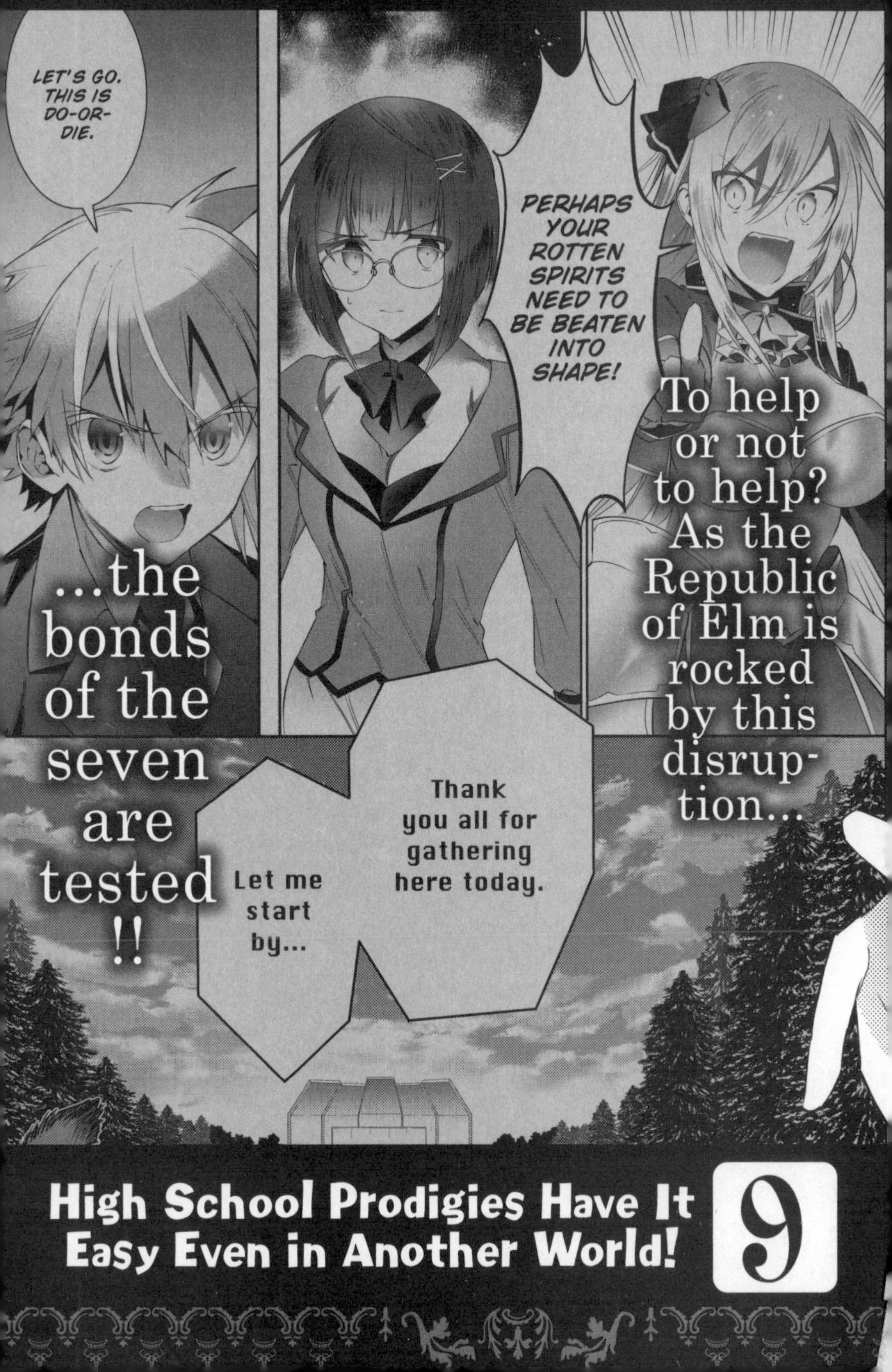
PERHAPS YOUR ROTTEN SPIRITS NEED TO BE BEATEN INTO SHAPE!
To help or not to help? As the Republic of Elm is rocked by this disruption...
LET'S GO. THIS IS DO-OR-DIE.
Thank you all for gathering here today.
Let me start by...
...the bonds of the seven are tested!!

High School Prodigies Have It Easy Even in Another World! 9

High School Prodigies Have It Easy Even in Another World! 8

STORY BY Riku Misora   **ART BY Kotaro Yamada**

CHARACTER DESIGN BY Sacraneco

Translation: Caleb D. Cook
Lettering: Brandon Bovia

CHOUJIN KOUKOUSEI TACHI WA ISEKAI DEMO YOYU DE IKINUKU YOUDESU! vol. 8
© Riku Misora / SB Creative Corp.
Original Character Designs: © Sacraneco / SB Creative Corp.
© 2019 Kotaro Yamada / SQUARE ENIX CO., LTD.
First published in Japan in 2019 by SQUARE ENIX CO., LTD.
English translation rights arranged with SQUARE ENIX CO., LTD.
and Yen Press, LLC through Tuttle Mori Agency, Inc.

English translation © 2020 by SQUARE ENIX CO., LTD.

Yen Press
150 West 30th Street, 19th Floor
New York, NY 10001

Visit us at yenpress.com

facebook.com/yenpress
twitter.com/yenpress

yenpress.tumblr.com
instagram.com/yenpress

First Yen Press Edition: August 2020

Yen Press is an imprint of Yen Press, LLC.
The Yen Press name and logo are trademarks of Yen Press, LLC.

The publisher is not responsible for websites (or their content) that are not owned by the publisher.

Library of Congress Control Number: 2018948324

ISBNs: 978-1-9753-0892-6 (paperback)
978-1-9753-0893-3 (ebook)

10 9 8 7 6 5 4 3 2 1

BVG

Printed in the United States of America